THE NATURAL VET'S GUIDE *to*

PREVENTING and TREATING CANCER in DOGS

THE NATURAL VET'S GUIDE to

PREVENTING and TREATING CANCER in DOGS

SHAWN MESSONNIER, DVM

New World Library
Novato, California

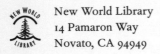

New World Library
14 Pamaron Way
Novato, CA 94949

Interior design by Tona Pearce Myers

Library of Congress Cataloging-in-Publication Data
Messonnier, Shawn.
  The natural vet's guide to preventing and treating cancer in dogs / Shawn Messonnier.— 1st ed.
    p. cm.
Includes bibliographical references and index.
ISBN 1-57731-519-7 (pbk. : alk. paper)
  1. Dogs—Diseases—Alternative treatment. 2. Cancer in animals.
3. Holistic veterinary medicine. I. Title.
SF992.C35M47 2006
636.7'0896994—dc22   2005030337

First printing, March 2006
ISBN-13: 978-1-57731-519-2
ISBN-10: 1-57731-519-7

New World Library is a proud member of the Green Press Initiative.

Distributed by Publishers Group West

10 9 8 7 6 5 4 3 2
Printed in Canada

CONTENTS

APPENDICES

FOREWORD

THE OLD SAYING that an ounce of prevention is worth a pound of cure is especially true with cancer prevention. It is infinitely easier to prevent cancer than it is to treat it. Having written a book on using nutritional science to treat human cancer, I am honored to write the foreword to Dr. Messonnier's guide to preventing and treating cancer in dogs. Dogs, among many animal species, have been used extensively in cancer research, so we have considerable direct evidence about what works and what doesn't.

The field of nutritional oncology (treating cancer with food and supplements) has virtually exploded over the past three decades. Our knowledge of the cancer process in particular, especially on a molecular basis, has expanded exponentially. Paralleling this has been a greatly improved understanding of how nutrition affects cell function and the cancer process. Dr. Messonnier reviews this new knowledge in such a way that the reader can easily understand and apply it.

Within this explosion of knowledge about nutritional cancer treatment lies a vast number of ways to prevent cancer from ever developing. Some of these methods entail special nutritional supplements, but the most important step is adhering to a scientifically based anticancer diet for your dog. By switching to such a diet, you will be not only preventing cancer but also vastly improving the general health of your dog and extending his or her life in the process.

One of the great revelations in oncology research is that cancer is a chronic inflammatory disease. As many as 70 percent of people who develop cancer have suffered from an inflammatory disease for a decade or more before the cancer developed. The same is true in animals. And, as Dr. Messonnier points out, 50 percent of dogs will develop cancer in their advanced years. When we examine these dogs we see a long history of various inflammatory diseases, such as arthritis and chronic viral or parasitic diseases. Particularly important is the connection between chronic inflammation and chronic overactivation of the immune system. We know that the two systems work together to produce the conditions necessary for cancer development.

I am particularly pleased to see that Dr. Messonnier pinpoints the problem of excessive vaccination of dogs and its connection to various diseases. The same is true in humans. There is growing evidence that excessive vaccination can produce prolonged states of inflammation, just as we see in arthritis, autoimmune disorders, and other degenerative diseases. In addition, vaccines often contain toxic doses of mercury and aluminum, both of which accumulate in the body and remain for a very long time.

So, what is the connection between inflammation and cancer? Inflammation is a powerful generator of free radicals. It is these free radials that damage the animal's DNA. And when a particular pattern of damage occurs, cancer genes are turned on. Recently, we have learned that these same free radicals can stimulate cancers to grow faster and become more deadly and aggressive. Likewise, they cause the cancers to grow and spread throughout the animal's body.

A number of recent studies have shown that reducing inflammation dramatically reduces the likelihood that cancer will spread. The nutrients discussed in this book primarily reduce inflammation and prevent immune system overactivation and do so with greater safety and efficiency than anti-inflammatory drugs. Even more exciting are studies showing that certain nutritional extracts can actually cause cancer cells to revert back to normal cells.

One myth perpetrated by oncologists is that antioxidants may interfere with conventional treatments such as chemotherapy and radiation. In fact, a growing number of new studies indicate the exact opposite is true. Special mixtures of nutritional supplements can greatly enhance the effectiveness of conventional treatments and dramatically reduce the complications they cause.

As Dr. Messonnier points out, one big problem with chemotherapy is that after initially responding to the treatment, the cancer will suddenly become resistant to it. Studies show that a number of nutritional extracts can completely reverse this and even make the cancer cells more sensitive to the chemotherapy drugs. Because normal cells are physiologically and biochemically different from cancer cells, these same nutrients can dramatically increase the resistance of normal cells to the powerful chemotherapy drugs, reducing the harmful side effects of the treatment. Because these special nutrients dramatically enhance the effectiveness of chemotherapy and radiation, your veterinarian can use lower doses of these conventional treatments, with much greater safety for your dog.

It is also important to keep in mind that combining certain

nutrients can make anticancer drugs significantly more effective. A number of newer studies have shown that by mixing specified vitamins, minerals, and plant chemicals called flavonoids, one can eradicate a number of cancers in animals, even advanced cancers.

One of the most exciting discoveries concerning radiation treatments was made by Dr. Levenson and co-workers, who found that animals implanted with highly malignant cancers and fed large doses of beta-carotene experienced complete resolution of their tumors when treated with radiation, while the majority of the animals not fed the beta-carotene died. Even when the tumor was not completely destroyed by the radiation treatment, as long as the animal remained on beta-carotene, the tumors did not grow or spread.

One reason animal studies are so much more successful than human studies is that it is much easier to control the animal's diet. This is the key to success. I find that many people feed their pets the same sort of cancer and disease-causing diet as they themselves eat. Dog foods devoid of anticancer plant flavonoids, oils, and a proper balance of nutrients are common. These poor diets also increase the incidence of many other diseases.

Conversely, a number of studies have shown that anticancer diets in dogs can dramatically reduce rates of cancer as well as of other crippling diseases. For example, omega-3 oils, magnesium, and antioxidants dramatically reduce the incidence of seizures in animals. Likewise, omega-6 oils (corn, safflower, sunflower, peanut, soybean, and canola oils) greatly increase both seizures and cancer growth.

The anticancer diet and special supplements can also reduce the incidence of atherosclerosis, heart failure, diabetes, arthritis, autoimmune diseases, brain disorders, and eyesight failure. The reason is that all these diseases have been shown to be caused by the same process: free radical damage caused by chronic inflammation.

Dr. Messonnier also brings up the very significant danger of exposing your pet to chemical carcinogens. Like human bodies, pets' bodies accumulate chemicals from their environment, such as pesticides, insecticides, fungicides, and herbicides, many of which are powerful carcinogens, especially in combination. Newer studies are showing that some chemicals may have a low cancer-causing potential when tested alone but can be very powerful carcinogens when combined.

Your dog is exposed to all the pesticides used in your house and all the pesticides, fungicides, and weed killers used in your yard. Few people are aware of the studies showing that both children and pets exposed to chemically treated lawns have a dramatically increased risk of developing both leukemia and lymphomas. The risk is even greater if these chemicals are used both indoors and outdoors in the yard or garden.

There is little question that the aggressive use of anticancer nutrition, especially when combined with conventional treatments, offers a tremendous opportunity for dog owners to save their pets from a terrible affliction. Even for those dogs that cannot be cured, anticancer nutrition can extend their lives and make them infinitely more comfortable. Dr. Messonnier's book will show you how to apply these practices for the well-being of your own dog. I applaud Dr. Messonnier for providing this vital information to both dog owners and the veterinarians who treat their dogs.

Russell L. Blaylock, MD,
neurosurgeon and visiting professor of biology,
Belhaven College, Jackson, Mississippi,
and author of *Natural Strategies for Cancer Patients*

ACKNOWLEDGMENTS

THERE ARE MANY VETERINARIANS who have shared their thoughts after reviewing this book — thank you all. A very special thanks to veterinarians Dr. Kevin Hahn, Dr. Steve Marsden, Dr. P. J. Broadfoot, Dr. Karen Brown, Dr. Rob Silver, and Dr. Russell Blaylock (MD) for their willingness to contribute to this book. Dr. Hahn helped with the editing and contributed information to chapter 5 on conventional therapies; Dr. Broadfoot also helped with the editing and contributed information on homotoxicology. The contributions of all of these fine doctors make this a great book containing the latest information on preventing, diagnosing, and treating cancer in dogs.

Thanks to all of the members of the email group of the American Holistic Veterinary Medical Association; by generously sharing their ideas with me, they have also made this a better book. Thanks also to my local veterinary oncologists and internal medicine specialists, particularly Dr. Cheryl Harris and Dr. Kelly Nitsche.

As always, thanks to my clients, who challenge me to develop the best treatments for their pets with cancer. And last but not least, thanks to my beautiful wife, Sandy, and my lovely daughter, Erica, for all of their support and encouragement.

INTRODUCTION

CANCER IS AMONG THE DISEASES most feared by pet owners and is appearing in dogs with increasing frequency. For
many owners, the diagnosis brings grief, uncertainty, fear, and
a general feeling of hopelessness.

While it is true that cancers can result in the untimely
death of our pets, not all cancers carry a poor prognosis. For
example, many solid tumors, if diagnosed early, respond quite
well to surgical removal before they have spread. In these
instances, surgery in the early stages of the disease may be
curative.

Other cancers, such as osteosarcoma and hemangiosarcoma, often are not diagnosed until they have already spread.
In these instances, treatment may not cure the pet but instead
make the pet as comfortable as possible during its final months
and weeks. In these cases, the goal isn't to prolong life but to
ensure that the pet is comfortable, free of pain, and therefore

experiencing a good quality of life during the treatment of its cancer. For most pets, the diagnosis of cancer is not an immediate death sentence but rather the chance to begin therapy. Few cancers spread so quickly as to prevent treatment. By keeping up with regular veterinary examinations that include laboratory tests, pet owners can rest assured that any cancer that might appear will be diagnosed early and treated more effectively.

This book presents a lot of information on treating cancer, but it is also about preventing cancer. While there are never any guarantees, some types of cancer can be prevented by following commonsense recommendations. For example, cancers of the reproductive organs may be prevented in most pets by spaying and neutering pets before they reach sexual maturity. Additionally, I believe there is substantial evidence that most if not all cancers can be minimized, if not totally prevented, by reducing the chances of chronic inflammation, oxidation, and DNA damage. There are several steps a pet owner can take for cancer prevention: feed your pet a diet that does not contain by-products or harmful chemicals, avoid unnecessary vaccinations, minimize your pet's exposure to common but toxic yard products, and reduce the amount of conventional medications and parasite-preventing drugs prescribed to your pet.

Of course, the bulk of this book explores the most common treatment options available for the dog with cancer. By wisely combining conventional and complementary treatment options, we can properly treat the pet's problem and minimize the chances of side effects.

There are many complementary therapies that can be used to treat a pet with cancer, including antioxidants, herbal preparations, homeopathic remedies, glandular supplements and raw food, and occasionally even acupuncture. Which therapy or therapies will be of most help to your pet depends upon a number of factors and should be chosen only after careful consultation with your veterinarian.

While there are many therapies, no one therapy is right for every pet. As a rule, complementary therapies are designed to be used with conventional cancer treatments (in an integrative mode), such as radiation therapy, chemotherapy, and surgery. The complementary therapies are designed to boost the immune system or reduce the severity of side effects that may occur with conventional therapies. For most pets, conventional therapies must be used to provide the pet with the best chance of being completely cured of cancer, or if cancer cannot be cured, of returning to an acceptable quality of life while the growth of the cancer is slowed. For those owners who decline conventional therapy for whatever reasons, or in those rare cases where there is no proven conventional therapy for the pet's type of cancer, various complementary therapies may be useful in place of conventional therapies for the treatment of cancer. Ultimately, consulting with both a board-certified veterinary oncologist and a holistic veterinarian will give pet owners the best selection of therapies for their pets.

Throughout this book I try to present information in a truly holistic fashion, remaining as objective as possible. I am very grateful for the help of veterinary cancer specialist Dr. Kevin Hahn, whose own work in the field of cancer treatment is detailed throughout this book. His efforts make sure that the information presented in the chapters on the types of cancer and the treatments of cancer is up to date and accurate. Dr. Hahn is instrumental in developing new cancer treatment strategies, known as protocols, based upon his ongoing clinical trial research at Gulf Coast Veterinary Specialists. (Your veterinarian can see if your pet might qualify for inclusion in a clinical trial by visiting www.gcvs.com.) Additionally, his expertise in cancer therapies and his open-minded approach to integrating complementary therapies with carefully selected conventional treatments make him the very best source for the latest, most accurate information currently available in the field of veterinary medicine. His contribution to *The Natural Vet's Guide to Preventing and Treating Cancer in Dogs* has been invaluable.

For some complementary therapies, there exists a large body of well-designed, scientifically coordinated research studies. For other therapies, we do not currently have these controlled studies but rather rely on clinical experiences. Still, some complementary therapies show promise in people, and while their effectiveness in pets is clinically unknown, it gives us hope; until there are more controlled studies, these therapies may need to be extrapolated from the human studies for use in pets.

My hope is that you and your doctor will find the right combination of conventional and complementary therapies that can help your pet. *Each pet is an individual and must be treated as such, and what works for one pet may not be helpful for another pet.* I am confident that your doctor will find something that can help your pet.

As you read this book, you may find some of the information quite technical. I include this information — and try to make it user-friendly — for the following reason: I want you to be able to work with your veterinarian and specialist when treating your pet with cancer. In providing you with accurate information, my hope is that you will share it with your doctors and they will understand *why* a treatment is recommended as well as *how* the treatment is purported to work. Having this information makes it more likely that your cancer team will be open to the ideas presented throughout the book.

While I would love to assure you that your pet will be cured of cancer, with rare exception that is not the case. Usually, the goal of therapy (either conventional or complementary) for a pet with cancer is to lengthen its life by increasing the amount of time the pet is in remission. This is not meant to discourage you but rather give you a realistic expectation of cancer treatment.

Information is always changing, and new treatments are popping up as I write this book. Future editions will update you with important and promising new therapies for your pet.

I would appreciate hearing from any of my readers about how I can improve future editions so that we can make the world a healthier, more holistic place for our pets.

ABOUT NATURAL SUPPLEMENTS

THROUGHOUT THE BOOK I mention a number of natural supplements for your pet with cancer. I try to be as objective as possible by refraining from promoting any particular products. Every holistic doctor has favorite supplements that have worked best in his or her practice, and I mention my favorites when appropriate. Since there are many products available to help your pet, I encourage you to work with your doctor to find the best products that are most suitable for your pet.

Keep in mind that many companies distribute dietary supplements. In the United States, dietary supplements are regulated as foods, not drugs. Therefore, pre-market evaluation and approval by the Food and Drug Administration (FDA) are not required unless these products make specific disease-prevention or treatment claims. Because dietary supplements are not formally reviewed for manufacturing consistency, there can be considerable variation in potency and quality from lot to lot. For this reason, it is important to choose only supplements manufactured and distributed by companies with good reputations for quality control. Ideally, companies bearing the seal of approval from the National Animal Supplement Council (NASC) are preferred. Most holistic doctors have done the research and can recommend the higher grade, better quality supplements. If you prefer to do your own research, contact the manufacturer and ask about its quality control and whether any studies have been conducted concerning its supplements (in most cases, manufacturers do not have clinical studies using their supplements because of the cost involved, although this is slowly changing). When in doubt about quality, you can't do better than consulting with a holistic veterinarian with experience in prescribing supplements.

For more information about supplements, please see the appendix entitled "Supplement Manufacturers" on page 245.

CHAPTER ONE

UNDERSTANDING *the* HOLISTIC APPROACH *to* TREATING CANCER

WHEN TREATING A DOG WITH CANCER, owners truly have many options. The reason for the large number of options is that there is no one "best" treatment for every pet. I share the holistic belief that each pet is an individual, and must be treated as such. I discuss this philosophy with owners right from the start. What worked for the last dog I treated may not work for their pet. Additionally, each owner is unique and has different wants and a different budget for their pet's medical care. Some owners want to do everything possible for their pet. Money is no object, and they will often allow us to experiment and try quite a number of unique treatments. Others opt for a bit less, and may choose only surgery or one round of chemotherapy. Still others never want any conventional medications, and will opt for only natural therapies such as herbal therapy or homeopathy.

I should point out before proceeding that the truly holistic view, desired by most pet owners, involves looking at all options and choosing what works best with the fewest side effects. I'm a conventional doctor by training and use many conventional therapies in my practice. Whenever appropriate, I like to integrate as many different therapies as possible, as the best results occur when conventional therapies are combined with complementary therapies. Chemotherapy, as used in veterinary medicine, is not as harmful as it is in people, and significant side effects are uncommon in pets. This is because maximum tolerated dosages are used in people, leading to complications in nearly every patient. For pets, most chemotherapy dosages are 10–20 percent lower than the maximum tolerable dosage, leading to fewer than 5 percent of treated pets having significant dose-limiting side effects such as bone marrow suppression (low white blood cell counts leading to increased risk of bacterial infection) or gastrointestinal upset (nausea, vomiting, or diarrhea).

The true goal of chemotherapy is to chemically reduce the burden of cancer and provide symptom-free quality of life. Having no *evidence* of cancer (by examination or X-ray evaluation) and no *symptoms* from cancer is called remission.

Once in remission, pets are prescribed supplements to help boost their immune systems as well as to counteract side effects of chemotherapy. In some cases chemotherapy may be the only treatment option, as the cancer patient may not be able or willing to take all of the recommended supplements. Some pets are easy to medicate and can take many herbal and homeopathic supplements several times a day, whereas others will never take anything by mouth, complicating our effort at developing the best treatment plan. The holistic approach simply means looking at all of the available treatment options and choosing what works best for each specific patient.

The best treatment for many dogs with cancer is often a sensible combination of both conventional and complementary therapies. I believe that by offering the two kinds of therapy to owners, I can give them the best of both worlds. By knowing the pros and cons of both types of medical care, owners can work with me to pick the therapies that they are most comfortable with, and that are most beneficial to their pets.

Keep in mind, too, that "holistic" doesn't necessarily mean "alternative." A truly holistic approach tries to heal the entire pet, and not just treat symptoms. A truly holistic approach chooses what's best for the pet, providing the pet relief while minimizing side effects. Conventional therapy can be a part of the holistic approach to the treatment of cancer *if* the goal is to help the pet become healthier and not just cover up symptoms or ignore the pet's overall well-being.

> *Combining complementary and conventional therapies offers the best of both worlds.*

Here's an example of the harm that can come to a pet with a treatable cancer when owners refuse to be truly holistic and consider conventional chemotherapy. I once treated a friendly shih tzu named Radar for lymphosarcoma, a cancer that is very responsive to conventional chemotherapy with minimal side effects in most instances. In cases like this, I usually prescribe supplements and homeopathy to help boost a pet's immune response to conventional therapy. Unfortunately, Radar's owners were totally opposed to chemotherapy because they could not overcome unfounded fears that he would suffer during chemotherapy. Despite two weeks of supplements and homeopathy, Radar rapidly worsened and was euthanized shortly thereafter. This case was frustrating, as I believe that

Radar could have done quite well if only his owners had agreed to a quick round of chemotherapy in addition to other therapies. In this instance, homeopathy and other supplements did not have any chance of success against the aggressiveness of Radar's cancer. The moral: whenever possible, don't decline treatments that work without serious thought and rational judgment. Remember that for many pets with cancer, complementary therapies alone rarely achieve the same results as conventional therapies. It is best to use them as they are intended, to complement the conventional treatments for the pet with cancer.

On the flip side, there are problems with the strictly conventional approach of diagnosing and treating cancer. *Often, by ignoring the holistic approach to treatment, we are treating the cancer and not the pet.* As one of the contributors to this book, cancer specialist Dr. Kevin Hahn likes to point out, *Don't forget that there is a pet attached to the tumor!* The only way to win the war against cancer is to make the pet as healthy as possible while we're treating the cancer. This may mean using supplements to support the liver, the gastrointestinal system, and any other organ or system of the body. Simply choosing conventional cancer therapies without regard for the overall health of the pet is not in the pet's best interest. Nutritional support is important — we must provide the pet with the best diet possible (see chapter 8 for more on the best diet for a pet with cancer). Nutritional supplements may be useful, to boost the immune system and help the pet recover its natural ability to fight cancer. Also, using complementary therapies such as glutamine supplementation may reduce the side effects, such as vomiting or diarrhea, that may occur with some types of chemotherapy or radiation therapy.

Finally, I cannot stress enough the importance of a full

diagnosis. Many doctors take a "wait and see" approach when an owner points out a suspicious lump on the pet. A diagnosis is often made by the doctor simply looking at and feeling the lump. *Fatty tumor* and *cyst* are the terms often applied to a benign (noncancerous) lesion. While it is true that most suspicious lumps are benign, some are malignant cancers. With rare exceptions (such as commonly observed warts, technically called papillomas, usually seen in older dogs), *no one* can adequately diagnose a tumor simply by looking at it and feeling it. I have removed too many malignant cancers that were originally diagnosed as fatty tumors or cysts to know that full diagnostic testing is essential, usually by examining under the microscope the aspirate taken from a tumor with a tiny needle.

Not too long ago I made an initial diagnosis of an infected cyst on the abdomen of Lizzie, a five-year-old spayed female black Labrador retriever. At first I was not concerned about this lesion. However, when it didn't get better after two weeks of topical antibiotic therapy, I suggested removal and biopsy. Imagine my surprise when this infected piece of skin was identified as a malignant mast cell tumor — a cancer notorious for looking like a benign cyst or fatty tumor! Thankfully, I had removed the entire tumor with that surgery and no further treatment was needed for Lizzie. Because of this and other similar cases, I have become convinced that mast cell tumors can look like almost anything. (You'll learn more about the ability of mast cell tumors to masquerade as benign fatty tumors and other lumps and bumps on pages 19–21 in chapter 2.)

Unless a lesion is an obvious old-age wart, I recommend removal and testing of all lesions. The lesson is simple: any lumps seen or felt under the skin or above the skin surface should be aspirated or in some way biopsied before a conclusive diagnosis of a benign fatty tumor or cyst is reached.

> *No one can adequately diagnose a tumor simply*
> *by looking at it and feeling it.*

It is quite troubling that so many pets I see have not received a proper diagnosis. A good number of these pets have not had any diagnostic tests done. Yet often a simple aspirate of the lesion, radiograph (X-ray) of the abdomen when a suspicious mass is felt during examination, or blood test of a pet with unexplained clinical signs, such as lethargy and a lack of appetite, will reveal the cause of the pet's problem. There is simply no excuse for failing to obtain a proper diagnosis. The bottom line is this: to prevent a misdiagnosis of the true cause of a pet's lumps and bumps, we need proper diagnostic tests to make sure that our treatment choice is correct.

CHAPTER TWO

UNDERSTANDING CANCER

COMMON QUESTIONS AMONG OWNERS of dogs with cancer include "What causes cancer?" "Why does my dog have cancer?" "Did I do anything to cause this?" and "Could I have prevented this?" This chapter attempts to answer these central questions. Following this discussion, I'll explain some of the more common cancers that occur in dogs. You can also refer to the index and turn to pages that address the cancer type that is most applicable to your pet's situation.

PREVENTING CANCER

In most cases, you did not cause your pet's cancer nor could you have prevented it. However, using holistic preventive care is the best approach to minimize the chance of your pet (or you, for that matter) developing cancer or any other diseases. One important step is vaccinating your pet on an "as-needed" basis, rather than giving your pet every possible vaccine every

. It's also important to feed your pet a healthy diet free of ɟ-products and chemicals, supplemented with quality nutritional supplements called *nutraceuticals* (Healthy Diet + Nutraceutical Supplementation = Health). Keeping your pet at an ideal weight may also reduce the incidence of cancer and other health problems, as obese pets are more likely to develop medical problems, including cancer, than pets maintaining a normal weight. If you find a lump on your pet, insist that your veterinarian aspirate it with a tiny needle and syringe so it can be tested for cancer; if the test indicates cancer, have the lump removed as soon as possible. Using more natural insecticides, when possible, to control fleas, ticks, and other parasites will lower your pet's exposure to carcinogenic toxins. In short, doing all of these things, which define the term *holistic*, will minimize your pet's chances of developing cancer.

Many types of cancer, such as ovarian, breast, and testicular cancer, are preventable by early removal of the reproductive organs. Specifically, early spaying and neutering (ideally between four and six months of age) reduces the incidence of or prevents most genital cancers. Some skin cancers, such as squamous cell carcinoma and cutaneous hemangiosarcoma, can be prevented by minimizing a dog's exposure to the sun, especially in breeds with lighter skin and sparse hair. For a holistic approach to increasing longevity for our pets, we may also consider natural therapies that have been shown to inhibit cancer during the aging process. We will explore these therapies further in chapter 6.

The holistic approach to cancer is concerned with prevention as well as treatment, and maintaining a good quality life until the very end of that life. By adopting a holistic approach to the care of your pet with cancer, you can be assured that it is the most loving approach to the care of your special friend.

Holistic healing supports the immune system and nutritional needs of patients from the very beginning of their fight against cancer. Holistic care includes providing natural supplements, antioxidants, herbs, and homeopathics in addition to proven conventional therapies.

Unfortunately, cancer is common in pets, killing up to one-half of those more than ten years old. When cancer develops in a pet, the battle to save that pet's life will require a combination of efforts.

WHAT CAUSES CANCER IN DOGS?

In most pets, the exact cause of cancer is not known. Basically, cancer is often a fatal disease that is caused by mutations in the genes of certain susceptible cells (see boxed text on pages 10–12). These genetic mutations, usually caused by inflammation or excessive oxidation, convert normal cells into cancer cells that divide rapidly and grow uncontrollably, pushing their way into the surrounding tissues composed of otherwise normal cells. Because oxidation and inflammation can lead to the development of most if not all cancers, an important part of cancer therapy includes prescription of medications and/or supplements that decrease inflammation and oxidation. Any preventive measures that reduce inflammation and oxidation, such as feeding natural diets and using nutritional supplements, may also help reduce the incidence of cancer in your pet.

The battle against cancer is often won or lost at this microscopic stage; if the pet's immune system is functioning well, it can identify and eliminate these altered cancer cells. Most cells are programmed to live for a limited period of time, but this is not always true with cancer cells. For example, studies have shown that a gene called Apaf-1 that causes cell death (a normal aging process called *apoptosis*) is inactivated in cancer, allowing the cells to live, reproduce, spread, and eventually kill the patient.

With a healthy immune system, cancer cells are killed at this early stage before they start growing and begin spreading, also known as metastasizing, throughout the body. However, sometimes the immune system, for reasons not always apparent, fails to wipe out these abnormal cells. If the abnormal cells are allowed to continue dividing, they may develop into small cancerous lumps that create tumors, which may be located anywhere in the body.

Cancers of the blood cells may prevent the bone marrow from developing normal cells, predisposing the body to infection, anemia, and blood-clotting problems. For cancerous cells that form solid tumors, the most obvious tumors appear in the skin, on the surface of the skin, or just under the skin. Cancer may also take the form of ulcers or nonhealing sores or red spots anywhere on the pet's body.

THE DEVELOPMENT OF CANCER

(Adapted from *New Developments in Phytoprevention and Treatment of Cancer*, Russell Blaylock, MD, Annual Conference of the American Nutraceutical Association, 2000.)

	Repeated Damage (a)		Abnormal Messages to Cell (b)	
Cell with Protooncogenes	⟶	Oncogenes	⟶	Cancer cell

a. Protooncogenes, which cause cell division in normal cells, may be damaged by repeated exposure to oxidizing agents (reactive oxygen and nitrogen molecules). This repeated damage causes DNA breaks in the protooncogenes, which transforms them into oncogenes.

b.   Oncogenes send abnormal messages to the cell, transforming it into a cancer cell.

These abnormal messages produce various hormones and enzymes in high quantities that:

1.   Prevent normal cell death (apoptosis), allowing the cancer cell to live indefinitely.
2.   Suppress the immune system (by stimulating LOX and COX enzymes, which increase the production of inflammatory and immune-suppressing chemicals such as PGE [prostaglandin E]).
3.   Allow the cancer cell to spread (metastasize) through the production of chemicals such as MMP-9, which destroy surrounding collagen and prevent normal cell-to-cell communication (normal cells don't grow and spread uncontrollably due to cell-to-cell communication).
4.   Replace fatty acids in the normal cell membranes with cholesterol, which prevents the cells from being attacked by the immune system (the immune system forms free radicals to attack the fatty acid components of cell membranes, but these free radicals are not effective at attacking cholesterol).
5.   Allow the cancer cells to produce their own blood supply (angiogenesis) via the formation of vascular

endothelial growth factor so they can grow and spread.

6. Allow the mutation of the p52 suppressor gene, which normally slows down cell growth and cell division, so that damaged DNA can be repaired or the cell can die if repair is not possible; when the gene mutates, it can't function properly and the cancer cell lives forever.

While we can't identify the cause of every cancer, there are certain predisposing factors for some types of cancer. For example, some types of tissues may be susceptible to certain cancers. Pale skin is susceptible because it has no pigment to protect it from sun damage. Heavy exposure to the sun in dogs with minimal hair coat or pale skin may result in ulcers and sores with subsequent inflammation that can lead to skin cancer.

Lymph nodes and reproductive organs are at greater risk of developing cancer because they have cells that are constantly growing and reproducing. The lymph nodes have follicles that make new white blood cells called lymphocytes. The reproductive organs of intact dogs are metabolically active, especially during the heat cycle in females. After a dog is spayed or neutered, the hormones that may predispose the dog to breast cancer, testicular cancer, or perianal tumors are no longer present in large amounts, which decreases the chance of reproductive cancers. Dogs that are spayed and neutered early in life (prior to the first heat period in females, which usually occurs around six months of age in most dogs, and prior to six months of age in males) rarely if ever have genital cancer, although neutering does not protect male dogs against prostate cancer.

Smoking predisposes people to lung cancer and cancer of the oral cavity. While few studies have been performed, there is a suggested link between secondhand smoking and lung cancer in cats, but not in dogs.

Cancer can also develop after infection by certain viruses, called retroviruses. These viruses enter the body and cause mutations in the DNA of susceptible cells. For example, the feline leukemia virus (FeLV) creates mutations in the white blood cells (lymphocytes) of cats that cause lymphoma. Also, exposure to feline immunodeficiency virus (FIV) may lead to oral cancer in cats. To date, there are no reports of similar viruses in dogs.

Environmental toxins may also damage DNA and cause cancer. Dogs exposed to the common weed killer 2,4-D have been shown to be at increased risk for lymphoma. This chemical is considered highly carcinogenic for dogs and should be avoided completely. Check the label if you are purchasing weed killer and avoid this product. Ask your gardener not to use it on your property. Scottish terriers exposed to pesticides also have an increased incidence of bladder cancer.

HOW CANCER KILLS

Cancer kills in one of several ways. First, locally aggressive cancers can cause large, infected, disfiguring wounds and sores. Depending upon the tumor's location in or on the body, an owner may elect euthanasia due to the poor quality of life the pet experiences as a result of severe local disease.

Second, cancer may cause secondary (paraneoplastic) syndromes that cause illness or death in the pet. For example, some cancers, such as anal sac tumors, may cause the pet's blood calcium levels to become dangerously high, which are not compatible with life.

Third, cancer often kills (or leads to euthanasia of the pet) as a result of the primary tumor spreading to other parts of the body. For example, a tumor may spread to the pet's brain, causing seizures or even death. Many cancers spread to the lungs, which causes difficulty in breathing and respiratory arrest. In order for cancer to spread, the tumor must develop its own blood supply (a process called *angiogenesis*) and destroy surrounding tissue. It does this using a variety of enzymes, including some called metalloproteinases. Current research is focused on finding new drugs to decrease or stop angiogenesis and inhibit metalloproteinase enzymes; one drug that is often used in pets to try to inhibit the development of the blood supply for the cancer and the spread of the cancer is the antibiotic doxycycline.

Fourth, cancer kills by using the pet's nutrition for itself, literally starving the patient.

It is crucially important to have early diagnosis and aggressive treatment in order to minimize the spread and side effects than can occur with cancer.

TYPES OF CANCER

The veterinarian who initially examines a dog with cancer often determines the fate of that dog. Therefore, it is important that pet owners have a basic understanding of veterinary cancer medicine in order to influence that fate. Up to one-half of the senior dogs in a veterinary practice will die of cancer. There are many types of cancer, and it is beyond the scope of this book to discuss all of them. In this chapter we will discuss some of the most common types of cancer and present sample treatment strategies, called protocols. (There are many treatment protocols, so if your doctor's recommendations vary from those presented here, that's okay.) If your dog's cancer is not included in this book, do not worry. The general principles of the conventional therapies discussed in chapter 5 apply to most cancers. The complementary therapies discussed in chapters 6 and 7 apply to the pet with any type of cancer.

Pet owners who understand cancer will appreciate the value of an early cancer diagnosis and will seek more options for treatment to obtain a longer-term survival and better quality of life for their pets. There is usually a period of time between the diagnosis of cancer and death or euthanasia. It's important for pet owners to understand that cancer is usually more treatable, and occasionally curable, when diagnosed early.

COMMON SKIN TUMORS IN DOGS

Skin tumors are usually obvious and easily seen or felt by pet owners. All skin tumors require fine needle aspiration (FNA) cytology for diagnosis, which answers the questions all owners ask: "What is this lump?" "Is this lump a problem for my dog?" "Should it be removed?" Fine needle aspiration is easily performed on most awake dogs with a tiny needle and syringe; minimal discomfort is involved.

If blood is aspirated during FNA from a skin tumor without a history of trauma, the tumor should be removed for histopathologic examination to identify common tumors such as hemangiomas, hemangiopericytomas, or hemangiosarcomas. If the skin mass is firm or fixed and cells are not loose enough to aspirate, to obtain representative cells, the doctor can use a larger needle in an attempt to pull out more cells that can then be examined microscopically. If no cells are obtained during aspiration, then a surgical biopsy is the next step. The veterinarian may recommend a sedative or short-acting anesthetic for this type of biopsy procedure to reduce pain and stress for the patient.

Lipomas

Lipomas are benign (noncancerous) fatty tumors and are the most common soft skin tumor in dogs. They are soft and very easy to confirm by fine needle aspiration (FNA). Surgery is not needed for most lipomas unless the lipoma enlarges so much as to interfere with the mobility or comfort of your pet, or is unpleasant to look at (large ones can be removed for cosmetic reasons).

Papillomas

Papillomas (warts) are firm, and smaller than lipomas; a pet can have one or multiple papillomas. They may appear in puppies as tufts of pink cauliflower-like tissue growing on the lips and in the mouth. In puppies but not older dogs, these lesions are viral in nature and usually disappear in a couple of months as the puppy's immune system matures. Warts and singular papillomas are found on the skin of older dogs and are easy to identify visually. If necessary, the diagnosis of papillomas can be confirmed with FNA cytology or surgical biopsy. If they are small (less than 2–3 mm) and look like mushrooms on a stalk or just fingerlike, they are typically nothing to worry about. However, if they grow in size or ulcerate, they should be removed and biopsied to make sure they are not cancerous, such as mast cell tumors. If they are black and are growing on the eyelids or lips, they should be removed and biopsied to rule out the possibility of malignant melanoma.

Melanomas

Melanomas are common skin tumors. They are usually pigmented and appear as black tumors on the skin. While melanomas are often feared in people because they can be deadly if malignant, many of them are benign in dogs. In general, they account for approximately 5–7 percent of all skin tumors in dogs. As is true with most tumors, melanomas are most common in older dogs (the average age is nine years). Most melanomas that occur in miniature schnauzers and Doberman pinschers are benign; most melanomas that occur in miniature poodles are malignant.

In general, benign tumors are smaller than malignant tumors, and are well defined and deeply pigmented. More than 85 percent of melanomas in dogs that occur on haired skin are benign; most of the melanomas that appear in the oral cavity and one-third of melanomas that occur on the nails are malignant (for more discussion of oral melanomas, see pages 38–42 in this chapter).

Treatment is usually surgical. Surgical removal of small benign melanomas, especially those arising from the haired skin (regardless of microscopic grade), is curative. The prognosis for pets with malignant melanoma arising from the mouth, digits, and eye is guarded due to the high incidence of metastasis, and cure is unlikely. However, control of the visible tumor may be possible by using injections of chemotherapy (cisplatin) into the tumor, or the use of photodynamic therapy, local hyperthermia, or local radiation. These approaches give immediate and long-term relief of symptoms of the mass. Systemic chemotherapy is helpful in delaying the growth of metastatic tumor sites and in relieving symptoms caused by metastases, but newer approaches (such as vaccines against tumor cells) continue to be investigated as veterinarians seek to find ways to extend the lives of pets with malignant melanomas.

Squamous cell carcinoma (SCC) is another malignant skin cancer. It is most commonly seen as a result of sun damage, especially to light-skinned pets or the lighter skinned areas (such as nose, ears) of any pet. The lesion resembles a raw ulcer or nonhealing sore. This cancer rarely spreads until later in the course of the disease, but it can be locally aggressive. Early diagnosis and surgical removal, when possible, is important. Responses to radiation therapy are very good for those lesions where removal is incomplete or not possible.

Cutaneous hemangiosarcoma is also seen in light-skinned dogs; breeds commonly affected include boxers, whippets, Italian greyhounds, Harlequin Great Danes, and beagles. This tumor often looks like a blood blister. A benign form called hemangioma is also seen; biopsy is needed to tell the difference.

Minimizing sun exposure and using sunscreen on the skin can help prevent skin cancer in dogs.

MISCELLANEOUS BENIGN SKIN TUMORS

Other common nonmalignant skin tumors are the wax gland cyst (adenoma), basal cell tumor, and hair follicle tumor. Occasionally, these common benign tumors can become cancerous and must be surgically removed, but they generally have a good prognosis for cure once removed.

> *All dogs with skin tumors should have a fine needle aspirate (FNA) for cytological evaluation. It is impossible to diagnose a tumor by look or feel.*

While many skin tumors in dogs are benign lipomas or cysts, occasionally a fine needle aspirate will be inconclusive or suggest a cancerous tumor. In these cases, the next step is to remove the mass and submit it for a biopsy. Once a diagnosis is made, proper recommendations for treatment and supportive care can be suggested.

While many skin lumps are simply benign cysts, fatty tumors, or warts, sometimes they are very malignant tumors. Mast cell tumors, which arise from tissue mast cells, are the most common fatal skin cancer in dogs. (Mast cells are normally present in all tissues of the body and function in allergic reactions.) The exact cause of mast cell tumors is unknown, but heredity may play a role. Like other cancers, mast cell tumors can occur at sites of previous inflammation. Mast cell tumors are known as "the great imitators" because their appearance mimics fatty tumors (lipomas) and other benign lesions. While many dogs can be cured if diagnosed and treated early, the ability of mast cell tumors to resemble other benign skin lesions means that often these dangerous tumors are not diagnosed until later in the disease, which usually means a worse prognosis for the pet.

> *Mast cell tumors can look and feel just like any other tumor.*

Boxers and bulldogs are at greater risk than other breeds. In dogs, the mean age for mast cell tumors to appear is eight years, although they can occur in dogs of all ages and have been reported in animals less than one year of age. There is no known sex predisposition to developing mast cell tumors in dogs, although in cats, males may be more commonly affected than females.

Mast cells can release chemicals from storage granules located inside the mast cells. One such chemical is histamine, which causes inflammation and itching. One in three pets that have mast cell cancer may have ulcers in the gastrointestinal tract that develop from histamine release. These ulcers cause mild to severe bleeding; occasionally, severe bleeding from a gastrointestinal ulcer causes an emergency and fatality. Other chemicals that can be released by mast cells have a heparin-like action and cause local bleeding if the tumors are scratched by the pet. Certain factors, even a change in temperature, can cause the mast cells to release their chemicals.

The behavior of mast cell tumors is variable; some are rapidly fatal and others are benign. While a mast cell tumor normally occurs as an isolated tumor of the skin or subcutaneous tissue, sometimes multiple tumors involving all the skin are seen.

> *Half of all mast cell tumors are malignant;*
> *up to 50 percent recur after surgical removal.*

Surgery often cures small mast cell tumors when diagnosed early. If the surgical margins are clean with adequate borders, and the tumor is a Grade I (low-grade malignancy) mast cell tumor, a cure is usually expected. If cancer cells are still seen at the surgical margins, the pet will need a second surgery, radiation therapy, or both to kill the remaining cancer cells.

If the mast cell tumor appears in the armpit area (axilla), mammary tissue, groin, perineum, genitals, or in the lips, anus, eyelids, or body openings, it is more likely to be malignant.

In addition to surgery for malignant mast cell tumors, radiation therapy and local injections of corticosteroids may be recommended. Also helpful in some cases is chemotherapy, using prednisone or prednisolone, vinblastine or vincristine, chlorambucil, and cimetidine (Tagamet).

Radiation may be helpful for a patient with a skin tumor in a location that does not allow aggressive surgical removal.

Mast cell tumors located on an extremity respond better to radiation therapy than do tumors located on the trunk.

Early diagnosis and aggressive treatment are most effective against this common cancer. A patient who has had more than one cutaneous mast cell tumor is predisposed to developing new mast cell tumors.

SOFT TISSUE TUMORS (SARCOMAS)

Soft tissue tumors arise from the fiber-producing cells, which are wrapped around nerve endings, blood vessels, and muscle along the skin and deeper tissues of the foreleg. Examples of soft tissue sarcomas include neurofibromas, neurofibrosarcomas, schwannomas, hemangiosarcomas, angiosarcomas, hemangiopericytomas, liposarcomas, and fibromas/fibrosarcomas (the suffix "oma" implies a benign tumor, whereas the suffix "sarcoma" implies a malignant tumor). In general, they are tumors with long "tentacles" that wrap around tissues, making complete surgical removal rare. They are very slow-growing tumors with spread (metastasis) uncommon to rare. Without additional treatment following surgical removal, it is common for tumors to reappear over a period of nine to eighteen months. To prevent this, one option is to consider a wider and deeper surgery to remove additional tissue layers that surround the tumor site (for tumors on the limbs, amputation may be the best option). When this is not possible or appropriate, another option is radiation therapy. The chance of tumor regrowth following surgical removal (complete or incomplete) and radiation therapy is less than 10 percent during the pet's remaining lifetime, and complication rates are low. When tumors regrow or cannot be reduced by surgical or radiation measures, other alternatives include chemotherapy (carboplatin or 5-fluorouracil) or an immune stimulant (Regressin) injected directly into the tumor mass. These will not cure the tumor but could significantly delay the harm the tumor may cause to the surrounding tissues.

Other alternatives that are not best for cancer cure but provide cancer control and prevent regrowth of microscopic cancer include low-dose medications such as antibiotics (doxycycline, once daily) and pain relief medications (piroxicam, daily or every other day) that inhibit the growth of blood vessels around cancer sites and improve an immune response.

> *Soft tissue tumors can be benign*
> *or highly malignant cancers.*

The cause of soft tissue tumors is usually unknown, although some sarcomas have been associated with radiation, tissue trauma, and the esophageal parasite *Spirocieca lupi*. There is no breed or sex predisposition (except for synovial sarcomas, which affect the synovial membranes lining joints, which occur more often in males). Most tumors are reported in large breed older dogs (although rhadbomyosarcoma, a cancer of the skeletal muscle tissue, has been reported in dogs as young as four months of age).

As a group, soft tissue sarcomas share certain characteristics:

- They occur anywhere in the body.
- While they appear encapsulated, in fact they have poorly defined margins. It is very common for them to infiltrate surrounding tissues as they send out "tentacles" of cancerous cells. This means that surgical removal must be aggressive and take extra tissue around the tumor site because these tumors will grow

back aggressively. It is very difficult to remove all of the tumor in most cases.

- When they spread, these tumors usually do so via the bloodstream rather than lymph nodes.
- Local recurrence is quite common.
- Death usually results from side effects of the local tumor rather than spread of the tumor.
- Chemotherapy and radiation can be used to provide significant delay in tumor growth (or regrowth).
- Diagnosis of the exact tissue type is often difficult even with microscopic analysis. Often the diagnosis is simply "soft tissue sarcoma."

Aggressive surgery is the main treatment recommended for these tumors, whenever possible. Using preoperative imaging techniques, such as an MRI scan, will help define the true extent of the tumor and aid the surgeon in its complete removal. Often, limb amputation is necessary for tumors occurring on the legs in order to assure total tumor removal.

The glycoprotein acemannan (see pages 194–196 in chapter 7) has been used in some cases of fibrosarcoma. Early studies offered hope that this natural therapy would be a useful tool in treating fibrosarcoma. However, currently most cancer specialists do not feel that acemannan is as helpful as the early studies suggested. If your pet has a fibrosarcoma, I suggest talking with an oncologist to see if acemannan might be a useful adjunctive therapy in your pet's treatment.

Keep in mind that even benign tumors can harm or even kill your pet. Even though benign tumors typically do not spread, any tumor can grow large enough to result in disability or even death to the pet.

BREAST TUMORS IN DOGS
(MAMMARY ADENOMAS, ADENOCARCINOMAS)

Breast cancer is one of the few cancers that is almost totally preventable. Almost 100 percent of female puppies spayed before their first heat cycle (which occurs, on average, at six months of age) will never develop breast cancer. Intact female dogs are highly prone to developing breast tumors. In women, one out of seven will develop breast cancer; for female dogs that are not spayed the incidence is much higher: one out of four will develop one or more breast tumors.

> *Breast cancer in female dogs is preventable.*

Unfortunately, half of all breast tumors in dogs are malignant, and half of those cancers will kill the dog by spreading to the lungs within one year. Hormones (estrogen, progesterone) produced by the ovaries during the dog's six-month reproductive cycles cause a harmful sensitization (programming) of the breast tissue cells. This hormonal influence ultimately causes point mutations in the genes of the breast tissue cells that dictate tumor growth. A female dog may develop tumors in any one of her ten mammary glands. While fine needle aspiration of tumors can easily diagnose many types of cancer, this is not always the case for breast tumors. Often, only red or white blood cells, indicating the formation of inflammation or infection within the tumor, are aspirated with a small needle and syringe.

However, it is still wise to test the aspirate to rule out other causes for the breast lump (such as fatty tumor, mast cell tumor) before assuming the lump is a breast tumor.

> *Half of all breast tumors in female dogs are malignant.*

If cancer is suspected based upon the aspirate of the mass, at least three radiographic views should be made of the chest to see if the cancer has already spread to the lungs before scheduling surgery.

All breast tumors should be promptly removed and biopsied. If the dog is not spayed, this should also be done. Whenever possible with breast cancer, a more aggressive surgery is preferred over the conservative procedure of lumpectomy. This ensures that the entire tumor is removed with a normal gland above and below the mass.

WHICH SURGERY IS BEST: LUMPECTOMY OR RADICAL MASTECTOMY?

In women with breast cancer, there is often a choice of removing just the tumor (a lumpectomy) or removing the entire breast and surrounding tissue, including the regional lymph nodes (a radical mastectomy). In dogs with suspected malignant breast cancer, a more aggressive surgery rather than a simple lumpectomy is usually recommended.

Because about half of all breast tumors in dogs are malignant, it is probably better if surgery is planned to completely remove the mass along with at least some normal surrounding tissue. This more aggressive approach ensures that the entire tumor is removed and may avoid the need for a second surgery. If there are multiple tumors in one gland, the surgery should include the removal of a normal gland above and below the mass to ensure complete removal of all of the cancer. Since all the breast tissue in intact females is pre-programmed to make tumors, it is better to remove the tumor and the surrounding breast tissue, which already may have been infiltrated by cancer cells.

If the biopsy report indicates that a malignant tumor has invaded the lymph system, or if the surgical margins contain cancerous cells (also known as "dirty margin"), a second surgery may be needed.

Surgery plus intraoperative radiation or follow-up radiation therapy may help reduce local recurrence. Radiation therapy is the second most commonly used treatment for breast cancer in women who have had surgery to remove the primary mass. In animals, radiation therapy is less commonly used.

Treatment with chemotherapy may reduce the ability of the circulating cancer cells to establish colonies in the lungs.

In women, the drug tamoxifen is often recommended as part of the therapy for breast cancer. The drug shows some potential for use in dogs as well.

In the past, the drug Adriamycin was commonly used to prevent metastases from malignant breast cancer. However, many oncologists now prefer to use mitoxantrone as a first-line drug and then Adriamycin or carboplatin for resistant disease. These drugs are usually given every twenty-one to thirty days in four to six treatments, then every six weeks in four to six treatments depending on the severity of the malignancy.

In women, the drug tamoxifen is often recommended as part of the therapy for breast cancer. The drug shows some potential for use in dogs as well. A more thorough discussion of tamoxifen can be found on pages 87–88 in chapter 5.

BONE CANCER: OSTEOSARCOMA (OSA)

Bone cancer is among the most common cancers seen by veterinarians. While any dog can get bone cancer, OSA more frequently occurs in large and giant breeds; dogs weighing more than 75 pounds are at a greater risk to develop bone tumors than dogs weighing less than 75 pounds.

> *Dogs that weigh more than 75 pounds were found to be at sixty-one to one hundred eighty-five times greater risk of developing skeletal tumors than dogs weighing less than 75 pounds.*

Most primary bone tumors are found in the appendicular skeleton (legs and arms) and first appear as swollen areas, with or without pain. The most common sites for bone cancer are at the far end of the radius bone above the wrist in the front legs or just above or below the knee in the rear legs. Other bone tumors are found in the flat bones such as the scapula, sinuses, skull, face, pelvis, vertebrae, and ribs.

In dogs, 70–85 percent of bone tumors are osteosarcoma (OSA). Other types of bone tumors include chondrosarcoma, fibrosarcomas, giant cell tumors, hemangiosarcomas, liposarcomas, and multicentric or myelogenous tumors.

The cause of bone cancer is not entirely known. One study in purebred rottweilers showed that the risk of OSA was 65 percent greater for neutered males and 34 percent greater for spayed females. The risk was greater in dogs spayed or neutered before one year of age. It is not clear what, if any, impact spaying or neutering has on the development of OSA. This does not mean that dogs should not be spayed and neutered. Early spaying can almost totally eliminate breast cancer, and early neutering prevents testicular cancer and reduces the incidence of some types of perianal tumors. More research needs to be done in this area before current recommendations for early spaying and neutering are changed.

The cause of bone cancer is not entirely known.

ARTHRITIS OR BONE CANCER?

While most dogs with arthritis show signs of lameness or limping, not all dogs that limp have arthritis. It is far too common for a limping dog to be initially treated with a non-steroidal anti-inflammatory drugs (NSAIDs, such as Rimadyl, EtoGesic, or Metacam), not improve, and then be shown to have bone cancer weeks to months later, and often late in the course of the disease.

Large breed dogs that limp need radiographs (X-rays) to confirm that they have arthritis *before* they are prescribed NSAIDs or joint supplements for long-term therapy. NSAIDs are helpful in cases of arthritis; unfortunately, they may hide aggressive bone cancer. It is easy to assume a diagnosis of arthritis in older pets, but it is best to know what type of orthopedic condition is afflicting your pet. While it's okay to treat lameness with NSAIDs for a week or so, be sure to quickly follow-up with your veterinarian if the lameness is not resolved. Many cases of bone cancer have a delayed diagnosis and worsened prognosis due to the excellent pain control afforded by the new powerful NSAIDs. Any delay in the diagnosis of bone cancer in a pet hurts that pet's chances for successful treatment.

Sadly, some dogs are diagnosed with bone cancer only after the affected leg breaks (also called a pathological fracture). The fractured leg cannot be repaired because it won't heal due to the bone cancer.

The radiographic appearance of bone cancer, as seen on X-ray film, is fairly characteristic. Usually a diagnosis is based on the pet's medical history, a physical examination, and radiographic findings. Very rarely, bacterial or fungal infection (osteomyelitis) can appear to be bone cancer in X-rays. In areas of the country where fungal disease is common, blood tests are recommended to rule out a fungus as the cause of lameness. In areas where fungal disease is rare, OSA is the cause approximately 99 percent or more of the time when bones appear moth-eaten.

Without treatment, osteosarcoma usually kills dogs within four to six months from diagnosis, usually by spreading to the lungs or by growing in the bone and causing uncontrollable pain or bone fracture. Dogs don't limp until pain is present; this may not occur until the cancer has been present for some time, and some dogs with bone cancer never appear to be in pain.

Whenever bone cancer is suspected, three radiographic views of the lungs should be taken to see if the cancer has already spread there. If it has, the prognosis is poor in most cases and life expectancy at this stage is from one to three months. If no cancer is seen in the lungs, the prognosis is better. However, in most cases, even if the lungs don't show signs of cancer at this stage, we know that it is probably present in the lungs in a microscopic form due to the aggressive nature of OSA.

*Without treatment, osteosarcoma usually kills
dogs by within four to six months from diagnosis,
usually by spreading to the lungs.*

While OSA is the most common bone cancer, other cancers may occur, such as tumors of the cartilage called chondrosarcomas. These are much less common and are less likely to be fatal.

With the exception of chondrosarcoma, all bone or non-bone-forming tumors appearing in the leg of a dog (regardless of size of tumor, intensity of pain, and duration of symptoms) usually grow rapidly, destroy the bone structure, and spread to many other body locations, resulting in loss of appetite and weight, breathing difficulty, or pain. These symptoms can become life threatening within three to six months of confirmed diagnosis.

DIAGNOSING BONE CANCER:
IS A BIOPSY NECESSARY?

With most solid tumors, a biopsy is needed to determine the type of tumor and whether or not the tumor is cancerous. However, bone cancer is a rare exception to the need for biopsy in most cases. Most oncologists believe that there are few reasons to do a bone biopsy in order to diagnose osteosarcoma. Usually, clinical signs, history, and the appearance of a lesion in radiographs is sufficient to diagnose OSA. Additionally, the biopsy of a bone tumor often does not contain cancer cells but may only show "reactive bone." In these cases the dog has gone through a surgery that may have weakened and fractured the bone without a definitive diagnosis. If no cancer cells are found, the diagnosis is still in doubt.

Even when the biopsy comes back positive for bone cancer, this only confirms the initial diagnosis without gaining anything for the pet.

However, whether to biopsy suspicious bone lesions is an individual decision that must be made by the owner after consultation with the oncologist. If there is any question about the nature of the lesion in the bone, a biopsy may be necessary, but it is important to appreciate the limitations in diagnosing bone cancer.

The best plan for a pet with bone cancer is to manage leg pain and prevent or delay tumor spread to other body sites. The best options for pain relief include medications (such as Rimadyl, EtoGesic, piroxicam, Deramaxx, Metacam, Tramadol, Fentanyl patches on the skin, or combinations of these), radiation to the bone site (every one to two weeks for a duration of six weeks), the use of monthly biphosphonates (injectable Pamidronate, which diffuses and inhibits pain in many bone sites), or amputation of the leg. The best approach for overall survival is amputation, but the other measures can allow the pet to use the leg for several months to possibly one year during chemotherapy.

If chemotherapy is chosen for treating osteosarcoma, the best plan for improving quality of life for as much time as possible is to induce control of the cancer (using high-dose chemotherapy such as Adriamycin every two weeks for five treatments) and maintain control of the cancer, or keep it dormant (using oral medications regularly for life). This cancer cannot be cured, but chemotherapy following amputation can provide for up to 60 percent of pets a full year of life and for up to 40 percent two years of life. In general, oral maintenance drugs (daily doxycycline, piroxicam, Tagamet; weekly Cytoxan) are safe and provide immune support and prevent cancer growth and spread. In some pets, the use of a nutritional supplement called Artemisinin may control cancer growth and spread (for more information, see pages 142–144 in chapter 6).

In general, the recommended treatment for all bone tumors is amputation of the affected leg followed by chemotherapy. Limb-sparing surgery may be considered in some cases as an alternative treatment. Limb sparing is a procedure that saves the cancerous leg by removing the diseased bone and replacing it with a cadaver bone from a donor dog bone bank. The procedure, which was pioneered at Colorado State University Veterinary School, is performed in specialized clinics around the country. The best candidates for limb sparing are dogs with small lesions in the far end of the radius or ulna. The wrist joint is then fused.

Polymer sponges (OPLA sponges) containing cisplatin are placed around the bone to deliver the chemotherapy. Additional chemotherapy might be used later if needed. While limb sparing is an alternative to amputation for some pets, it is not without its drawbacks: dogs that undergo this procedure show an infection rate of 44 percent, with a local recurrence rate for cancer of 25 percent.

When OSA is diagnosed late in the course of the disease, and the cancer has already spread to the lungs, very few remissions are obtained with chemotherapy. If only a few tumors are found in the lungs, removal of a lung lobe (lobectomy) may extend a pet's life; in some cases, life may be extended by one to two years for those pets undergoing lung lobectomy and chemotherapy, according to Dr. Steve Withrow at Colorado State

University Veterinary School. In cases where many lung tumors are seen, treatment for these pets consists of palliative therapy to keep the pet comfortable and supplements to boost the immune system and improve appetite and attitude.

Dogs with OSA should have chest radiographs (X-rays) taken every two to four months to allow early detection of the spread of the cancer to the lungs.

HEMANGIOSARCOMA (HSA)

Hemangiosarcoma is a common soft tissue tumor (sarcoma) of the support tissues that surround blood vessels. It commonly arises from the spleen or liver. Other organs that are less frequently affected with HSA include the heart, skin, subcutaneous tissue, and muscle tissues. The cancerous cells invade the endothelial cells lining the walls of the blood vessels in the spleen and liver. Because blood vessels exist in every tissue, HSA has been found as a primary tumor in most tissues.

> *Most hemangiosarcomas involve the spleen or liver.*

While several benign splenic conditions occur in dogs (hemangiomas, hyperplastic nodules), the most serious tumor is the malignant hemangiosarcoma, which makes up 2 percent of all tumors in dogs. Most splenic tumors occur in middle-aged to older larger breeds of dogs. The average age of affected dogs is eight to ten years. The medical literature shows a possible male sex predisposition.

Many of the warning signs of HSA of the spleen and liver in dogs are easy to overlook. Affected pets may show only reduced activity and energy, have pale gums (due to anemia), or an enlarged abdomen, but some may suddenly collapse due to shock from rupture of the affected organ. Other warning signs, not specific for HSA, include weight loss, weakness, lameness, seizures, dementia, and paralysis.

There is no known cause for hemangiosarcoma, but genetic factors are suggested by its presence in certain breeds. Hemangiosarcomas in people have been linked to exposure to arsenical chemicals, vinyl chloride, and thorium dioxide; methyl nitrosamine has been implicated in these types of tumors in minks.

> *There is no known cause for hemangiosarcoma, but genetic factors are suggested by its presence in certain breeds.*

Early diagnosis of HSA can be made with regular X-rays or ultrasound examinations of the chest and abdomen. Owners of large breed older dogs should consider having these procedures done every six months after six or seven years of age as part of an annual geriatric evaluation. Diagnosis is also made using blood tests.

Typically, hemangiosarcoma is a cancer that rapidly spreads throughout the body, and without treatment beyond surgical removal it can cause significant harm to other body sites such as the kidneys, liver, lungs, or other organs within two to four months. For those pets with a confirmed diagnosis of hemangiosarcoma, chemotherapy on a regular basis following surgery can extend a pet's good quality of life for nine to eighteen months. Regrettably, there are few treatments that effectively reverse this condition, so the best approach is to prevent further harm from tumor growth or spread through a combination of chemotherapy and other agents to keep the disease dormant for as long as possible.

As with the management of other high-grade malignancies,

such as osteosarcoma, our best approach to HSA is to use a cycle of anticancer drugs, beginning with Adriamycin every two weeks for up to five times, followed by a monthly combination of oral medications to keep the cancer from doing additional harm. Oral medications include a combination of doxycycline (an antibiotic that inhibits cancer cell growth, cancer cell spread, and may improve the action of some chemotherapy agents), Cytoxan (chemotherapy taken once a week), piroxicam (a daily pain relief medication that helps the immune system contain cancer), and Tagamet (a daily antacid to protect the stomach). Nontraditional approaches might include use of nutritional substances to minimize vessel injury, or bleeding, and inflammation.

The first step is surgery to remove the tumor (spleen, liver lobe), which usually provides dramatic results. Unless performed as a lifesaving emergency procedure, surgery should be postponed until an ultrasound examination is done to see if there are lesions in the organs of the chest and abdomen, in order to determine a prognosis. Liver surgery to remove tumors confined to one or two lobes of the liver can be performed. However, if the entire liver is cancerous, surgery should not be performed.

BLADDER CANCER

While bloody urine in dogs most commonly indicates the presence of bladder stones, occasionally it is a symptom of bladder cancer. Most bladder tumors are transitional cell carcinomas (TCC). Benign tumors or other bladder lesions are rare and are commonly associated with chronic urinary tract disease.

Older dogs are more likely to develop bladder cancer than younger dogs, and female dogs may be at greater risk for bladder tumors, possibly because they urinate less frequently, which may increase exposure to carcinogens in urine. Bladder cancer is more commonly found in smaller female dogs that weigh 22 pounds or less. Male dogs may be at greater risk for urethral tumors, due to prostatic urethral irritation that is secondary to prostatitis in intact dogs.

Beagles have a predisposition for developing TCC in the urethra and in the prostatic urethra, which has tiny openings that pass into the prostate. Shetland sheepdogs (Shelties), Scottish terriers, and Airedales are reported to be at higher risk for TCC than other breeds. Insecticidal dips (more than two times per year), exposure to insecticidal sprays for mosquitoes in marshland environments or to cyclophosphamide, and obesity are associated with development of bladder tumors, especially in Scottish terriers.

Pets with bladder cancer are rarely cured and always treated with palliatives. Very rarely, complete remissions are achieved.

Transitional cell carcinomas usually affect the neck of the bladder in the area called the trigone. Because both ureters from the kidneys empty urine into the bladder in the trigone area, it is easy to see why tumors in this location are usually inoperable, but tumors located in the upper part of the bladder are usually more easily removed by surgery.

> *Pets with bladder cancer are rarely cured.*

Clinical signs of bladder cancer include straining while trying to urinate, blood in the urine (hematuria), urinary incontinence, and recurrent urinary infections.

Persistent blood in the urine should always be investigated with ultrasound, cystoscopy, and fine needle aspiration for cytology. A diagnosis can be confirmed in more than 90 percent of cases through aspiration cytology with minimal risk of tumor seeding, and is preferred to urethral washes or urine sediment cytology.

> *Pets that have recurrent urinary infections*
> *should be screened for bladder cancer.*

Spread of cancer (metastasis) has occurred in more than half of dogs at the time of diagnosis; the lumbar vertebrae, pelvis, and regional lymph nodes are common sites of cancer spread, but complications arising from metastatic sites are uncommon and late in onset. Abdominal ultrasonography and thoracic radiography should be performed to check for metastasis. If not treated, complications from urinary tract obstruction and/or metastases (usually to regional lymph nodes) often occurs within three to six months of presentation.

CAN WE SCREEN DOGS FOR BLADDER CANCER?

The makers of a tumor antigen test called V-BTA originally claimed their product could diagnose TCC in its early stages. Unfortunately, blood in the urine causes false positives, and because bloody urine is the chief symptom in TCC, the test has limitations. Most doctors do not feel this test has any merit or usefulness in diagnosing bladder cancer.

Traditional chemotherapy is unrewarding given the slow, chronic, progressive nature of TCCs. However, alternative chemotherapy treatments — such as mitoxantrone, cisplatin, carboplatin, doxorubicin, and piroxicam — show promise. It is reported that lives have been extended after treatment with cisplatin, carboplatin, or doxorubicin, with median survival time of

37

five months in a range of four to seven months. Piroxicam has shown a median survival time of six months in a range from one to twenty-four months, and mitoxantrone has shown a median survival time of nine months in a range of six to twelve months.

If severe bloody urine is seen, an infusion into the bladder of a 1 percent solution of formalin (mixed with one vial of the topical DMSO solution Synotic) may be useful; the solution is kept in the bladder for ten to fifteen minutes, and then removed.

Palliative radiation (one to three treatments) can be used for local control of bladder cancer with a median survival of nine months in most reported cases. Side effects such as fibrosis, cystitis (bladder inflammation), and stranguria (difficulty urinating) are uncommon during palliative treatments. Higher dosages usually result in complications but survival times can be significantly extended, maybe by more than two years, for dogs undergoing surgical removal of the bladder mass and palliative radiation.

An aggressive approach combining surgery, radiation, and chemotherapy is also an option for selected patients. In studies at Gulf Coast Veterinary Specialists, surgical removal of as much of the tumor as possible (called debridement) and the use of localized radiation and concurrent platinum chemotherapy has resulted in a median survival of 375 days in a preliminary clinical trial in twelve dogs.

ORAL CANCER

Cancer of the mouth, tongue, and tonsils occurs with some frequency in dogs; older pets are more commonly affected. The most common tumors of the oral cavity include melanoma (probably the most common), squamous cell carcinoma (SCC), and fibrosarcoma. Benign tumors also occur, including fibromas and epulides, a common gum tumor.

Malignant melanomas most commonly appear as dark lumps inside the mouth, usually on the lower gums. These tumors often involve the bones of the jaw as well as the gums.

> *While any type of tumor could occur in the mouth, malignant melanoma is probably the most common.*

Clinical signs of oral cancers include excessive drooling, a bad odor from the mouth, bleeding from the mouth, decreased appetite, and chewing on one side of the mouth. These are the same signs as severe dental disease (periodontal infections). Because cancer of the oral cavity can be easily mistaken for dental disease, any pet with clinical signs should be sedated or anesthetized so that a thorough oral examination can be performed. In my practice I've found that an oral tumor may not show any clinical signs and only be diagnosed during a regularly scheduled dental cleaning. *This is yet another reason your pet should have regular dental cleanings while under anesthesia at the veterinarian's office.*

Treatment of oral cancer depends upon the location of the tumor and the type of cancer. If the tumor occurs on the hard palate or soft palate, the prognosis is generally poor because the procedures to surgically remove or irradiate the mass are more complicated and may not be effective.

While melanomas in dogs have a high metastatic rate, the effects of the spread of the cancer frequently are not observed until late in the course of the disease; local tumor control is important to extend the life of the pet. Most dogs are euthanized because of progression or recurrence of local disease rather than due to the actual spread of cancer.

Surgical removal of the affected part of the lower jaw (hemimandibulectomy) and the affected part of the upper jaw (hemimaxillectomy) is curative for benign tumors such as acanthomatous epulides and may be an excellent treatment for oral fibrosarcomas and SCCs that can be completely removed. If the surgeon can remove at least 1 cm of normal tissue at all margins of the tumor, then surgery is a good choice for treatment. The further forward in the jaw the mass is located, the better the chances for wide, clean margins and cure. Aggressive surgery is the best chance for cure or longer survival times.

Surgery to "debulk" the soft tissue part of the mass is only useful for local control and not cure, because the roots of the tumor will not be removed.

Radiation therapy can be used to assist in local control if clean margins could not be obtained with surgery. Chemotherapy with carboplatin is often chosen as a follow-up treatment for cancers that have spread far from the primary site. Interferon and piroxicam may also be used.

Melanoma of the oral tissues that is malignant will rapidly spread to the regional lymph nodes along the neck and to the lungs. In general, the prognosis of melanoma is poor, but occurrence in the lip is not as certain, and some pets may survive years with surgical removal alone. However, the more common scenario for most dogs is rapid regrowth and spread. Even if the tumor is removed completely from the mouth, enlarged lymph nodes along the neck are usually found within three to six months and lung disease within six to nine months. Likewise, even after treating the oral site with radiation therapy, the cancer may shrink but inevitably spreads to the lymph nodes, lungs, and other sites. The one-year survival rate after local treatment only (surgery, radiation, or both) is 10–20 percent. When weekly chemotherapy (carboplatin) is combined with either surgical removal of the tumor or radiation therapy to the tumor site (weekly for six weeks), nearly 50 percent of treated pets survive for one year or longer and 40 percent survive two years or more.

Other approaches such as immune therapy are not as successful but still helpful. Some of these medications include doxycycline (to inhibit tumor spread and blood vessel growth) and piroxicam (to promote the immune response against the cancer). Recently, it has been found that low doses of Lomustine (CCNU) chemotherapy, administered weekly or every other week, causes melanoma of the mouth, lymph node, or lung to shrink over time. In general, the best approach to extend survival and ensure good quality of life should include the use of surgery or radiation therapy to manage the oral disease in combination with weekly carboplatin chemotherapy; all other approaches will help improve quality of life, but the prognosis beyond one year is less certain.

> *In dogs diagnosed with oral malignant melanoma, a combination of localized radiation and low-dose chemotherapy can significantly improve the prognosis.*

Cancer of the tongue in dogs is usually squamous cell carcinoma (SCC). These tongue tumors may be operable if the lesion can be removed without taking more than one-third of the length of the tongue or no more than half the width of the tongue. The submandibular nodes generally show metastases within a year following initial diagnosis. The prognosis for malignant melanoma of the tongue is similar to that for any oral location — poor. Significant palliation is usually needed for oral discomfort, ulceration, and infection within the first or second week of a weekly radiation protocol running six weeks total. Survival is also improved using carboplatin or Lomustine chemotherapy.

While cancer of the tonsils is rare in dogs, tonsillar squamous cell carcinoma is almost always fatal in dogs in about four to five months of diagnosis. Radiation therapy delivered to the tonsils and submandibular nodes two to three treatments a week can be tried. Another option is chemotherapy rotating mitoxantrone and carboplatin every twenty-one days for two hours prior to radiation therapy. Piroxicam can be given once daily with meals for pain control and as a potential anticancer agent.

LYMPHOMA (LYMPHOSARCOMA, LSA)

Cancer of the lymphatic system is a common cancer in dogs, making up approximately 7–25 percent of all dog cancers. While any dog may develop lymphoma, golden retrievers, boxers, Labrador retrievers, rottweilers, St. Bernards, Scottish terriers, Airedale terriers, bulldogs, and bassett hounds are commonly affected. Breeds with lower risk include dachshunds and Pomeranians. Lymphoma is considered a cancer of the immune system, because the lymphocyte, which is the affected cell, plays an important role in defense of the body against infections. Lymphoma can rapidly ruin the health of the internal organs and without treatment can become life threatening to the pet within four to eight weeks.

The cause of lymphoma is unknown, although there is an increased risk in dogs exposed to the herbicide 2,4-D.

While lymphoma can involve any organ in the body, most commonly the lymph nodes are affected. Owners may notice a painless enlargement of the pet's lymph nodes; fever is typically absent, and most dogs do not feel sick (unless there are other problems, such as elevated blood calcium, which is associated with lymphoma). Sometimes the affected lymph nodes will enlarge, then regress to normal size, then enlarge again.

Diagnosis is obtained by aspiration cytology of the affected organ (usually a lymph node) and biopsy.

Some dogs develop enlargement of other lymphatic organs, such as the thymus gland, spleen, or liver. Occasionally, lymphoma will affect a dog's bone marrow or central nervous system. Because the lymphatic system is located alongside the vascular system (bloodstream), lymphoma is considered a systemic or whole body disease and may strike in any location, including the skin. Surgery plays almost no role in controlling the cancer, but it does assist in the diagnosis.

There are many good options for managing lymphoma and inducing remission for as long as possible while also providing for the best quality of life. Most treatment options, or protocols, begin with the regular use of chemotherapy, which includes several anticancer medications such as Elspar (asparaginase), Adriamycin (doxorubicin), Oncovin (vincristine), Cytoxan (cyclophosphamide), and prednisone. In general, the longest period of first remission occurs after multiple drugs are used at regular intervals (every two, three, or four weeks) for six months to one year; eight in ten pets will be in remission for the full year and one in three for as long as two years.

One of the best protocols is weekly chemotherapy using a cycle of Oncovin (week 1), Cytoxan (week 2), and Adriamycin (week 3), then a week without treatment before repeating this cycle of three drugs for a duration of four to six months. With this approach it is possible to achieve a period of four to ten months of drug-free remission before relapse occurs. Another good option is a conservative monthly treatment of Oncovin and Cytoxan (given indefinitely), with Asparaginase used every three months to boost remission duration.

Monoclonal antibody therapy has been used in the past as an adjunctive therapy in dogs with lymphoma. It has not lived up to expectations, is no longer available, and is not being man-ufactured.

Radiation therapy is seldom recommended for lymphoma because palliative chemotherapy is considered the standard of care. However, an increasing number of oncology centers are recommending and using novel approaches that may include half-body irradiation (whole-body radiation is used in people but requires bone marrow transplantation). With the half-body approach, each body half (above or below the thirteenth rib) is treated four weeks apart; studies have shown that at least one in three pets with lymphoma do not relapse during a three-year observation period. Side effects may include prolonged mar-row suppression, short-term dizziness, and diarrhea. Radiation to a single node or to all nodes (total nodal radiation) has been used in drug-refractory (drug-resistant) patients as rescue pro-tocols, resulting in additional periods of remission lasting two to six months.

During chemotherapy, regular blood testing is needed to monitor for decreased white blood cell counts, also known as drug-induced myelosuppression. Ideally, the blood should be tested before each treatment. If the white cell count is too low (fewer than 3,500 cells) and if the neutrophil count (neutrophils are specific types of white blood cells that help fight infections) is below 1,800, antibiotics may be needed and the dose of the chemotherapy may need to be reduced or the treatment post-poned. Medications can be given to stimulate red and white blood cell production in pets that develop anemia or myelosuppression. In the future, similar medications may be helpful for patients who have low platelet counts as a side effect of chemotherapy.

The dosages and sequence of chemotherapy protocols for lymphoma must be personalized for each pet and depend upon the severity of disease and the status of organ function.

As previously mentioned, the steroid prednisone (or prednisolone) is often part of the chemotherapy regimen for dogs with lymphoma. Despite the fact that some holistic practitioners and owners hesitate to use steroids of any type, the benefits far outweigh the risks. The initial use of prednisone typically shrinks the cancerous lymph nodes and stimulates the pet's appetite. Some pet owners prefer not to use chemotherapy but will allow the use of prednisone as the sole conventional treatment. When only prednisone is used against lymphoma, a dog will not usually survive any longer than three months. Some oncologists feel that the use of prednisone alone for more than two weeks may predispose lymphoma patients to develop resistance to future chemotherapy. Unless you are totally opposed to any other chemotherapy treatments, it is wise to avoid prednisone as the sole therapy for your dog.

While there is no one right approach for the pet in extended remission, I personally prefer to stop chemotherapy and rely on nutritional supplements to maintain a healthy immune system. My hope is that a strong immune system will keep the pet in remission. Of course, I always discuss the pros and cons of my recommendation with the pet owner, who must make the final decision.

When a dog treated with chemotherapy comes out of remission, the decision must be made regarding further chemotherapy (so-called rescue protocols). Some owners will choose another round of chemotherapy; others will choose euthanasia at this point. Rescue protocols can induce second and even third remissions. However, the cancer cells that have survived prior chemotherapy treatments are more resistant to being killed with further chemotherapy. Usually, other medications, often more toxic, must be used for these rescue protocols. Expected survival times with rescue protocols are usually shorter than expected first remissions.

In general, a pet that is in good health with an otherwise normal physical examination and blood laboratory profile will have few side effects from chemotherapy. However, if they should occur, signs may include appetite loss, excessive salivation (nausea), vomiting, watery or bloody diarrhea, and lethargy.

Dogs with cancer such as lymphoma may have chronic pain. Butorphanol helps in these situations as an analgesic (painkiller). Piroxicam is well tolerated as an analgesic in most patients, but it can't be used if the chemotherapy protocol uses corticosteroids or side effects include gastrointestinal ulceration. Fentanyl patches may provide analgesia for up to seventy-two hours. Subcutaneous nalbuphine hydrochloride administered at 0.5–1 mg/kg every three to four hours may also be used for pain and usually doesn't cause the lethargy associated with some other analgesics.

The role of diet has been studied in dogs with lymphoma. Cancer cells don't use proteins and omega-3 fatty acids as easily as they use sugars and carbohydrates for energy. Hill's Prescription Diet Canine is a specialized diet for dogs with cancer (see pages 231–233 in chapter 8). Studies have shown increased life expectancy for dogs eating this diet when combined with conventional chemotherapy as compared to dogs eating a standard commercial dog food during conventional chemotherapy. More information on diet and cancer can be found on page 229 in chapter 8.

While this chapter has not been an exhaustive discussion of all types of cancers, its aim has been to help you develop a greater appreciation for the more common cancers that affect dogs. In the next chapter, I will discuss some of the more common diseases whose clinical signs mimic cancer.

CHAPTER THREE

NOT CANCER, *but* SOMETHING ELSE

IT'S EASY FOR OWNERS to jump to the wrong conclusion and think "cancer" whenever their pets become ill. While the frequency of cancer in pets does seem to be increasing, most ill pets do not have cancer! However, any time a pet has an illness that does not respond well to treatment within four to eight weeks, the possibility of cancer must be considered.

> *Cancer can mimic signs of other disorders such as kidney disease, inflammatory bowel disease, or urinary tract infections.*

Some common physical complaints for which cancer may be suspected, but which are commonly caused by diseases other than cancer, are vomiting, diarrhea, weight loss, coughing, sneezing, lumps under and on the skin, and changes in appetite, thirst, and urination.

47

GASTROINTESTINAL SIGNS:
VOMITING, DIARRHEA, WEIGHT LOSS

Chronic gastrointestinal signs such as vomiting, diarrhea, and weight loss can occur as a result of cancer of the gastrointestinal tract, or cancer anywhere else. However, the most common cause of weight loss, vomiting, or diarrhea that persists for more than one month is usually inflammatory bowel disease (IBD). IBD is rarely caused by gastrointestinal cancer and most often caused by an infiltration of white blood cells into the pet's intestines. Very rarely, an infection (usually fungal) of the intestines can cause IBD. Early diagnosis and treatment of IBD is very important because chronic inflammation can progress to cancer. Chronic vomiting, weight loss, or diarrhea should be investigated by endoscopic examination (examining the intestinal tract with an endoscope while the pet is anesthetized) and biopsy of the intestines to determine the exact cause. A hormonal disease affecting the adrenal glands called Addison's disease can also cause chronic gastrointestinal signs, especially intermittent vomiting, and should be considered as a possible cause.

RESPIRATORY SIGNS:
COUGHING AND SNEEZING

Acute coughing is usually the result of allergies or an infection, such as the infection that causes kennel cough. Chronic coughing can also result from heart disease, heartworm infection, lung infections (usually fungal if the problem is chronic), and chronic irreversible bronchial disease (which is especially common in small breed older dogs), but *rarely* lung cancer. Unlike in people, primary lung cancer is rare in dogs. When cancer of the lungs occurs, it is usually the result of metastatic disease after a cancer somewhere else in the body spreads to the lungs.

Sneezing is usually the result of allergies or a respiratory infection. Cancer should be suspected if the pet has a nasal discharge that is confined to one side of the nasal cavity and if the discharge contains blood. Dogs with longer noses, usually characteristic of large breeds, are more prone to nasal and sinus cancer than other breeds.

LUMPS AND BUMPS

As discussed in the previous chapter, there are many forms of cancer that can appear on an animal's skin. Fortunately, most lumps and bumps (technically referred to as *nodules* or *tumors*) are benign fatty tumors or epidermal cysts. However, these lumps and bumps are sometimes cancerous tumors, including mast cell tumors or connective tissue tumors such as fibrosarcomas. Dogs with multiple lumps on their bodies that appear suddenly may be afflicted with a type of cancer called lymphosarcoma, also referred to as lymphoma. These lumps usually occur in areas where the lymph nodes are located, such as under the jaw, in the armpits, in the groin, and in front of the shoulder blades. Owners should also keep in mind that any lumps and bumps that appear, then decrease in size or even disappear, and finally reappear and enlarge are more likely to be cancer (often lymphoma) than benign lumps or infectious lesions.

The only way to tell for sure if a lump or bump is a benign or malignant tumor is to examine the tissue microscopically. Extracting the aspirate of the lump is easy, painless, inexpensive, and can be done right in the doctor's office using a tiny needle and syringe. While the aspirate will usually tell the doctor if the mass is something other than a fatty tumor (lipoma) or cyst, occasionally it fails to indicate if the cells are cancerous. Sometimes no cells other than blood cells are aspirated, which is more common in cancerous than benign lesions. If there is any doubt after aspiration, the lump should be surgically biopsied (see pages 72–74 in chapter 4 for a more thorough discussion of these biopsy procedures).

CHANGES IN APPETITE, THIRST, AND URINATION

The most common causes of changes in appetite, thirst, and urination are diseases other than cancer that are commonly diagnosed in older dogs. These include diabetes mellitus, kidney disease, liver disease, bladder infections, urinary incontinence, and bladder stones. These diseases are so commonly diagnosed that I believe all dogs, but especially those five years of age and older, should be checked at least twice yearly with simple blood and urine tests, in addition to a thorough physical examination, to ensure early diagnosis and treatment of these conditions; most pets with these conditions can live comfortably by using a holistic approach to treatment.

ABNORMALITIES IN BLOOD OR URINE TESTS

Unlike in people, leukemias and blood cancers are very rare in pets. Most commonly, changes in the red or white blood cell counts occur as a result of anemia (often secondary to any chronic disease), infection, or inflammation somewhere in the body. When the counts for several different cell types (red cells, white cells, and platelets) increase or decrease on the complete blood count, a bone marrow aspirate should be performed to investigate if cancer may be the cause.

While a blood test will not usually tell if a pet has cancer, elevated calcium levels are often seen in pets with cancers such as lymphoma or anal sac cancer (adenocarcinoma). Pets with high calcium levels must be carefully examined for cancer if no other cause of the elevated calcium is apparent from the pet's medical history and physical examination. One cause of elevated calcium is vitamin-D rodenticide poison.

A urinalysis will also not usually tell us if a pet has cancer. However, the urinalysis can point to other diseases, such as diabetes or kidney disease, that may mimic signs of cancer. Likewise, urine abnormalities such as blood or protein in the urine may increase the suspicion for cancer, which should prompt other tests. *It is for these reasons that I recommend an annual blood and urine test for pets less than five years of age and twice annually for pets five years of age and older.*

Recently, a tumor antigen test (V-BTA) became available that purported to help screen for TCC in its early stages. Unfortunately, blood in the urine causes false positives in this test, and because bloody urine is the chief symptom in TCC, the test is not felt to be useful at this time.

> *Unlike in people, leukemias and blood cancers are very rare in pets.*

CLINICAL SIGNS THAT MIGHT INDICATE CANCER IN DOGS

- Lumps and bumps (especially new ones; those that grow quickly; those that appear, decrease in size or disappear, and then reappear or enlarge; and those that change color or easily bleed)

- Skin sores or irritated areas

- Red spots on the skin, gums, or mucous membranes

- Wounds that do not heal

- Weight loss or gain

- Lack of appetite or decreased appetite

- Abdominal enlargement (potbellied appearance)

- Weakness or exercise intolerance

- Excessive panting or heavy breathing

- Collapse

- Pale gums or mucous membranes

- Bad breath

- Bleeding or chronic discharge from wounds or any body orifice

- Change in bowel habits (chronic diarrhea, vomiting, or both)

- Change in urinary habits (blood in the urine or urinary incontinence)

NOTE: While cancer can cause these signs, so can many other diseases.

I remind pet owners not to suspect cancer every time a pet becomes ill. Having a pet examined early in the course of any illness will usually allow for a prompt diagnosis and the correct treatment. In the unfortunate event that some type of cancer is in fact responsible for the pet's illness, early diagnosis ensures quick intervention, which can extend the pet's life and, in some cases, totally cure the pet of cancer.

CHAPTER FOUR

WORKING *with*
YOUR VETERINARIAN

WHAT SHOULD YOU EXPECT when you visit your veterinarian with a pet showing signs that might indicate cancer? Unfortunately, that depends upon your veterinarian. A wholly conventional doctor who is close-minded toward complementary therapies will have one approach, while a wholly alternative doctor who is closed-minded toward conventional therapies will offer a totally different approach. The strictly conventional doctor won't consider therapies such as homeopathy, herbal medicine, and the use of nutritional supplements, opting to use only chemotherapy, radiation, or surgical therapies. Some of these doctors will unfortunately not offer much in the way of diagnostics for suspicious lumps and bumps, instead preferring to try various medications and take a "wait and see" approach.

Conversely, the strictly alternative doctor might be completely opposed to using medications for treating cancer and any form of conventional therapy. These doctors also may not use a lot of conventional diagnostic testing, instead preferring to treat your pet based upon clinical signs or alternative diagnostic techniques.

I believe the best doctor is one who is truly "holistic," that is, one who offers both conventional and complementary therapy options (integrative therapy), which is my approach in *The Natural Vet's Guide to Preventing and Treating Cancer in Dogs*. By being open-minded to both types of therapies in order to do whatever is in the pet's best interest, we are truly offering the pet the best of both worlds. There are a variety of terms associated with natural pet care, including *holistic care, alternative therapies, complementary medicine*, and, of course, *natural care*. What do all of these terms mean, and how can you use them to evaluate which doctor should care for your pet? Before I give you my definition of *holistic care*, let me briefly define the terms often applied to nonconventional therapies.

Alternative therapy means any therapy that is an alternative to conventional allopathic medical treatment. This would include treatments such as homeopathy, acupuncture, herbal medicine, and nutritional medicine, to name a few common ones. Complementary therapies include the same therapies mentioned under the heading alternative therapies. The term *complementary therapy* is often used interchangeably with *alternative therapy*, but this practice is not really correct. *Alternative* implies "something other than." The term *complementary therapy* implies the chosen treatment is "complementing" the standard treatment, and not necessarily replacing it. Because most holistic doctors are open-minded to both forms of treatment, the preferred term *complementary therapy* is more accurately defined as treatment, such as acupuncture or homeopathy, that is used in conjunction with and is complementary to the traditional medical therapy. The term *integrative therapy* is used interchangeably with *complementary therapy*. *Natural care* refers to using treatments other than traditional drug therapies.

In my practice I will often use a conventional therapy for a pet when it is in that pet's best interest, but also supplement my treatment with a few well-chosen complementary therapies. When treating cancer, a blending of conventional and complementary therapies is a wonderfully effective, truly holistic approach. *In my experience, pets with cancer respond best to this integrative approach, which combines as many therapies as possible.*

Your goal as a pet owner is simple: do what is in the best interest of your pet. If that includes conventional therapies such as surgery, radiation, or chemotherapy, so be it. If your dog is better treated with a complementary therapy such as herbal medicine, homeopathy, or acupuncture, that's great too. To repeat, *most pets with cancer benefit from a combination of complementary and conventional therapies.* If you keep in mind that most dogs with cancer will not be cured, and that our ultimate goal is to keep the pet healthy and alive as long as possible, you can easily appreciate the need for combining complementary and conventional therapies in most cases. And that is what holistic medicine is all about: simply keeping our minds open to doing what is best for our four-legged friends.

In order to do what is in the pet's best interest, veterinarians and pet owners alike must develop a holistic frame of mind. Remember that *holistic care* refers to a way of thinking. The holistic doctor and pet owner view the dog in its entirety, rather than just focusing exclusively on a specific set of problems or signs and symptoms. (Again, don't forget that your dog is attached to that tumor!) Another goal of holistic care is disease prevention (this is discussed in more detail in chapter 8). As a holistic doctor, I prefer to "treat the pet" (actually "heal" the pet) rather than "treat a disease" (at best) or "treat signs and symptoms" (at worst).

> *The true holistic mind-set considers all options for cancer treatment, and then chooses those that are in the pet's best interest.*

Let me share with you a true story, about a person, not a pet, that highlights this attitude toward integrative medicine. I had the good fortune to hear a well-known naturopathic doctor speak about treating patients. He received a call from a new patient who wanted his help treating her cancer. She said that one of her friends had referred her to his practice and wondered if he could treat her cancer. She was quite surprised when he said no. He said that he doesn't treat *cancer*, but he treats *patients with cancer*. This is such an important difference. Many doctors treat diseases, but *holistic doctors treat patients with diseases* (and of course, when possible, prefer to prevent diseases from ever occurring).

By changing our thought processes and becoming more holistic, everyone, especially our pets, benefit. Simply put, we must be open-minded and always put the dog's interest first. With every treatment performed, we must always ask, "Is this in the dog's best interest?" Having a holistic attitude means that doctors and owners refuse to focus just on the problem at hand, but instead prefer to focus on total wellness for the pet.

> *Holistic veterinarians don't treat cancer, they treat pets with cancer.*

I'm often asked why more doctors don't practice holistic medicine. There are several answers to this question.

First, we really aren't trained to be holistic doctors. Few if any veterinary schools truly teach about wellness programs and disease prevention. The focus is on diagnosis and treatment of diseases through recognition of signs and symptoms. While it certainly is important to diagnose and treat diseases, it's more important to prevent as many of these problems as possible. We are just now beginning to see a focus on wellness and holistic care in medical schools; I believe the veterinary schools will eventually adapt to this philosophy, although it will take some time.

Traditional pharmacology courses focus only on traditional drug therapies and ignore the more natural treatments, such as herbal remedies. While it is vitally important to know about the many amazing medications we can use to help our patients, a few lectures on the more natural treatments would help expose the young doctors-to-be to these exciting therapies.

Second, practicing holistic medicine takes time, and a lot of it. While many doctors find it possible to schedule four or more appointments per hour, thanks to a well-trained, fully leveraged support staff, a holistic practice such as mine schedules at most one or two appointments per hour on a typical day! It takes time to develop a complete patient history and personalize a wellness or disease prevention program for each patient.

Third, there are still a large number of doctors who believe that doctors who practice anything other than conventional medicine are quacks. I get a lot of mail from doctors who are upset that I propose treatments that have not been subjected to double-blind studies. While I also hope for the day when more of our complementary therapies can receive funding to undergo these rigorous trials, I must accept the clinical data we have now and do what I can to help my patients. I don't think I need to run expensive tests to show, for example, that the ten-thousand-year-old practice of acupuncture has merit. This is one therapy that has stood the test of time. The benefits from supplements are well documented in the medical literature. While my colleagues and I wish clinical trials on specific supplements would be funded to formally document their benefit in pets with cancer, there is no reason not to use them in our treatments while waiting for studies that may never happen. I can't always prove these therapies will help my patients simply because they have shown their effectiveness in people, but common sense tells me that it is certainly worth considering their use when appropriate. While it is true that there are certainly some charlatans in practice and there are some complementary treatments of questionable value, there is considerable evidence for the success of many mainstream complementary therapies.

FINDING A HOLISTIC VETERINARIAN

It can be difficult to find a good doctor who has this much-needed holistic philosophy. So how do you go about finding a holistic veterinarian for your pet?

First, evaluate your pet's current veterinarian. Is he or she open to complementary therapies? Many are, even if they don't offer these specialized therapies themselves. Your current doctor can treat your pet's basic needs with a holistic approach, and refer you to a doctor who performs complementary therapies, if those are needed. (As an aside, most veterinarians, even those who do not offer services such as acupuncture and herbal medicine, use nutritional supplements, such as fatty acids and antioxidants, as part of their therapy for pets with cancer. This means your current veterinarian might be able to offer your dog some basic complementary therapy prior to referral to someone more qualified to put together a holistic plan for your pet. Hopefully, this trend toward using supplements as part of the treatment of various diseases will continue.)

Second, ask friends for referrals. If you know someone who uses a holistic veterinarian, ask that person for a referral.

Third, try asking for a referral at the local health food store, pet store, or natural grocery store. These places get requests for referrals all the time (a number of my clients were referred to my own practice in this way). Also, stores often have directories with ads of holistic doctors and holistic veterinarians.

Fourth, consult your phone book for veterinarians advertising holistic care.

Finally, you can contact the American Holistic Veterinary Medical Association at 410-569-0795, or visit its website at www.altvetmed.com. Ask the association for referrals to doctors in your area.

> *The American Holistic Veterinary Medical Association is a good resource for locating holistic veterinarians in your area.*

None of these methods of tracking down a holistic doctor is foolproof; rather, use these as a starting point. Compile a list of as many names as possible from these sources, and then make an appointment to visit with each doctor on your list. Make sure you and the doctor get along, because your relationship with your pet's doctor is key to your pet's health. Make sure the doctor is open to a variety of conventional and complementary therapies, and places your pet's interests first.

Finally, and perhaps most important, treating cancer is a

specialty unto itself. I never treat a pet with cancer without the input of specialists. It's not uncommon for me to use the services of a local oncologist for chemotherapy, a radiation specialist for radiation therapy, and a surgeon who can skillfully remove tumors. I think it's imperative to realize that your doctor can't do it all; none of us is a jack-of-all-trades. *Make sure your doctor refers you to a proper cancer specialist.* If none are available, inquire about a referral for a telephone consultation, or visit the website of the American College of Veterinary Internal Medicine (www.acvim.org), and use its "Find a Specialist Near You" link to help you locate a veterinary oncologist or internist. If your doctor is comfortable administering chemotherapy, at least make sure he or she is doing so in cooperation with a cancer specialist who can devise a specific protocol for your pet and advise your veterinarian on how to proceed.

> *Cancer is a special disease. Make sure you utilize the services of specialists to help fight it.*

QUESTIONS TO ASK THE VETERINARIAN

Here are some sample questions to ask the prospective holistic doctor who might end up treating your pet for cancer (following the questions are my preferred answers):

Q: "How do you make a definitive diagnosis of cancer?"

A: Ideally, this is done by fine needle aspiration or by performing a biopsy on solid tumors, combined with other diagnostic tests (radiography, blood testing, ltrasonography, endoscopy) as needed for pets with vague clinical signs such as weight loss and lack of appetite.

Q: "What are your feelings about using chemotherapy in dogs with cancer?"

A: Chemotherapy, while not without risks, usually has fewer side effects in pets than in people. When necessary to quickly achieve remission, chemotherapy should be considered by the holistic pet owner.

Q: "What are your feelings about using complementary therapies in dogs with cancer?"

A: While not always backed by strong clinical studies, a number of supplements may benefit dogs with cancer by boosting the immune system, decreasing tumor growth and spread, and minimizing side effects from other therapies, such as radiation and chemotherapy. As long as the complementary therapy does not interfere with another therapy, it should be considered for the pet with cancer.

Q: "What type of diet should my pet eat?"

A: The most naturally prepared food or homemade diet is recommended. (Dogs with cancer may benefit from a specific diet discussed in detail on pages 229–237 in chapter 8).

Q: "What do you recommend for the dog with lumps and bumps on the body?"

A: The best approach is to aspirate the lump or bump with a tiny needle and examine the aspirated cells or fluid microscopically. If necessary, the lump or bump can be surgically biopsied to give a definitive diagnosis. With the exception of an obvious wart or a lump too tiny to biopsy or aspirate, the doctor should not just "wait and watch." *There is no reason to watch cancer grow and spread!*

For the best results with holistic medicine, you must be an active partner with your pet's veterinarian.

Once you've found the perfect doctor for you and have arrived for your appointment, it is important to understand what should happen during your visit. If this is your first visit, expect to spend anywhere from thirty to sixty minutes or more for the initial evaluation and diagnostic testing. The visit is divided into three parts: the medical history, physical examination, and laboratory evaluation.

The Medical History

The history you provide during an office visit is vital in helping the veterinarian properly assess your pet. It guides the doctor in knowing what areas of the body to pay particular attention to during the examination, and helps in selecting only those laboratory tests needed to arrive at a proper diagnosis. It is not uncommon for my clients to bring pages of notes they have made at home, as well as notes and medical records from a prior doctor, to aid me in making the correct diagnosis and in deciding on the proper course of treatment.

Here are some typical questions your doctor may ask you about your pet:

- What is your pet's diet?
- Is your pet current on its annual needs? (Vaccinations or preferably vaccine titers when necessary, parasite control programs, including heartworm medications if needed. Pets with cancer should *never* be immunized again in order to minimize the chances of the pet coming out of remission.)

- Are there any other problems that concern you in addition to the reason for this visit? (Other problems may indicate the likelihood of a disease other than cancer, or may indicate the potential that a solid tumor has spread, indicating a poorer prognosis; other problems may also simply indicate additional medical problems in your pet, which are not uncommon and must also be treated. *Remember, we want to treat the pet and not just the cancer!*)

- If your pet has been to another doctor, what was the diagnosis? How was the diagnosis made? Was any diagnostic testing done? Was any treatment prescribed? If so, what was it, and did your pet improve? (To help answer this question, always bring in any medicine containers, even if empty, so the doctor can assess the prescription. Many times I find that the wrong dosage or dosing interval was prescribed, and this may account for the pet failing to improve.)

- Have you done any home treatments (medicines or supplements?) If so, what were they (once again, bring in the containers), and did they help?

- Has your pet been vaccinated recently? (In my experience, many pets with cancer have been recently immunized. While I'm not saying that vaccines will cause cancer, although this can happen, I believe they may unmask cancers. Pets with cancer that have recently been immunized can be treated with additional therapies to reduce vaccinosis, a condition of illness caused by vaccines.)

63

The Physical Examination

After asking these and any other questions concerning your pet's medical history, your veterinarian will commence with the physical examination.

> *The holistic examination for the pet with cancer focuses not just on the primary complaint but on the whole pet and all of its body systems.*

The general physical allows me to properly examine the pet from head to toe. During this exam, I usually ignore the primary complaint (e.g., solid tumor, lethargy) so that I can detect whether other problems exist. Sometimes these other problems are related to the original complaint; other times they are only incidental to the primary reason for the visit. By thoroughly checking the patient over I am truly offering holistic care. For example, during my overall physical examination on Sasha, an older female collie who was originally brought in for evaluation of a solid tumor, I discovered that she had a heart murmur, indicating heart disease. My recommended diagnostic testing and therapy had to take into account possible heart disease. Other pets might show clinical signs indicating cognitive disorders or periodontal infections. These problems can't be ignored and might actually take priority over the original problem. Therefore, all of my patients receive a thorough physical examination whenever possible.

When applicable, the second part of the examination involves evaluating any solid lumps or bumps the owner has noticed. Occasionally, there are additional masses unknown to the owner that I have discovered during the examination. One pet I recently examined for a second opinion about a single large breast tumor actually had four additional breast tumors unnoticed by the owner or the other veterinarian! I examine tumors to determine how easy removal will be if their aspirate indicates the possibility of cancer (see The Laboratory Evaluation on the next page). This examination also lets me plan how much healthy tissue will need to be removed if surgery is indeed indicated; for benign tumors (such as fatty tumors), removal of only the tumor is usually adequate, but for malignant cancers, a certain amount of normal tissue that surrounds the tumor (also referred to as "clean margins") must be removed to ensure that all cancerous tissue has been removed.

DIAGNOSTIC TESTING
OF THE PET WITH CANCER

1. Medical history

2. Physical examination

3. Aspiration of solid tumors / tumor biopsy

4. Diagnostic imaging: X-rays, MRI, CT scan, ultrasound

5. Blood tests: basic blood count and profile, bone marrow analysis

6. Urinalysis

The Laboratory Evaluation

The laboratory evaluation is critical in allowing veterinarians to distinguish subtle clues that are detected during the physical examination. It is often the most neglected part of the evaluation of a pet with solid tumors, as evidenced by the number of pets in my practice with solid tumors that have never had any laboratory testing done to reveal the true status of the masses. The various tests that might be necessary to help the doctor fully evaluate your pet include diagnostic imaging, such as X-rays, MRI and CT scan, and bone scan; urine evaluation; blood tests; bone marrow evaluation; aspiration cytology; and biopsy.

> *The laboratory evaluation is critical in helping determine the extent of your pet's cancer, ability to withstand treatment, and presence of other diseases.*

DIAGNOSTIC IMAGING

The tests used by most veterinarians for diagnostic imaging are conventional radiography, MRI (magnetic resonance imaging), CT scan (computerized tomography scan), and bone scan and nuclear imaging.

Conventional Radiography (X-rays)

The basic type of diagnostic imaging for evaluation of the pet suspected of having cancer is a conventional radiograph. This two-dimensional picture, using X-ray irradiation, allows the doctor to evaluate the patient's chest, abdomen, and bones. When radiographs are made correctly, most pets will not need other types of diagnostic imaging to properly evaluate them for cancer.

Radiology is not usually necessary for pets with solid skin tumors, but this will vary depending upon the pathologic diagnosis after a biopsy or aspirate is examined. For example, a dog with a benign skin tumor does not need radiographic evaluation for cancer because there is no chance of it spreading throughout the body. (However, I believe that all pets, especially older ones, can benefit from complete evaluations once to twice yearly, including radiographs, because other problems, such as bladder stones or other internal cancers, may be detected before clinical signs are seen.) A dog with a tumor of the bone, such as an osteosarcoma, will need radiographic evaluation of the primary site (bone) as well as three radiographic views of the chest to determine if the primary tumor has spread. If metastasis is seen at the time of initial diagnosis, the prognosis is very poor. This information is important so that the doctor can properly discuss the outlook and potential therapies with the owner.

Even if the lungs are clean and free of tumors at the time of the initial diagnosis, follow-up radiographs (usually done every two to three months) are necessary for early detection of metastasis, and to help the doctor consistently evaluate the pet and modify the prognosis for the owner. Additionally, further treatments can be recommended based upon the findings of these follow-up visits.

Modern X-ray machines are very safe and are calibrated to expose patients to only the minimum X-ray energy needed to produce high-quality pictures. Most often two views are taken to allow the doctor to assess the tumor site from two perpendicular sides: a front-to-back view and a side-to-side view. To evaluate for spread of tumors to the lungs, three views are necessary: front-to-back and both left and right side-to-side views.

Because even the best-trained pet will not usually lay still while placed in odd body positions, many pets will need to be sedated for proper positioning and to minimize the need for multiple X-ray exposures (in some states, anesthesia is required because it is against the law for medical personnel to be in the same room when X-rays are taken). Modern sedatives are safe when used properly and the pet is monitored carefully. In my practice the sedative is reversed at the completion of the X-ray procedure, and the pet can leave fully awake within minutes.

> *Pets are often sedated to allow technicians to place them in the best position for the X-ray evaluation.*

MRI and CT Scans

Occasionally, a plain radiograph fails to reveal any abnormalities, and the doctor may order a more specialized test. This is especially true when cancers of the face, sinuses, brain, and spinal cord are suspected.

The MRI scan makes use of powerful magnets to detect magnetic fields in the body; a computer analyzes these magnetic fields and turns them into a picture. This test is especially useful in looking at soft tissues that a regular radiograph often won't reveal. It is also recommended to evaluate the extent of some soft tissue tumors to help the surgeon plan the most complete surgical removal possible.

The CT scan, formerly called CAT scan, uses X-ray energy to produce a more detailed picture than that produced by regular X-ray.

Because patient movement must be avoided during each of these special procedures, pets are usually put under full anesthesia.

Bone Scan and Nuclear Imaging

While not used as commonly in pets as in people, bone scans and nuclear imaging might be needed if other tests fail to detect the cause of the pet's clinical signs and the clinician suspects cancer. In these procedures, which must also be done under full anesthesia, a radioactive isotope is injected into the blood. A special scanning camera is used to detect accumulations of the isotope in the body where there is inflammation, infection, or a tumor. A computer assembles information from the camera and produces an image for evaluation.

URINE EVALUATION

Tumors of the urinary and reproductive tracts can cause clinical signs that mimic bladder infections or bladder stones. These signs include urinary incontinence, straining to urinate, frequent urination, and the passing of blood in the urine. A urinalysis is useful to evaluate the dog's health as well as provide information that can identify the cause of the animal's symptoms. Because bladder cancer is often not treatable after clinical signs are seen, I recommend an annual or semiannual screening of the dog's urine. Persistent blood in the urine should be evaluated with radiographs (to rule out bladder stones) and an ultrasound (to allow early detection of bladder tumors). As stated previously, the tumor antigen test (V-BTA, created by Bion Diagnostic Sciences, Redmond, WA) is not useful in screening pets for bladder cancer. Early diagnosis increases the likelihood that bladder surgery can cure the pet.

BLOOD TESTS

A blood count and blood profile are often useful for diagnosing diseases that might be the cause of the pet's symptoms. The pet with cancer might have nonspecific symptoms, such as lethargy and reduced appetite. Other diseases, such as thyroid disease, may also cause similar signs, and blood testing helps the doctor narrow the diagnosis. With the exception of rare types of bone marrow or lymphatic cancers (leukemias), blood tests alone cannot currently diagnose most cancers; some cancers, such as lymphoma and anal sac adenocarcinoma, may cause an extremely elevated blood calcium level, which can direct the doctor to look for cancer in the pet. But blood tests can also tell the doctor if other diseases, such as liver or kidney disease, might be causing the clinical signs seen in the pet. These tests can also let the doctor know if certain treatments, such as chemotherapy, can be safely administered to the pet; some chemotherapy drugs may not be safe to use in pets with disorders of the liver or kidneys, for example. Because some chemotherapy medications can cause alterations in the red cell, white cell, and platelet counts, it is important to evaluate these levels prior to and during chemotherapy.

Blood tests also provide information on the general health of the pet, and tell the doctor if alterations in prescribed medications need to be made. For example, a blood test might reveal diabetes. While diabetes does not cause cancer, early detection of this hormonal problem will extend your pet's life if treatment begins before clinical disease is present.

> *The blood profile is an important tool for monitoring the possible side effects of chemotherapy.*

Often, a potent nonsteroidal anti-inflammatory medication called piroxicam (Feldene) is prescribed for pets with solid tumors. In very rare instances, pets taking piroxicam also have had their cancers miraculously disappear, which is one reason it is used for dogs with cancer.

Pain is caused when chemicals (prostaglandins) are formed by an enzyme called cyclooxygenase. These prostaglandins also inhibit the immune response, decreasing the dog's ability to fight cancer. Piroxicam, and possibly other NSAIDs, have been shown to inhibit the formation of prostaglandins, which prevent a proper immune response against cancer. The most notable example is the control and shrinkage of bladder tumors in dogs. A response may take weeks or longer, depending on the growth rate and behavior of the tumor; also, chronic illnesses oftentimes respond better than acute-onset illnesses.

However, NSAIDs like piroxicam also can cause side effects typical of nonsteroidal medications, such as gastrointestinal ulcers, kidney disease, and liver disease. (A medicine called Cytotec® can be prescribed to minimize the potential for gastrointestinal ulcers.) In my practice, I have not needed to use Cytotec, but I wouldn't hesitate to do so in any dog prone to NSAID side effects, especially one with a sensitive stomach. Regular blood and urine testing lets the doctor monitor your pet for any side effects that could occur with piroxicam administration.

Once a dog has been started on treatment for cancer, regular follow-up examinations and laboratory testing are necessary at least every two to three months, to monitor treatment and allow early detection of any side effects.

BONE MARROW EVALUATION

To determine the extent of a dog's cancer, your doctor may recommend a bone marrow biopsy. This test, done under sedation or anesthesia, will show if the bone marrow is affected, which may explain the presence of any abnormal blood counts, such as decreased red cell, white cell, or platelet counts.

ASPIRATION CYTOLOGY

Aspiration cytology, or fine needle cytology (*cytology* means "the study of cells"), is a quick and easy test to determine the status of suspicious lumps and bumps. In the procedure, the doctor gently inserts a tiny needle, attached to a syringe, into the suspicious mass to extract, or aspirate, a tiny amount of fluid or cells by pulling back on the plunger of the syringe. The material is placed on a slide, treated with a special stain, and looked at under the microscope. Most doctors can perform the procedure in the office; those not trained in cytology can send the slide to a laboratory for evaluation by a pathologist, with results normally available within twenty-four to forty-eight hours. The procedure is only slightly uncomfortable for most pets (similar to what an injection feels like), and sedation or anesthesia is usually not needed.

In most cases an exact diagnosis can be made and treatment planned while you wait in the office. Sometimes an exact diagnosis can't be made because the tumor cells look similar to normal cells when examined by aspiration cytology. Some tumors, such as soft tissue sarcomas, rarely give up any cells when aspirated. In these cases a surgical biopsy is needed to give an exact diagnosis.

I prefer aspiration cytology because I can usually give the pet owner an exact diagnosis shortly after the procedure. Even if an exact diagnosis is not possible, I can at least tell the owner if the mass is a cyst, fatty tumor, or possibly something more serious that may require a surgical biopsy.

With rare exception, I believe *all lumps and bumps should be aspirated*. I have seen too many malignant cancers in pets that were not originally diagnosed because the veterinarian did not perform aspiration cytology but only felt the tumor and diagnosed it a cyst or fatty tumor. While many lumps and bumps are in fact cysts or fatty tumors, some are cancer. The sooner these cancers are diagnosed and treated, the better the prognosis. Whenever possible, make sure lumps and bumps are aspirated. You cannot definitively diagnose cancer or exclude cancer simply by feeling at a lump. There is no reason to take a "wait and watch" approach for lumps and bumps, because cancer could already be spreading and kill your pet.

Most tumors are surgically removed (an excisional biopsy) and then a portion of the mass is sent to a pathologist for a histopathological evaluation. The mass is placed in paraffin, sliced very thin, and then stained and examined microscopically. The pathologist can usually tell if the mass is benign or malignant, or something that resembles a cyst, abscess, or granuloma.

Occasionally, the veterinarian may decide to remove only a tiny piece of the tumor for diagnosis (an incisional biopsy), and then plan a complete surgical removal if the histopathology indicates cancer. This is most commonly done when the doctor is not sure of the exact diagnosis prior to biopsy or when a major surgery (such as amputation) is needed to remove the entire tumor. Getting the correct diagnosis first allows the doctor to prescribe the proper form of therapy for the patient that might need a major surgical procedure.

Most tumors should be biopsied for an accurate diagnosis.

Because biopsies are surgical procedures, sedation or anesthesia is needed. While biopsies can usually identify whether a tumor is benign or malignant, occasionally all the pathologist sees are signs of infection or inflammation in the submitted specimen. This is quite common in cases of bone cancer (especially osteosarcoma) and breast cancer (mammary adenocarcinoma), because these tumors often contain areas of infection and inflammation and do not contain uniform areas of cancer cells. If a second biopsy is recommended, you can be sure it is needed to help the doctor make the proper diagnosis for your dog.

After your veterinarian has verified the presence of cancer through the medical history, physical examination, and diagnostic tests, he or she can review the various treatment options with you. The next chapter discusses the most commonly used conventional therapies, followed by a chapter presenting various complementary therapies that your veterinarian may prescribe for your dog.

CHAPTER FIVE

CONVENTIONAL THERAPIES *for* CANCER

MANY PET OWNERS have preconceived notions about cancer and conventional treatment. Biases and negative feelings regarding cancer and conventional therapies may discourage owners from pursuing therapies that can make the pet feel better, put the cancer in remission, and give the pet a few more months or even years of quality life. Pet owners should understand that in most instances the best treatment for cancer will use not only a variety of natural therapies but also some combination of conventional therapies, which includes surgery, chemotherapy, and radiation therapy.

In general, cancer affects older dogs, usually seven years of age and older. It is important for pet owners and veterinarians to consider what constitutes an "old" pet, as many equate old age with decreased health. Age is a condition rather than an illness; many senior pets are quite healthy while others are afflicted with many ailments. If we think of each pet as an individual, we give that dog the ultimate in personal, holistic care. Many of the best candidates for cancer therapy are elderly dogs that were denied treatment by other doctors because they were "too old." Owners should take comfort in knowing that most pets with cancer can be treated successfully and live normal lives until the cancer comes out of remission. Pets can live quite comfortably with cancer. In most cases there are not the kind of side effects from treatment (specifically with chemotherapy) typically seen in people undergoing cancer treatment. While we usually cannot cure most cancers, there is no reason the diagnosis of cancer should be an immediate death sentence for most pets.

In choosing a therapeutic protocol for a pet with cancer, owners should consider three important questions:

- What is the very best treatment to provide a chance for cure? (While a cure is never guaranteed, it's at least a goal to consider.)

- What is the very best treatment to ensure the pet's quality of life? (It may not always be appropriate to pursue the most aggressive treatments for an older dog, say, one with congestive heart disease, that would be suitable for a younger dog in otherwise good health.)

- What is the best choice for the family's quality of life? Can the pet's family handle the emotional stresses of chemotherapy or radiation therapy? Will a surgery disfigure the pet? How much will it all cost?

Since cancer has usually been in the pet's body for some time when it is finally discovered, the more methods we use to fight the cancer, the more successful we can hope to be with our treatment. The most important consideration is that we must treat the whole patient with a true holistic approach to avoid causing additional illness or discomfort in the pet. That is why it is important to monitor the patient's blood counts, weight, activity, and general well-being, as well as address any other problems. Talk with your pet's oncologist about providing a "supportive care package" of medications and supplements that might counteract the rare side effects (such as lack of appetite, vomiting) that may occur in some pets in treatment. Finally, the use of supportive remedies, antioxidants, dietary supplements, herbs, homeopathic remedies, and good cancer-fighting nutrition will provide the best chance for successful treatment for the pet with cancer.

CONVENTIONAL (WESTERN) THERAPIES

The conventional cancer therapies common to Western medicine, for humans and their pets, are surgery, chemotherapy, and radiation therapy. I'll address each of these three main therapies and their most common side effects throughout this chapter.

Surgery (Cut Out the Cancer)

For many years, surgery was the only conventional treatment available for pets with cancer. Surgical removal of a tumor can sometimes cure a pet. Chemotherapy or radiation therapy may also be used because surgery by itself may not be curative, as in the case of very large tumors located on parts of the body in which total removal is not possible. Surgery is usually performed safely with modern anesthetics and monitoring equipment; however, no surgery is without risk. Your veterinarian will explain the risks to you prior to surgery.

Surgery is usually performed safely, regardless of the pet's age, with modern anesthetics and monitoring equipment.

While complications are rare, the most common ones following surgery are bleeding, infection, and seepage from the surgical wound. Some surgeries may leave the pet with loss of function, such as difficulty eating after oral surgery, incontinence after colon or bladder surgery, or reluctance to walk after amputation. In the case of the amputation of a limb or part of the jaw or nose, the owner faces the complication of having to adjust to the pet's appearance (this is actually less of a problem for the pet!).

Maybe the most important consideration for the pet owner is whether surgery will cure the pet of cancer. *Cure* means the successful treatment of a disease. For some tumors that are diagnosed early and completely removed with surgery, a cure is possible. In other instances a true cure does not occur; surgery and other therapies give pets cancer-free or tumor-free intervals even if the cancer is expected to return at a later date. If free of cancer for one year, a dog may be considered "cured" for some cancers but not others.

No veterinarian can guarantee that every cancer cell has been removed, even following thorough microscopic examination of the excised tissue. There are clues that may suggest a "curative intent," such as the pathologist not finding cancer cells at the surgery edges of the removed tumor, the tumor cells appearing almost normal (low grade of cancer), and a history of slow tumor growth prior to the time of removal. The only test to prove cure is time, and depending on their type, some tumors may grow unnoticed for one to five years.

Consult with your doctor or preferably an oncologist to

understand the chance of curing your pet with surgery or any cancer therapy. In general, if the tumor is removed and the pathology report shows "clean margins," chances are fairly good for a cure for many tumors. If your doctor can only partially remove the mass or debulk it, or if the biopsy shows cancer cells extending to the margins of the tumor, then some of the cancer remains and will require chemotherapy or radiation therapy.

For tumors that are difficult to remove by a general practitioner, it's best to get a referral to a board-certified surgeon who understands the principles of surgical oncology and reconstructive surgery. A cancer may be considered inoperable in one hospital but operable in another, depending on the skill and experience of the surgeon. Delaying the proper therapy or making incorrect decisions at the onset of the pet's cancer often means a pet's survival time is shortened; while quick decisions should be made, waiting one to two weeks to consider all the options rarely harms the pet in most instances.

> *A cancer may be considered inoperable in one hospital but operable in another, depending on the skill and experience of the surgeon.*

While surgery can easily cure most small tumors, in other instances additional therapies are needed to increase the cancer-free interval and extend the pet's life. For example, the successful removal of a malignant hemangiosarcoma of the spleen or a malignant melanoma in the jaw, or the amputation of a leg due to osteosarcoma, will not cure the dog. Surgery can make the pet feel better, but after surgery for bone, spleen, bladder, prostate, and most malignant breast and oral cancers, follow-up chemotherapy is the standard recommendation to fight any remaining cancer cells. Without follow-up treatment, the chances for a cure or an extended life span are greatly decreased. Chemotherapy, radiation, and complementary therapies can play a huge role in protecting the dog from spread and recurrence of the cancer, or can at least slow down the progression of the cancer.

Occasionally, additional surgical procedures are needed. Some tumors recur at the original site of the surgery because cancerous cells remain. The first surgery should be as aggressive as possible in removing tissue to minimize the need for additional surgeries. If additional surgeries are not feasible, radiation or chemotherapy may be useful for some types of cancer.

Sometimes surgery is used not to cure the pet but only to help it feel better and improve its quality of life. For example, in most cases of bladder cancer, surgery is not curative and does not increase the survival of the dog, but it may be used to clear an obstructed urinary passage and make urination more comfortable for the pet. Debulking large tumors is very useful when it restores compromised functions such as breathing, swallowing, eliminating, or walking.

Sometimes surgery is used not to cure the pet but only to help it feel better and improve its quality of life.

SURGERY TO CORRECT
THE IMMEDIATE PROBLEM

Sometimes surgery will not alter the ultimate course of the disease but will give the pet extra time with the owner. For example, in one case I treated a dog with a malignant breast tumor. Following surgical removal of the tumor, the owner declined additional conventional therapies but did use nutrition and herbs to help boost her dog's immune system. As I expected, the tumor returned within six months and quickly became ulcerated and infected. Chest radiographs taken at that time showed there was no obvious spread of the cancer to the lungs. I recommended another surgery to remove the infected tumor. In this instance, the owner clearly understood that removing the tumor would not ultimately affect the outcome. The dog would still die at some future point when the cancer appeared in the lungs. However, if we did not remove the tumor a second time, then euthanasia would be recommended that same day due to the decreased quality of life for the pet (and the owner, who did not want to witness an oozing, bleeding, smelly tumor). The owner agreed to another surgery, which prevented the dog from dying *that day* and made the dog and owner feel better. In this case, multiple surgeries enabled the pet to live longer than it would have without intervention, but the surgeries did not alter the expected outcome of the disease. Owners should consider multiple surgeries to improve the quality and quantity of life for their pets, as long as they are realistic about the ultimate outcome of the cancer.

Chemotherapy (Poison the Cancer)

Chemotherapy consists of treatment with potent medications that interfere with the ability of the cancer cells to grow, reproduce, and spread. Remember that our primary goal is to control the cancer so that the pet has a good quality of life. Few cancers can be completely eliminated by chemotherapy, but many cancers are put into long remissions after chemotherapy. With proper treatment, pets with cancer can recover from the cancer and not get sick from the chemotherapy.

In people, chemotherapy drugs often have toxic side effects. Many people are cured with chemotherapy and do not have to remain on treatment for the rest of their lives. For pets however, chemotherapy in high doses won't work because the side effects are unacceptable to most owners.

> *With proper treatment, pets with cancer can recover from the cancer and not get sick from the chemotherapy.*

Combination Chemotherapy

The most successful chemotherapy protocols for various cancers use a combination of drugs that attacks various stages of the cancer cell's life cycle. Normal cells need to be spared for the pet to have minimal side effects and a good quality of life. The higher the dose of drug used, the greater the risk of dangerous side effects to these healthy cells. Combination chemotherapy uses lower doses of each drug so that the cancer can be attacked while reducing the incidence of side effects. Each drug in the combination attacks the cancer in its own way.

While chemotherapy may cure some cancers, we often use chemotherapy for palliation, to make the pet feel better and live longer, but not to cure the pet. Sometimes chemotherapy is used to shrink tumors before surgery or to enhance the effects of radiation therapy.

BONE MARROW TRANSPLANTS

Pet owners often ask me about bone marrow transplants to help their pets with cancer. In people, this procedure is performed after high doses of chemotherapy have killed most of the cells in the body, including the bone marrow. The bone marrow must be replaced via transplant before the person can again make red blood cells, white blood cells, and platelets. While this procedure has been done in dogs, veterinarians can't routinely offer clients bone marrow transplants for their pets because of the high cost and serious side effects that accompany this therapy. However, if you are interested in this therapy for your pet, be sure to discuss it with your veterinary oncologist.

WHY CHEMOTHERAPY WORKS

Chemotherapy drugs are designed specifically to damage cancer cells as they grow and divide; the drugs work best on rapidly growing cancer cells. Because some normal cells also multiply quickly, chemotherapy drugs may damage them as well. The normal cells most commonly affected are the blood cells developing in bone marrow, cells lining the stomach and intestines, and the cells lining the hair follicles. The temporary damage to these normal cells accounts for much of the toxicity, and the side effects, of chemotherapy. Fortunately, the lower dosage of chemotherapy given to dogs is designed to minimize damage to normal cells; when damage occurs, it is almost always temporary. Also, chemotherapy is given at intervals to allow the bone marrow to recover on its own.

In most chemotherapy regimens, more than one drug is used, either simultaneously or sequentially. This is called combination chemotherapy and it works for a number of reasons:

- As cancer cells grow, they pass through several stages of cell division known as the *cell cycle*. Different chemotherapy agents stop cell growth at different stages in the cell cycle. By giving a combination of drugs, each of which may interfere with cell growth at different stages of the cell cycle, more cancer cells are likely to be killed.

- Different drugs have different side effects. Because of this, drugs with different side effects are combined to give as much treatment as possible with minimal toxicity.

- Combination chemotherapy may reduce the chances of the cancer cells becoming resistant to specific chemotherapy agents. Clinical trials have shown that combination chemotherapy is more effective than single-agent drug therapy for many types of cancer. Because only a small percentage of cells in a cancerous or malignant tumor or any tissue are dividing at any one time, multiple treatments are also more effective. With repeated treatments, more cancer cells are attacked in the process of dividing.

TYPES OF CHEMOTHERAPY

Most oncologists use several different chemotherapy medications for their patients. (While none of these drugs are officially approved for animal use, oncologists have developed successful protocols using these medications.) There are six basic classifications of chemotherapy drugs. These include alkylating agents, antimetabolites, antitumor antibiotics, plant alkaloids, hormones, and miscellaneous chemotherapy agents.

Alkylating Agents

Alkylating agents include cyclophosphamide (Cytoxan), chlorambucil (Leukeran), melphalan (Alkeran), busulfan (Myleran, Busulfex), cisplatin (Platinol), and carboplatin (Paraplatin). These drugs work by cross-linking DNA, preventing the cells from reproducing. The possible side effects of these drugs include bone marrow suppression, lack of appetite, vomiting, nausea, bleeding from the bladder (sterile hemorrhagic cystitis in dogs treated with cyclophosphamide), and pulmonary fibrosis (in dogs treated with busulfan).

Antimetabolites

Antimetabolite drugs include cytosine arabinoside (Cytosar-U), methotrexate, 5-fluorouracil (5-FU), 6-thioguanine (6-TG), 6-mercaptourine (Purinethol), and azathioprine (Imuran). These drugs mimic natural metabolites that can substitute for purines or pyrimidines in the cancer cells, interfering with cell synthesis. They work best when given repeatedly at low doses or as a continuous intravenous infusion. Side effects are the same as those seen with alkylating agents (see above).

Antitumor Antibiotics

These drugs work by causing oxidative damage in DNA by the production of free radicals. The most common examples include doxorubicin (Adriamycin), bleomycin (Blenoxane), actinomycin-D (Cosmegen), and mitoxantrone (Novantrone). Side effects are the same as those seen with alkylating agents (see previous page). However, some drugs — such as doxoru-bicin, vincristine, vinblastine, mustargen — can cause tissue damage if the drug leaks out of the vein during treatment. Doxorubicin also can cause a dose-related toxicity to the heart. Complementary therapies, such as coenzyme Q-10 (see pages 177–182 in chapter 7), may be helpful in minimizing cardio-toxicity. Bleomycin can cause pulmonary fibrosis. The anti-oxidants curcumin, green tea extract, rutin, hesperidin, and quercetin may help limit damage to the lungs.

Plant Alkaloids

These drugs, derived from the periwinkle and may apple plants, act by disrupting the mitotic spindle apparatus during selected periods of cancer cell division. Examples of medications are vincristine (Oncovin), vinblastine (Velban), and etoposide (VP-16, VePesid). Tissue damage can result if the medications leak out of the vein during treatment.

Hormones

Hormones include glucocorticoids (such as prednisone and prednisolone) and testosterone. These therapies work in a variety of ways. Glucocorticoids (steroids) may cause side ef-fects such as increased thirst, increased urination, increased appetite, and weight gain. Potentially serious short-term side effects of high-dose glucocorticoid therapy include pancreati-tis and gastrointestinal ulceration. Using adrenal glandular supplements (see pages 189–191 in chapter 7) during steroid administration can support the adrenal gland. Using medica-tions such as Cytotec can decrease the chance of gastrointesti-nal ulceration when steroids (or NSAIDs) are used.

Miscellaneous Chemotherapy Medications

The most common drug in this category is L-asparaginase (Elspar), which works as an enzyme that destroys the amino acid asparaginine. Rapidly reproducing lymphoblasts need this amino acid to grow and survive, which makes L-asparaginase useful in pets with lymphosarcoma. The main side effect is a hypersensitivity reaction that may occur in some dogs, especially when multiple treatments are given.

Another drug that may be useful for dogs with cancer is tamoxifen, which is commonly used to treat women with breast cancer. Tamoxifen is a synthetic antiestrogenic medication. While the precise mechanism of action of tamoxifen is uncertain, it is thought to block estrogen receptors and suppress the genetic material of the breast cancer cells. Not all dog breast tumors are estrogen-receptor positive, so tamoxifen may not help all dogs with breast cancer.

While tamoxifen might be effective in the management of canine mammary neoplasia in some dogs, it is not widely prescribed. Caution should be exercised in prescribing tamoxifen because of the high percentage of dogs demonstrating estrogen-like side effects (uterine stump pyometra, vaginal hyperplasia).

Tamoxifen may also be useful in other types of cancers in which chemotherapy is an adjunct medication. Recent biochemical effects of tamoxifen that have gained increased attention of researchers include interaction with protein kinase C, stimulation of human natural killer cells, and reversal of the P-glycoprotein (Pgp) membrane-associated multidrug-resistance pump. Approximately 25 percent of malignant melanomas have demonstrable estrogen receptors. Many canine malignancies are known to express Pgp spontaneously or acquire Pgp during chemotherapy treatment.

Although the clinical significance of this is not known, occasional objective responses to tamoxifen have been reported in various human malignancies. Similarly, the presence of estrogen receptors and estrogen-binding proteins has been reported in normal and malignant tissues besides breast tissues.

It has been shown that tamoxifen can inhibit efflux of doxorubicin (through the Pgp membrane pump in canine drug-resistant cell lines) out of cancer cells. It has also been shown to enhance the reaction of platinum-containing compounds in laboratory and clinical studies of human melanoma. This suggests that tamoxifen might help increase the effectiveness of chemotherapy drugs in resistant tumor cells.

The studies on tamoxifen suggest that there are many indications for its use in the management of canine diseases. Further studies will likely suggest an adjuvant role for tamoxifen in cancer case care. However, the drug should not be used in intact female animals; severe pyometra and vaginal hyperplasia will occur.

> *Further studies will likely suggest an adjuvant role for tamoxifen in cancer cases.*

Another miscellaneous medication that may be helpful in treating some pets with cancer is the antibiotic doxycycline. Your doctor may recommend adding doxycycline, a tetracycline antibiotic, to your pet's protocol. This antibiotic (and some fluoroquinolone antibiotics) inhibits matrix metalloproteinase (MMP) enzymes. MMP enzymes are dissolving proteins that exist in the extracellular matrix, the fluid that is in between cells. For cancer cells to spread, they must invade other cells and vessels; one way they do this is to dissolve the cell walls of surrounding cells using adhesive molecules that interact with the MMP. Inhibitors of MMP may decrease the spread of cancer. (Omega-3 fatty acids have also been found to inhibit these MMP enzymes; a fuller discussion of omega-3's can be found on pages 215–218 in chapter 7) Cancers that have high amounts of MMP-2 and MMP-9 (such as malignant melanoma and osteosarcoma) often don't respond as well to chemotherapy treatments and usually cause death more quickly than other cancers.

The final class of miscellaneous medications that may be helpful for pets with cancer are the nonsteroidal anti-inflammatory medications (NSAIDs). The most commonly prescribed NSAID for cancer therapy is the drug piroxicam (Feldene), which reduces the level of prostaglandin E-2 (PGE-2) that is a strong inhibitor of natural killer cells.

Doxycycline and omega-3 fatty acids (fish oil) can inhibit the matrix metalloproteinase (MMP) enzymes that play a role in how cancer cells survive and spread in the body.

COMMON CLASSES OF CHEMOTHERAPY MEDICATIONS

CLASS	EXAMPLES
Alkylating agents	Cyclophosphamide (Cytoxan), busulfan (myleran, Busulfex), chlorambucil (Leukeran), melphalan (Alkeran), cisplatin (Platinol), and carboplatin (Paraplatin)

CLASS	EXAMPLES
Antimetabolites	Cytosine arabinoside (Cytosar-U), methotrexate, 5-fluorouracil (5-FU), 6-thioguanine (6-TG), 6-mercaptourine (Purinethol), and azathioprine (Imuran)
Antitumor antibiotics	Doxorubicin (Adriamycin), bleomycin (Blenoxane), actinomycin-D (Cosmegen), mitoxantrone (Novantrone)
Plant alkaloids	Vincristine (Oncovin), vinblastine (Velban), etoposide (VP-16, VePesid)
Hormones	Glucocorticoids: prednisone, prednisolone, testosterone
Miscellaneous agents	L-asparaginase (Elspar), tamoxifen, doxycycline, piroxicam (Feldene)

SIDE EFFECTS OF CHEMOTHERAPY

Cancer cells are, to some extent, similar to normal cells. Any drug that can damage or kill cancer cells carries the potential to damage normal cells as well. As a result, treatment with chemotherapy drugs may have significant side effects, such as nausea, vomiting, diarrhea, appetite loss, bruising, fever, and hair loss.

Nausea, vomiting, diarrhea, and loss of appetite are the

side effects of chemotherapy that cause the most discomfort. With the development of new antinausea medications, this problem can now be prevented in almost every patient. Chemotherapy drugs can stimulate and irritate key areas in the brain and cause nausea and vomiting. Chemotherapy will also decrease the number of cells that line the inner portion of the small intestine and colon about three to seven days after drug administration. This may cause a decrease in nutrient and fluid absorption, resulting in nausea, diarrhea, appetite loss, and possibly dehydration. You should call your veterinarian or an emergency clinic if these signs persist for more than twenty-four hours or if fresh blood is noted in the stool.

The lowering of platelets in the blood (thrombocytopenia) may also occur during chemotherapy, and if severe enough it can cause bleeding. It is normally due to impaired production of the platelets in the bone marrow, which can be damaged during chemotherapy. In mild cases, patients may have no symptoms at all. In moderate cases, red spots or bruising may appear on the skin, most commonly along the abdominal wall and along the legs. In severe cases, a low platelet count can cause bleeding at any site of the body and can be very dangerous. Bleeding may be obvious, like from the gums or vagina, or it could be hidden. If you see any of these signs, call your veterinarian or an emergency clinic immediately.

A decrease in the number of white blood cells that fight infection is known as *neutropenia* and is the most significant complication of chemotherapy. This condition is almost always due to impairment of the bone marrow to produce white blood cells and normally occurs three to seven days after chemotherapy. It is most severe in patients who receive aggressive treatments. Patients with even mild forms of neutropenia can develop major problems. The most severe cases of neutropenia may have no signs at all, or may show only minor problems, such as a fever and infection. A fever in patients who have received chemotherapy must be taken seriously, requiring a complete evaluation. When a low white blood cell count is combined with a fever (febrile neutropenia), it is a medical emergency and must be dealt with immediately. Any rectal temperature greater than 103.5°F (39.7°C) should be immediately reported to your veterinarian or emergency clinic. Hours and minutes are critical! If left untreated, this complication may become fatal in a matter of hours.

To minimize problems (infection, bleeding) associated with bone marrow suppression, the pet's blood should be tested on a regular basis during treatment. If abnormalities are detected, chemotherapy might be postponed until there's improvement. Occasionally, a very low white blood cell count necessitates the short-term use of antibiotics to prevent infection until the white cell count returns to normal.

Hair loss is the most noticeable side effect of chemotherapy. Severity of hair loss, as well as the timing of it, depends on the breed of the dog, the schedule of treatments, and the types of drugs and their dosage. Hair loss usually starts two to three weeks after initiation of chemotherapy, and it may involve just thinning and partial loss, or complete loss. Hair may be lost gradually over a period of a few weeks, or it may happen in matter of days. Every part of the body can be affected. Hair will start to grow back about a month after the completion of chemotherapy. The new growth may look exactly the same as before chemotherapy, or it may feel and look completely different. The color may be slightly different, and it may grow back thicker or thinner, less curly or more curly.

Most breeds of dogs don't lose their hair or show other side effects when treated with chemotherapy.

What should you do if you notice any of these side effects at home? Call your veterinarian or emergency clinic if any side effect persists for more than twenty-four hours, or if it worsens at any time. If nausea, vomiting, or diarrhea occurs, withhold all food for twenty-four hours. Always offer plenty of water, including ice chips. Reintroduce food slowly by feeding your pet frequent small meals versus one large meal. Bland meals, such as chicken or veal baby food, are good choices. If your pet is not drinking, offer chicken or beef broth.

The bottom line is this: if any thing bothers you about your pet's condition, don't hesitate to contact an animal emergency clinic veterinarian!!

Fortunately, side effects rarely occur in pets treated with chemotherapy.

CONTROLLING VOMITING AND NAUSEA DURING CHEMOTHERAPY

Unlike when people undergo chemotherapy, nausea and vomiting are very rarely seen in pets. Some chemotherapy medications are more likely to cause vomiting (emesis) than others (this is known as the "emetic potential" of the medication). The emetic potential is based upon the medication itself, as well as individual sensitivity to the medication and individual sensitivity to gastrointestinal upset. For example, a dog with a sensitive stomach that easily becomes nauseous has a higher emetic potential than another dog that rarely becomes nauseous.

LOW EMETIC POTENTIAL	MODERATE EMETIC POTENTIAL
carboplatin	actinomycin-D
corticosteroids	chlorambucil
cyclophosphamide	cisplatin
L-asparaginase	cytosine arabinoside
mitoxantrone	dacarbazine
nitrogen mustard	doxorubicin
vinblastine	methotrexate
	vincristine

Two conventional medications that are quite effective at controlling nausea and may be given during chemotherapy are Reglan and Anzemet. Reglan (metoclopramide), dosed at 0.2–0.4 mg/kg, is given at the time of chemotherapy and for several days following treatment. Anzemet (dolasetron) can be used by itself or with Reglan, and is dosed at 0.7–1 mg/kg and given once daily, administered by injection (subcutaneous, intramuscular, or intravenous). Supplements containing glutamine and probiotics also offer some relief from gastrointestinal side effects, as does the herb ginger.

While side effects are rare in dogs when compared to people, they can still occur. You should closely observe your pet's appetite, activity, and elimination. If any abnormality is noted, medications or supplements can be used. It may be helpful for you to have your doctor prescribe a first-aid kit of medications and supplements. The kit can include famotidine (Pepcid) for lack of appetite or nausea, metoclopramide (Reglan) to treat nausea or vomiting, and sulfasalazine, glutamine, and probiotics to treat diarrhea and colitis. Talk with your doctor about potential side effects of your pet's chemotherapy regimen.

COMMON SIDE EFFECTS ASSOCIATED WITH SPECIFIC CHEMOTHERAPY MEDICATIONS

DRUG	DOSAGE	TYPES OF CANCER	SIDE EFFECTS
Adriamycin	> 20 lbs = 30 mg/m² IV q 2–3 weeks (max 5) < 20 lbs = 1 mg/kg IV q 2–3 weeks (max 5)	Lymphoma, Soft tissue tumors	Myelosuppression, anaphylaxis, vomiting, cardiomyopathy (heart damage)
Bleomycin	2 mg/m² SC weekly	Carcinomas, lymphoma, leukemias	Myelosuppression
Busulfan	0.2 mg/kg PO daily	Myeloblastic leukemias	Myelosuppression
Carboplatin	300 mg/m² IV q 3–4 weeks 90 mg/m² IV weekly	Osteosarcoma, melanoma	Myelosuppression, vomiting

DRUG	DOSAGE	TYPES OF CANCER	SIDE EFFECTS
CCNU (lomustine)	90 mg/m² PO q 3 weeks	Relapse lymphoma, mast cell tumors	Myelosuppression, vomiting
Cisplatin	70 mg/m² IV q 3–4 weeks 30 mg/m² IV weekly	Osteosarcoma, melanoma	Myelosuppression, vomiting, kidney failure
Cytosar-U	100 mg/m² SC TID for 3 days 10 mg/m² SC q 12 hours until remission	Leukemias	Myelosuppression
Cytoxan	200 mg/m² PO or IV q 1–3 weeks	Lymphoma, leukemias, soft tissue malignancies	Myelosuppression, hemorrhagic cystitis (bladder inflammation and bleeding)
Dacarbazine	200 mg/m² IV daily for 5 days	Relapse lymphoma	Severe vomiting, myelosuppression
5-Fluorouracil	50 mg/m² IL in oil	Soft tissue malignancies	Seizures, ataxia
Gemzar	90 mg/m² IV q 3 weeks	Pancreatic and hepatocellular carcinomas	Myelosuppression, vomiting, anaphylaxis
Hydroxyurea	50 mg/kg PO SID until remission	Leukemias	Myelosuppression

DRUG	DOSAGE	TYPES OF CANCER	SIDE EFFECTS
L-Asparaginase	10,000 IU/m^2 IM q 1–4 weeks 400 IU/kg IM q 1–4 weeks	Lymphoma, leukemia	Anaphylaxis
Leukeran	0.2 mg/kg PO daily for 10 days then EOD	Lymphoma, leukemias, soft tissue malignancies, mast cell tumors	Myelosuppression
Melphalan	0.1 mg/kg PO daily for 10 days then EOD	Leukemia	Myelosuppression
Methotrexate	0.5 mg/kg IV q 3 weeks	Lymphoma, leukemia	Myelosuppression, vomiting
Mitoxantrone	6 mg/m^2 IV q 3–4 weeks	Lymphoma, soft tissue tumors	Myelosuppression, anaphylaxis, vomiting
Piroxicam	0.3 mg/kg PO daily or EOD with concurrent Misoprostil 3 mg/kg PO BID	Transitional cell carcinoma, melanomas, carcinomas	Gastrointestinal ulceration
Prednisone	40 mg/m^2 PO divided BID, SID, or EOD	Lymphomas, leukemias, insulinomas	Polyuria, polydypsia
Tamoxifen	600 mg/m^2 PO divided BID for 7 days, with chemotherapy administered on day 4	Mammary tumors, brain tumors, MDR tumors	Vaginal discharge, pyometra

DRUG	DOSAGE	TYPES OF CANCER	SIDE EFFECTS
Vinblastine	2 mg/m² IV slowly q 1–3 weeks	Lymphoma, leukemias, mast cell tumors, soft tissue tumors	Myelosuppression
Vincristine	0.5–0.75 mg/m² IV q 1–3weeks	Lymphoma, leukemias, mast cell tumors, soft tissue tumors	Myelosuppression

Notes: *Myelosuppression* means bone marrow suppression. *Polyuria* means increased amounts of urine produced. *Polydypsia* means increased thirst. Anaphylaxis means an immediate allergic reaction.

INTRALESIONAL CHEMOTHERAPY

Occasionally, an oncologist may recommend that chemotherapy be injected directly *into* the tumor. Soft tissue sarcomas that are not treated surgically (such as an inoperable tumor, in instances where conventional chemotherapy may not be affordable, or in those instances in which the pet is too ill to be safely treated with systemic chemotherapy) may also be treated in this fashion. Finally, intralesional chemotherapy can be used as an adjunctive therapy to increase tumor cell kill.

> *An oncologist may recommend that chemotherapy be injected directly into the tumor.*

No two oncologists treat their patients in the same exact way; talk with your veterinarian about the particulars of the drugs selected for treatment.

This overview of conventional therapies should serve only as an introduction to treating a pet with cancer; it is not a how-to book on the best ways to treat any particular cancer. It is up to the oncologist and pet owner to decide which treatments to use for a specific cancer.

Remember that chemotherapy may not agree with your pet, and that you can always stop the treatments or try a different chemotherapy drug. If the quality of life during your pet's treatment is not good, discuss it with your doctor, who will make adjustments to the dose, the schedule, and the type of medication. Most dogs do well when treated with chemotherapy, but if your dog is doing poorly, it may be wise to take a break or stop it and give supportive care. It may be time to try only complementary therapies until the dog feels better. With the guidance of your veterinarian and the consulting oncologist, an integrative program can be planned. *Remember that quality of life, not cure, is the goal for most of our pet patients.*

CHEMOTHERAPY RESISTANCE

In most cases, veterinarians don't cure cancer in pets but rather help them live longer by putting the cancer into remission for as long as possible. A main reason for this is that we use lower, less toxic doses of chemotherapy than are used in people. This is done specifically to minimize side effects; few pet owners would opt for chemotherapy if their pets experienced the same side effects commonly seen in people. The trade-off is that chemotherapy usually doesn't kill all the cancer cells, and remissions don't last as long in pets as in people.

Why do cancer cells develop drug resistance? The cancer cell is able to code its genes to make protein pumps on the cell surface membrane, which pump the drugs out of the cell. The pumps are called MDR pumps (for "multiple drug resistance"). This is a survival mechanism for normal as well as cancer cells; the MDR pumps move poisons (including chemotherapy drugs) out of the cell and in effect detoxify the cell. Stopping this process in cancer cells, which would allow chemotherapy drugs to accumulate in the cells and kill them, without harming normal cells and hurting the patient is major area of research study. Drugs such as calcium channel blockers can decrease the action of the pumps and may help patients whose cancer has develop resistance to chemotherapy.

HOW LONG SHOULD PETS UNDERGO CHEMOTHERAPY?

While it doesn't happen very often, occasionally a pet with cancer undergoing chemotherapy will live longer than expected. The question then arises: How long should we continue chemotherapy for this patient? Unfortunately, there is no right answer, and there's not any research data on this important question. One school of thought (usually expressed by conventional cancer doctors) suggests that since chemotherapy helped the pet recover from cancer and live longer than expected, chemotherapy should be continued to keep the pet in remission as long as possible. The other school of thought (usually expressed by holistic veterinarians, including me) suggests that chemotherapy should not continue indefinitely, because there is a chance, though rare, that it could lead to development of other cancers. Holistic doctors prefer to get the pet in remission and at some point (not everyone agrees when this "point" occurs) stop chemotherapy but continue immune-boosting supplements. The hope is that the pet's own body, helped by the supplements, will keep it in extended remission and no new cancers will develop. This is a personal decision to be decided by each pet owner after reviewing all of the facts.

RADIATION THERAPY
(BURNING THE CANCER)

In addition to surgery and chemotherapy, there's radiation therapy for the conventional treatment of pets with cancer. Radiation therapy became available for animals in the 1970s. It utilizes high-energy ionizing radiation to kill cancer cells. Because cancer cells are destroyed in the area being treated, radiation is generally considered a local therapy. Radiation breaks down one or both strands of the DNA molecule inside of cells, preventing cell growth and division. It does this by dislodging electrons from the atoms of the cells that are targeted by the radiation. The dislodged electrons (free radicals) cause oxidative damage to the cells, resulting in cell death.

> *Radiation therapy utilizes*
> *high-energy ionizing radiation to kill cancer cells.*

Normal cells in the area of treatment may be affected by radiation, but they are better equipped for repairing damage to DNA than the cancer cells. Cancer cells targeted with radiation cannot repair the damage adequately before reproducing, which kills the affected cancer cells. Radiation therapy is delivered with machines administering high-energy ionizing radiation. The machine used will depend on the tumor itself.

The dosage of radiation used for cancer treatment or palliative pain control (typically for dogs with osteosarcoma) is determined by several factors: the radiosensitivity of the tumor (some cancers are affected by radiation, whereas others are not), normal tissue tolerance, and the volume of tissue to be irradiated. Radiation therapy is planned according to clinical status. The desired dosage of radiation should be delivered in the smallest amount possible to ensure patient comfort. A simulator

(X-ray machine) is used to visualize and define the exact area to be treated. Healthy tissue may be protected from radiation therapy with customized shields (blocks). Reference points on the skin are marked with temporary dye or permanent tattoos, which is to ensure that the correct area will be treated. Each fraction of radiation is given from two to five times a week for three to five weeks, and each of these treatments requires sedation or general anesthetic. Radiation therapy may be used after surgery to kill residual cancer cells or before surgery to shrink tumors.

There are three main types of radiation therapy: external beam radiation, internal radiation, and palliative radiation.

External Beam Radiation

External radiation therapy (teletherapy) uses machines or sources that release high-energy beams such as X-rays, gamma rays, protons, and electrons. There is no pain or residual radiation coming from the patient after treatment.

Internal Radiation

Another less common form of radiation treatment uses short-range radiation therapy delivered by specially designed tubes, seeds, or implants (brachytherapy). Also, radiochemicals can be administered that release radiation into a known target field over time. This form of delivery is even less available for pets than the external beam delivery systems due to equipment and facility qualifications and regulatory limitations. In people, both internal and external radiation therapy may be used to treat cancer.

There is controversy regarding when radiation should be used. Some doctors prefer using radiation before surgery and others prefer using radiation after surgery for most soft tissue sarcomas of dogs and cats. When possible, intraoperative radiation with intralesional chemotherapy implants may be preferred.

PALLIATIVE RADIATION

Radiation therapy may also be used for palliative purposes to make pets more comfortable. Palliative radiation can shrink tumors that are inoperable, slowing down their growth and relieving pain. Palliative radiation schedules usually deliver higher doses of radiation over shorter periods of time than regular presurgical or follow-up radiation therapy protocols.

> *Palliative radiation therapy should be considered to help make dogs more comfortable.*

Palliative radiation therapy is often used to control pain from growing tumors, improving the quality of life for the patient. Radiation may enhance the effectiveness of painkilling (analgesic) drug therapies by directly targeting the cause of the pain. Noninvasive analgesic therapy should accompany or precede invasive palliative treatment of metastatic pain. In palliative radiation, high doses with small daily fractions are administered over one or two weeks; alternatively, low-dose, short-course radiation is just as effective as high-dose protocols, and may be preferred.

Radiation therapy is used for the relief of metastatic pain, especially metastatic bone pain. Symptoms from local extension of primary disease may also be controlled. Indications for radiation therapy in bone metastasis include pain relief and prevention of pathological fractures. Spinal cord compression from metastatic tumors requires immediate surgery, followed or preceded by radiation therapy and high-dose steroids. Radiation therapy is also used to relieve headaches caused by brain tumors.

External beam radiation therapy is used for localized bone metastasis. This may be directed locally, or if the pain is widespread, it may be treated with hemibody irradiation (one-half of the body at a time). Another way to deliver radiation is through the use of radiopharmaceuticals. Examples of these include Iodine-131, which is used to treat multiple bone metastasis from thyroid cancer; Phosphorous-32-orthophosphate, which is used for pain relief associated with bone metastasis from breast and prostate cancer; and Strontium 89, which is very effective for bone pain.

Radiation therapy for pain control is often recommended for dogs with osteosarcoma when amputation is not appropriate. Palliative radiation therapy should be considered in addition to chemotherapy to provide pain relief and additional use of the affected leg. In general, a nine- to twelve-month prognosis with full use of the leg could be considered.

RADIATION THERAPY FOR LYMPHOMA

Lymphatic cancers, known as lymphomas, are very sensitive to the effects of radiation therapy. In people, radiation is often used in treating lymphoma. Whole-body radiation therapy is used in people undergoing bone marrow transplants for various types of cancer, including resistant lymphoma. For dogs with lymphoma, radiation therapy to half of the body when starting and the other half one month into treatment with chemotherapy has been proposed in order to achieve longer remissions than would occur with only chemotherapy. This gives the dog a total whole-body radiation dose but protects the bone marrow from destruction because the untreated half remains functional. The side effects and the long-term results in a larger number of cases must be evaluated before this combination treatment becomes routinely recommended. Localized radiation therapy, rather than whole-body irradiation, has also been used to treat resistant lymph nodes in lymphoma for many years. More information on this topic is presented in chapter x in the discussion of lymphosarcoma on pages 42–46 in chapter 2.

SIDE EFFECTS OF RADIATION THERAPY

The most common side effect of radiation therapy is a localized burn, similar to a sunburn, in the area that is treated. Hair often falls out, but only in the area that was treated with radiation. The hair is generally expected to grow back within several months. The burn can be treated topically with aloe vera gel or another topical recommended by the oncologist. If the mucous membranes of the mouth, lips, or eyelids are in the treatment area, this tissue ulcerates, developing a condition called *mucositis*. The mucositis and sores in the mouth cause bad breath and excessive salivation, and can make eating painful. The use of mouth washes (diluted tea tree oil or aloe may be helpful, as may the homotoxicologic remedy Traumeel; medicated washes may be needed), the application of eye ointments, and the feeding of soft food generally takes care of the problem for most dogs. (Some dogs and many cats may need surgically placed feeding tubes for a short period of time to maintain adequate nutrition.) If the skin or mucous membranes show too much irritation, treatment may be postponed for a few days to allow healing, but the total radiation dose should still be used for optimal results.

> *The most common side effect of radiation therapy is*
> *a localized burn, similar to a sunburn.*

Unfortunately, when radiation therapy is used for nasal and brain tumors, the eyelids become irritated and tear production is often permanently diminished. This requires lifelong treatment with artificial tear ointments. Another hazard is that the lens of one or both eyes may be damaged, resulting in compromised vision or loss of vision. Ointments that soothe the eyes and skin are very helpful for these side effects. Complete healing of mucous membranes takes one month and healing of the skin takes two months after the last radiation treatment. The results of radiation therapy on an existing tumor may be evident after only two months. The tumor may not shrink but a biopsy of it may show that the cells are not active. If the tumor continues to grow or recurs during the therapy, it is considered resistant and the dog will need further evaluation for a new treatment plan.

Other side effects of radiation therapy include fatigue and lack of appetite (anorexia). These may occur with treatment to any site, while other toxicities are more specific to the site being treated. The amount of tissue being treated, total daily dose of therapy, method of treatment, and individual factors will influence the severity of side effects. Acute reaction to radiation occurs during treatment itself, while delayed side effects may occur months or years after treatment and may lead to chronic problems. Radiation may also affect the bone marrow, resulting in anemia, low platelet counts, and low white blood cell counts. Routine blood testing, as is done with chemotherapy, is recommended during radiation treatments.

Radiation therapy also has some long-term side effects, such as paralysis, bone marrow suppression, bone death, ligament or muscle contraction, and scarring of the skin. Because these long-term effects usually don't show up for two to three years, they are rarely a problem in dogs. As is true with chemotherapy, serious side effects occur rarely in pets treated with radiation.

Side effects of radiation therapy might be minimized by using various supplements, including glutamine, probiotics, fatty acids, and antioxidants. Proper nutrition is also important in maximizing health and minimizing side effects. While supplements are safe and effective, their use during radiation therapy and chemotherapy is controversial, especially the use of antioxidants (see pages 161–172 in chapter 7 for a more detailed discussion of this important topic).

While the goal of integrative therapy is to utilize conventional treatments only when absolutely essential, it's important to understand that for most cancers, some combination of chemotherapy, radiation therapy, and surgery will be needed. In most pets these therapies quickly reduce the presence of cancer without serious side effects. By reducing the number of cancer cells, the body's immune system can go into action and do its job to help the pet heal. The next chapter will consider complementary therapies.

CHAPTER SIX

COMPLEMENTARY THERAPIES *for* CANCER: ACUPUNCTURE, CHIROPRATIC, HERBS, HOMEOPATHICS

THERE ARE SEVERAL COMPLEMENTARY THERAPIES that have been recommended for pets with cancer. Most have not been proven beneficial in strict clinical trials. However, based upon laboratory testing and clinical experience over many years in people and animals, many of these therapies appear to have some benefit in supportive care. In my own practice I have seen positive benefits from complementary approaches in many patients. My personal belief is that if we treat with conventional therapies alone, and fail to include diet and complementary methods as part of our treatment, we are not doing a complete job for the patient. As we veterinarians learn more, our recommendations for treatments will change over time. Just as there are many opinions as to which conventional treatments should be used for pets with cancer, there are also many choices for complementary approaches. Regardless of which therapies are chosen, the ultimate goal is the same: slow the growth and spread of cancer, support the pet's immune system, encourage maintenance of body weight, and closely monitor and minimize side effects associated with conventional treatments. Some complementary therapies can be toxic or interfere with conventional treatments, so you should work with your doctor to decide which therapies might be of most value.

Whatever you do, do *not* go to the store and buy supplements on your own. Many pet owners who come to my office for consultation arrive with a big shopping bag with twenty to thirty different supplements! Often I have to tell them that their purchases will not be of use to their pets. Instead of wasting their money on supplements that may not help and could harm their pets, they should spend their money wisely by purchasing the supplements recommended by their veterinarian.

ARE SUPPLEMENTS SAFE FOR PETS WITH CANCER?

One question that arises frequently is whether or not the use of supplements (particularly antioxidants) will *hurt* pets with cancer by *interfering* with their conventional treatments?

This is actually a very controversial topic in both human and veterinary cancer medicine. Certainly, we don't want to do anything to interfere with a treatment such as chemotherapy or radiation therapy. If we're going to use these conventional treatments, we want them to work to the best of their ability (otherwise why even use them?). Supplements, particularly antioxidants, inhibit cellular oxidation. Too much oxidation causes inflammation and cell injury; if left unchecked, inflammation and cell injury can damage a cell's DNA and cause it to transform into a cancer cell. The good news is that any supplements that can dampen this process should be helpful to any patient, especially one with cancer. The bad news, and the reason for the controversy, is that some conventional therapies deliberately cause oxidation in the cancer cells as a way to kill them. If supplements inhibit oxidation, including the oxidation of cancer cells, a proposed theory is that the cancer cells won't die. Could supplements prevent chemotherapy and radiation from working properly and even make the cancer worse?

First, keep in mind that while radiation therapy kills cancer cells by causing oxidation, most chemotherapy drugs do not (they kill by other mechanisms, discussed in chapter 5). The only chemotherapy drugs that use oxidation as their main strategy for killing cancer cells are some of the antitumor antibiotics, the most common of which is bleomycin (see pages 85–86 in chapter 5). With rare exception, there is no need to worry about supplements, particularly antioxidants, interfering with conventional cancer treatments.

Second, at least in people, we know that diets high in antioxidants (particularly natural sources such as fruits, vegetables, and natural antioxidant supplements) are likely to minimize the formation of cancer (so-called cancer-preventing diets). This is due to the fact that antioxidants prevent excessive oxidation of cells; excessive oxidation leads to cell (DNA) damage, inflammation, chronic disease, and cancer.

Third, cancer cells do not behave like normal cells (if they did, cells would never become cancerous). So in theory, what we might think would happen to a normal cell doesn't happen to a cancer cell.

Fourth, patients who are nutrient deficient or who have poor immune systems do worse when treated with conventional therapies than patients who have stronger immune systems and better nutrient intake. In my own practice, patients who take supplements and improve their diets generally do much better than patients who do not when treated with chemotherapy and radiation. It's important to boost the pet's strength, health, and immune system to help it better withstand conventional therapies and help it stay in remission after conventional therapies are no longer used. The greater the pet's debilitation, the greater the chance that any therapy will fail.

Fifth and finally, the only reported studies that have shown that antioxdant supplements increase cancer growth are those where *individual, synthetic* vitamins were taken at *high* doses — in effect, the supplements acted like drugs. There have been no valid studies in people or pets that show that the use of supplements and diets, when properly prescribed and used under medical supervision, make the cancer worse or interfer with conventional treatments; there have been many studies, as well as my own clinical experience, that show the exact opposite.

The evidence is strongly in favor of using supplements (including antioxidants) and proper nutrition as part of the therapy of cancer patients. What should you do if your pet's doctor is opposed to using supplements and improving nutrition during conventional cancer treatment? This is a tough situation that unfortunately many pet owners face. In my own practice, I've had clients tell me that their oncologists have told them not to use supplements I have recommended. Here are your choices if you get conflicting advice from your holistic doctor and your general practitioner or specialist. Choice number one is to ignore your holistic doctor and not use supplements at all. Choice number two is to ignore the specialists and use the supplements prescribed by the holistic doctor. Choice number three is to use the prescribed supplements before or after conventional therapy, but not during the therapy.

I tell all of my clients that most conventional doctors, including specialists, simply do not know anything about the use of complementary therapies for treating cancer. While I appreciate that they don't want to do anything to hurt the pet, I don't want their lack of knowledge or aversion to what I'm doing to hurt the pet either. Obviously, I won't knowingly prescribe any therapy that might hurt the pet or interfere with the pet's conventional treatment. I research all of my recommendations and prescribe only those I think are most likely to help and not hurt my patients. In the final analysis, it is the pet owner who must decide what is best for the pet. I don't like to mislead other doctors who are consulting on a cancer treatment, but sometimes it is best for a pet owner to keep quiet and not argue with the specialist.

As long as one of your veterinarians is aware of all the treatments being used, I don't think it helps to create a situation where one of them refuses to treat your pet simply because you choose additional treatments he or she may not understand or approve of. Hopefully, some day all doctors will let go of their personal prejudices and work together (as most of my local specialists do with me) for the betterment of the patient!

> *There have been no valid studies in people or pets that show that the use of supplements and improved diets, when properly prescribed and used under medical supervision, make the cancer worse or interfere with conventional treatments.*

Even though the use of supplements remains controversial, I think the evidence clearly shows selected supplements, combined with an improved diet, help people and pets with cancer.

After considering all the facts and consulting with the pet's oncologist and holistic veterinarian, the final decision is solely the pet owner's.

ACUPUNCTURE

Acupuncture is not usually prescribed as a cancer treatment, as there are few clear-cut indications of its benefit. However, there are several instances in which acupuncture may be useful.

Because the immune system is depressed in cancer, both as a result of the cancer itself and possibly as a result of chemotherapy and radiation therapy, acupuncture may be useful to stimulate the body's immune response.

Acupuncture may also be useful to control the nausea that may accompany chemotherapy or radiation therapy.

A study published in the *Journal of the American Medical Association* found that electro-acupuncture may reduce nausea and vomiting during chemotherapy. The study evaluated 104 women with breast cancer. All of the women were undergoing high-dose chemotherapy (cyclophosphamide, carmustine, and cisplatin) and were receiving antivomiting medication (prochlorperazine, lorazepam, and diphenhydramine hydrochloride). Patients were randomized to receive daily low-frequency electro-acupuncture treatment at point PC6 (a classic antiemetic acupuncture point), daily minimal needling acupuncture at sites not indicated for nausea or emesis control, or no additional treatment. After a five-day study period, the group receiving electro-acupuncture at point PC6 had significantly fewer vomiting episodes than the control group, which did not receive acupuncture at PC6. The researchers concluded that the addition of daily electro-acupuncture to a regimen using anti-vomiting medications may be superior to acupuncture or medication alone for controlling vomiting.

> *Acupuncture may be useful to control*
> *nausea in pets with cancer.*

While acupuncture may be recommended for the pet with vomiting caused by chemotherapy or radiation treatment, most pets rarely suffer from nausea during treatment with conventional anticancer therapies, unlike the situation in people.

There is a continuing debate over whether acupuncture applied to tumors is beneficial or harmful. At this time, acupuncture is most useful for its ability to stimulate the immune system and counteract nausea.

CHIROPRACTIC

Chiropractic medicine attempts to improve health through spinal manipulation. Like other complementary therapies, chiropractic medicine is designed to work at the appropriate level of the healing process and to work with the normal inborn homeostasis of the body (the ability of the body to maintain its normal functioning and good health), rather than simply treat the symptoms. While chiropractic care has been used in human medicine for over one hundred years, only recently has this discipline been applied to animals. While few controlled studies have shown benefits of chiropractic therapy, a number of anecdotal reports have demonstrated positive benefits.

Chiropractic care focuses on the interactions between neurologic mechanisms (the nervous system) and the biomechanics of the vertebrae. In chiropractic theory, disease arises as a result of spinal misalignment that negatively influences the nervous system. Because all body systems are regulated by the nervous system, anything that interferes with nervous impulses to organs, spinal misalignment being the most common cause, could hinder the proper functioning of those organs and body systems. Chiropractic therapy seeks to realign the spine by a variety of manipulative techniques.

Spinal misalignments are called subluxations by chiropractors (not to be confused with the term *subluxation* used by conventional doctors, which means partial dislocation). A subluxation is technically defined by A. E. Homewood as a "disrelationship of a vertebral segment in association with contiguous (surrounding) vertebrae resulting in a disturbance of normal biomechanical and neurological function."

Chiropractic medicine seeks to cure the disease process by correcting these subluxations. Chiropractors determine which vertebrae are misaligned through clinical examinations and radiographic imaging. Once the location of the subluxation is determined, the veterinary chiropractor corrects the misalignment through spinal adjustment. The spinal adjustment is performed as needed to realign the subluxated vertebrae and ensure neurologic reprogramming of muscle contractions and healing of damaged ligaments. Usually multiple adjustments are needed as the body requires time to heal.

(Note: Because of the increase in popularity in many complementary treatment techniques such as chiropractic, a number of "animal therapists" have advertised chiropractic care, and massage and acupuncture/acupressure, as part of their specialty. Only veterinarians, or chiropractors using the technique under direct veterinary supervision, should perform chiropractic therapies on pets. Laypersons should not be allowed to practice any of these medical techniques on pets.)

Chiropractic therapy alone cannot cure cancer. However, chiropractic adjustments may improve functioning of the immune system, which improves the prognosis for pets with cancer. Additionally, chiropractic may help mitigate side effects of cancer or cancer therapy (such as pain and vomiting) through proper functioning of the nervous system.

There are many herbal remedies that can be helpful for pets with cancer. At this time, definitive controlled studies showing the effectiveness of most herbs in pets with cancer are lacking, and recommendations are made based upon extrapolation from human medicine and historical use. In many instances, the appropriate dosage of an herbal supplement for a dog is not known. Therefore, the following guidelines may prove useful. Nevertheless, a final decision about the proper dose should be made in consultation with your veterinarian.

Herbs that are prescribed for pets may be the whole herb or just the active ingredient in the herb. Products vary according to whether the whole herb or just part of the herb is included. Products using only the active ingredient may have advantages, because they do not include parts of the herbs that may contain toxins or other ingredients that may make the active ingredient less effective. However, by using only the active ingredient, some of the other ingredients that might act in conjunction with the active ingredient are lost. Which is better is up to debate, although most herbalists prefer remedies that contain the whole herb to take advantage of all of the ingredients contained within the herb.

There are a number of companies making herbs for the human and pet market, but standard quality controls that exist for pharmaceuticals is lacking in the supplement market (although the National Animal Supplement Council [NASC] reviews submitted products, and its seal of approval indicates a manufacturer who adheres to high standards). Studies have shown that some products have more or less, and sometimes even none, of the active ingredient listed on the bottle! For this reason, you should use only products from high-quality, reputable companies. The least-expensive generic herbal supplements are likely to be of lowest quality and questionable value.

Quality control is important when choosing herbs. You should only use herbs from companies with strict quality-control procedures. Because the potency of herbs deteriorates over time, it is best if the herbal preparation can be specially made for the pet and administered soon after it is prepared. Your veterinarian should keep only a small supply of herbs on hand, again because their potency fades quickly. As a rule, you should discard any herbal product you've had for more than one year.

While most herbs taken as complementary therapies are generally considered safe, many can be quite toxic if taken incorrectly. All medicines are potentially toxic; only the dosage and the length of treatment determine what is toxic and what is safe. Owners should refrain from diagnosing and medicating their pets and instead should rely upon advice from a knowledgeable holistic veterinarian. Because herbal remedies can interact, sometimes dangerously, with conventional medications, make sure you tell your veterinarian whatever medications your pet is currently taking.

While herbs are generally safe, their active ingredients can have powerful effects. Don't use herbal therapy on your pet without proper veterinary supervision.

Herbs are usually supplied in powder or capsule form; tinctures (alcoholic extracts) are also available. Many products made for humans can be used in pets. Unfortunately, the appropriate dosage for pets has not been formally established for many herbs, and clinical experience and extrapolation from human data is often the only way to determine how much to give a pet. It is hard to find good controlled studies for the use of herbs in pets because there is much less funding available compared with the support pharmaceutical studies receive.

The following guidelines serve as a starting point for herbal therapy.

WESTERN HERBS:

1–500 mg capsule/25 pounds of body weight, given 2–3 times daily

0.5–1.5 tsp of powder/25 pounds of body weight, given 2–3 times daily

5–10 drops/10 pounds of body weight, given 2–3 times daily

Alternatively, some herbalists recommend extrapolation based on weight. Since human doses are based on a 150-pound male, a recommended dose of three capsules given three times daily for this 150-pound male would extrapolate to one capsule given three times daily for a 50-pound dog.

CHINESE HERBS:

1 g concentrated herbs/20 pounds of body weight, given 2–3 times daily for dogs

4 g fresh herbs/20 pounds of body weight, given 2–3 times daily for dogs

The following discussion on specific cancer-fighting herbs has been adapted from my book *The Natural Health Bible for Dogs & Cats.*

*Alfalfa (*Medicago sativa*)*

Alfalfa contains many nutrients (protein, minerals, and vitamins, especially vitamin K) and chlorophyll, which serves as an antioxidant. Alfalfa possesses cancer-preventing properties by inactivating some of the chemicals that can cause cancer. It is often fed to animals that need to gain weight, making it helpful for pets with cancer who experience reduced appetites and weight loss. Alfalfa is generally regarded as safe; most owners simply add a super green food supplement containing alfalfa and other grasses, such as wheat grass, to the pet's food. If pets must be force-fed, adding a green food such as alfalfa to the food might also be helpful. Do not use alfalfa seeds because they can cause blood disorders. Animals sensitive to pollen may also be sensitive to fresh alfalfa.

Aloe Vera (Aloe spp)

Aloe is often used topically as a preparation or soothing rinse. Aloe contains a number of beneficial chemicals; the prostaglandins in aloe can reduce inflammation, minimize allergic reactions, and promote wound healing. Aloe has antibacterial and antifungal effects; the antibacterial effects have been compared to silver sulfadiazine. Aloe ointments may be useful for pets with ulcerated skin cancers or for pets with ulcers of the mouth as a result of cancer or chemotherapy or radiation treatments.

In people, oral aloe vera is sometimes recommended to treat AIDS, diabetes, asthma, stomach ulcers, and general immune weakness. While the clinical evidence for the benefits of aloe vera in these conditions is weak, one of its constituents, acemannan, does seem to possess immune-enhancing properties. Test-tube and animal studies suggest that it may stimulate immunity and inhibit the growth of viruses.

> *Aloe has bone marrow stimulating*
> *abilities and antioxidant actions.*

Acemannan, a polysaccharide immune stimulant found in aloe vera, may be helpful for pets with allergies, skin infections, and other diseases, including cancer, that suppress the immune system. Acemannan is approved for use as part of the therapy for treating fibrosarcoma tumors in pets. (Further discussion of acemannan and other glycoproteins can be found on pages 193–196 in chapter 7.)

Aloe may be helpful for pets with cancer due to its potent bone marrow stimulating abilities, as well as its antioxidant actions.

In people, aloe has been used internally as a laxative or tonic (lower doses) for the gastrointestinal system. In pets that don't have direct veterinary supervision, aloe should only be used externally; internal application can result in strong laxative effects due to its anthraquinone (aloin) content.

Do not give aloe to pregnant or lactating dogs. In people, oral aloe is not recommended for those with severe liver or kidney disease; the same warning is probably justified in pets.

Astragalus (Astragalus membranaceus)

Astragalus is a popular herb. Its roots are used to strengthen the immune system, and it possesses antibacterial and anti-inflammatory properties. Astragalus also boosts energy in debilitated patients. Many doctors prescribe this herb for pets with various infections and for those with chronic illnesses, including cancer. The mode of action is to stimulate T cell activity, raise white blood cell counts, and strengthen the liver. Astragalus can be used to help a patient recover from long-term steroid therapy, which is often part of the chemotherapy regimen for dogs with cancer. *Astragalus membranaceus* is safe, but other species of astragalus can be toxic. Similar to the concerns with echinacea, caution is warranted when administering astragalus to pets with diseases resulting from an overactive immune system or autoimmune diseases (see pages 124–127 for more information).

Burdock Root (Arctium lappa, Arctium minor)

Burdock root is used as a diuretic liver tonic and a blood cleanser. Its diuretic action removes toxins and wastes from the body. This herb is useful in any situation in which toxins have built up and need to be eliminated from the body, such as when pets have finished a period of chemotherapy or when pets are eating low-quality processed foods (pets with cancer should have proper diets and nutritional supplementation).

> *Burdock root's diuretic action removes toxins and wastes from the body.*

Burdock root may also be able to stimulate the bone marrow and may possess some antioxidant activity. Burdock root has been shown to contain chemicals that remove environmental toxins from the body, which has made it a popular herbal supplement during the treatment of cancer. It is also a primary ingredient in the Hoxsey and Essiac herbal cancer treatments (see pages 135–136). Burdock root is extremely safe and can be given to most adult pets on a long-term basis. It has not been established as safe to administer to young children, pregnant or nursing women, or people with severe liver or kidney disease; similar precautions are warranted in pets. (In 1978, the *Journal of the American Medical Association* caused a brief scare by publishing a report of burdock root poisoning. Subsequent investigation showed that the herbal product involved was actually contaminated with the poisonous chemical atropine from an unknown source.)

Cat's Claw (Uncaria tomentosa)

In people, cat's claw is used to treat cancer, diabetes, ulcers, arthritis, and infections, as well as assist in recovery from childbirth. In pets, cat's claw is used for the treatment of abscesses, arthritis, dermatitis, cancer, and urinary infections. It appears to have immune-stimulating and anti-inflammatory properties, and it may be useful for treating feline leukemia and feline immunodeficiency infections in cats.

Cat's claw appears to be safe for pets. However, European physicians believe that it should not be taken in conjunction with hormone treatments, insulin injections, or vaccinations. It has not been established as safe to administer to young children, pregnant or nursing women, or people with severe liver or kidney disease; similar precautions may be warranted in pets.

Dandelion (Taraxacum officinale)

All parts of the dandelion plant are useful in stimulating the liver and promoting diuresis (increased urination). In addition, all of the plant is efficacious for its anti-inflammatory properties. Dandelion, especially the fresh greens, is also a healthy green food, providing vitamins, minerals, and other nutrients to the pet. The most active constituents in dandelion appear to be eudesmanolide and germacranolide, substances unique to this herb. Other ingredients include taraxol, taraxerol, and taraxasterol, along with stigmasterol, beta-sitosterol, caffeic acid, taraxacin, terpenoides, inulin, and p-hydroxyphenylacetic acid.

Various parts of the dandelion are recommended for specific uses. In addition to serving as a nutritional supplements (leaves), it's useful for fluid retention (leaves), liver and gallbladder disease (root), constipation (root), and various forms of arthritis (root).

In pets with cancer, dandelion may be useful for providing

nutrients and for removing waste from the body by acting as a diuretic and by supporting liver function.

Dandelion can be used safely in pets; because it may lower blood sugar, it should not be used in pets receiving hypoglycemic therapy without veterinary supervision. There might also be some risk when combining it with pharmaceutical diuretics. Do not use dandelion in pets with diseases of the gallbladder or in animals with bile duct obstruction. Contact dermatitis and allergic reactions have been reported in people. Pets with known allergies to related plants, such as chamomile and yarrow, should use dandelion with caution.

> *Dandelion may provide nutrients and remove wastes from the body.*

Dandelion has not been established as safe to administer to young children, pregnant or nursing women, or people with severe liver or kidney disease. Similar precautions probably also apply in pets.

Echinacea
(Echinacea purpurea, E. angustifolia, E. pallida)

Echinacea is used as an immune-supporting herb and as an antimicrobial (antiviral and antibacterial) herb. There are a number of classes of pharmacologically active chemicals in echinacea, including polysaccharides, flavonoids (calculated as quercetin), caffeic acid, essential oils, alkylamides, and polyacetylenes.

Echinacea has strong immune-modulating properties that may make it useful for pets with cancer. This herb increases the ability of white blood cells to destroy invading organisms (phagocytosis), stimulates the lymphatic system to remove waste materials, and reduces the production of hyaluronidase, an enzyme that breaks down hyaluronic acid, which is needed to bind cells together to prevent infection. The reduction of hyaluronidase is responsible for tissue regeneration and decreased inflammation. Both test-tube and animal studies have found that polysaccharides in echinacea can increase antibody production, raise white blood cell counts, and stimulate the activity of key white blood cells. These positive benefits make echinacea an herb that may be useful for pets with cancer. The lack of effectiveness in *preventing* diseases when taken long-term suggests that echinacea does not actually strengthen the immune system overall, which means echinacea is not useful for preventing cancer.

> *Echinacea is best known for its strong immune-modulating properties.*

Echinacea works best with a healthy immune system, so its effectiveness is boosted with the use of other herbs, such as goldenseal (see page 131) and Oregon grape (see page 140), and a proper diet with nutritional supplements.

It remains controversial which species of echinacea is the best to use. Many experts consider the fresh-pressed juice of *Echinacea purpurea* to be the best preparation because it contains the greatest range of active compounds. Other experts recommend a minimum standard of 2.4 percent beta-1,2-fructofuranosides, which guarantees the plant was harvested in the blossom stage and was carefully prepared and stabilized. More research is needed to resolve the controversy.

Because the effectiveness of echinacea depends on a healthy immune system, some doctors do not administer it to pets with immune disorders. This is based on concerns in human medicine, but since these precautions date back to the 1950s, they may no longer be warranted. Germany's Commission E, which regulates herbal therapies, warns against using echinacea in cases of autoimmune disorders such as multiple sclerosis, lupus, and rheumatoid arthritis, as well as tuberculosis and leukocytosis. Also, there are rumors that echinacea should not be used by people with AIDS. These warnings are theoretical, based on fears that echinacea might actually activate immunity in the wrong way. But there is no evidence that echinacea use has actually harmed anyone with these diseases. In fact, it has been used in cancer therapy because of its potential immune-modulating properties. A recent study in *Alternative Medicine* disputes the claims that long-term use of echinacea is bad for the immune system or causes serious side effects such as liver damage and anaphylactic shock. Echinacea is now believed to be an immune modulator rather than immune stimulator, and there is no evidence that it worsens immune conditions (such as AIDS). As with all herbal therapies, consult with your holistic veterinarian *before* you give echinacea to your pet.

Echinacea appears to be safe. Even when taken in very high doses, it has not been found to cause any toxic effects. Side effects in people are uncommon and usually limited to minor gastrointestinal symptoms, increased urination, and mild allergic reactions. Prior recommendations were not to use echinacea for extended periods of time without a break before using it again. However, it appears that this recommendation was made without foundation and that echinacea can be used for extended periods of time (but always consult with your doctor). There are no known drug interactions. Echinacea has not been established as safe for young children, pregnant or nursing women, or people with severe liver or kidney disease.

The side effects and warnings that apply to people might also be applied to pets. Because wild echinacea is becoming endangered, cultivated echinacea or other immune stimulants (such as reishi) may be preferred.

Flax (Linum spp)

Flaxseed (linseed) has been proposed as an herbal therapy for pets with cancer due to its fatty acid and lignan contents. It contains both omega-3 and omega-6 fatty acids. While omega-3 fatty acids are of proven benefit to pets with cancer, flaxseed contains inactive omega-3's that must be converted by the pet's body to active omega-3's (fish oil contains the active omega-3s DHE and EPA). There is some evidence that pets may not be able to convert the inactive fatty acids to the active form. Therefore, I prefer to prescribe omega-3's via fish oil. However, flaxseed may have benefits for cancer therapy due to its lignan content (extra virgin olive oil also contains lignans; adding it to your pet's food or cooking your pet's homemade diet in olive oil will supply lignans as well). Lignans contain seoisoloriciresinol diglycoside and matairesinol, which are active cancer-fighting chemicals. Lignans also contain antioxidants and other chemicals that have antiproliferative, anti-estrogen, and antiangiogenesis properties, all of which may slow the growth and spread of cancer.

Garlic (Allium sativum)

Garlic contains several nutrients and sulfur compounds that have been shown to have medicinal properties, especially allicin and alliin. The sulfur compounds in garlic may increase phase 2 detoxification enzymes, which may significantly reduce the risk of many degenerative conditions such as cancer. Preliminary evidence suggests that regular eating of garlic may help prevent cancer, perhaps due to its antioxidant properties, its ability to stimulate white blood cell production in the bone marrow, and its ability to inhibit chemicals that are responsible for the growth of cancer. Garlic has been shown to prevent tumor formation in lab animals because of its diallyl sulfide component and its liver-strengthening chemicals. In people, several large studies strongly suggest that a diet high in garlic can prevent cancer. In one study, women whose diets included significant quantities of garlic were approximately 30 percent less likely to develop colon cancer. The potential benefits, with minimal chance of side effects when taken at the recommended doses, make garlic a common recommendation for including in the diets of pets with cancer. Too much garlic can be toxic, so be sure to follow your doctor's recommendations.

WHICH FORM OF GARLIC IS BEST?

Garlic contains two main medicinal compounds: allicin and alliin. Allicin contains the antibiotic properties of garlic. The "allicin potential" of the garlic compound is important for fighting infections. Because allicin is an unstable compound that is easily destroyed, fresh garlic or products with an identified allicin potential should be used when garlic is chosen for treating infections. Because it is difficult to know if a prepared formula has the amount of allicin listed on the label (unless the product comes from a reputable manufacturer), many herbalists recommend using fresh garlic cloves when the allicin dosage is important. Prepared products should provide a daily dose of at least 10 mg of alliin or a total allicin potential of 4,000 mcg (4–5 mg), which approximates one clove (4 g total weight) of garlic; in people, a typical dosage of garlic is 900 mg daily of garlic powder extract standardized to contain 1.3 percent alliin, providing about 12,000 mcg of alliin daily. This recommendation needs to be extrapolated for use in pets. Many manufacturers claim a specific allicin potential "at the time of manufacture," but this is not helpful because it does not reveal the allicin potential of the finished product and whether or not the product is stable. Read the label carefully.

Alliin is a relatively odorless substance. When garlic is crushed or cut, an enzyme called allinase is brought in contact with alliin, turning it into allicin. The allicin itself then rapidly breaks down into entirely different compounds. Allicin is most responsible for garlic's strong odor. It can also blister the skin and kill bacteria, viruses, and fungi.

Putting powdered garlic in a capsule is akin to cutting or crushing a bulb; the powdered garlic degenerates quickly. Alliin contacts allinase, yielding allicin, which then breaks down. Unless something is done to prevent this process, garlic powder won't have any alliin or allicin left by the time you buy it.

Some garlic producers declare that alliin and allicin have nothing to do with garlic's effectiveness in promoting health and simply sell products that contain none of either compound, such as aged powdered garlic and garlic oil. Other producers believe that allicin is absolutely essential. However, in order to make garlic relatively odorless, they must prevent the alliin from turning into allicin until the product is ready for consumption. To accomplish this feat, they use complex and proprietary manufacturing processes.

How well each of these methods works is a matter of controversy.

In most of the studies that found cholesterol-lowering powers in garlic, the daily dosage of garlic was at least 10 mg of alliin. Alliin-free aged garlic also appears to be effective when taken at a dose of 1–7.2 g daily.

Either form of garlic — allicin or alliin — will probably have benefits if the garlic has not been subjected to extreme heat, such as roasting. Whenever possible, it's probably best to eat raw garlic cloves to get the most out of its medicinal compounds.

Too much garlic can be toxic to pets; for commercially prepared products, be sure to follow the directions printed on the label. As a rule for feeding fresh garlic, I recommend one clove per 10–30 pounds of body weight per day. There do not appear to be any animal toxicity studies on the most commonly used form of garlic: powdered garlic standardized to alliin content.

Garlic should not be fed to pets with anemia or to those scheduled for surgery due to the possibility of increased bleeding; refrain from use at least one week before and one week after surgery.

Taking garlic at the same time as taking ginkgo or high-dose vitamin E might also cause bleeding problems.

Ginseng *(Panax ginseng, Panax quinquefolius)*

There are actually three different herbs commonly called ginseng: Asian or Korean ginseng (*Panax ginseng*, the species most commonly used), American ginseng (*Panax quinquefolius*), and

Siberian "ginseng" (*Eleutherococcus senticosus*), which is not truly ginseng at all, but the Russian scientists responsible for promoting it believe that it functions identically to ginseng. Asian ginseng is a perennial herb with a taproot resembling the human body. It grows in northern China, Korea, and Russia; its close relative, *Panax quinquefolius*, is cultivated in the United States. Because ginseng must be grown for five years before it is harvested, it is expensive. Dried, unprocessed ginseng root is called white ginseng, and steamed, heat-dried root is red ginseng. Chinese herbalists believe that each form has its own particular benefits.

Ginseng contains many chemicals, the most important of which are triterpenoids called ginsenosides. Different species of ginseng contain different concentrations of the various classes of ginsenosides.

Regular intake of ginseng may protect against cancer formation; the extract and powder have been shown to be more effective in preventing cancer in people than tea or juice made from ginseng or fresh sliced ginseng.

Ginseng may also have some antioxidant properties, which would make it useful for pets with cancer. Ginseng stimulates the immune system by enhancing white blood cell and antibody functions. It should not be used in high doses during acute infections because it may inhibit some immune functions.

Red ginseng in particular stimulates natural killer cell function, inhibits tumor invasion as well as the formation of blood vessels to a tumor (angiogenesis), activates apoptosis genes p53 and p21 (to encourage cell death), and stimulates cancer cell differentiation (to encourage cancer cells to revert back to a "normal" cell state).

Dosage in people varies based upon ginsenoside content. In general, tonic effects are seen when the product contains at least

10 mg of ginsenoside Rg1, with a ratio of Rg1 to Rb1 of 1:2. In people, the typical recommended daily dosage of *Panax ginseng* is 1–2 g of raw herb, or 200 mg daily of an extract standardized to contain 4–7 percent ginsenosides. *Eleutherococcus* is taken at a dosage of 2–3 g whole herb, or 300–400 mg of extract daily. Ordinarily, a two- to three-week period of using ginseng is recommended, followed by a one- to two-week rest period. Russian tradition suggests that ginseng should not be used by those under the age of forty. Finally, because *Panax ginseng* is so expensive, some products actually contain very little. Adulteration with other herbs, and even caffeine, is not unusual.

In people, unconfirmed reports suggest that excessive doses of ginseng can raise blood pressure, increase heart rate, and possibly cause other significant health problems. Ginseng should not be given to pets with hypertension, kidney disease, or cardiomyopathy. Pets with a history of bleeding, anxiety, hyperactivity, or nervousness should not be given ginseng. Do not use in pets taking hypoglycemic medications without veterinary supervision. There are several important reasons why ginseng should be administered only with the advice of a veterinarian and why long-term ingestion of ginseng should be avoided: (1) patient responses to ginseng are unpredictable, (2) various species of plants contain different quantities of ginsenosides, and (3) a lack of quality control among producers of supplements makes it difficult to know exactly how much ginseng a patient is getting. Ginseng may also increase levels of digitalis drugs.

The safe use of ginseng has not been established for young children, pregnant or nursing women, or people with severe liver or kidney disease. Chinese tradition echoes some of these guidelines, suggesting that ginseng should not be used by pregnant or nursing women. Similar precautions are probably warranted in pets.

Goldenseal *(Hydrastis canadensis)*

Goldenseal has shown potent anticancer properties in vitro against rat and human malignant brain tumors. Its berberine content has beneficial effects for patients who have decreased white blood cell counts as a result of chemotherapy or radiation treatment.

Goldenseal is used as a topical antimicrobial and anti-inflammatory herb. It can be applied topically to open sores or inflamed skin for its soothing effect on inflamed mucous membranes; this may be helpful for pets with cancer or ulcers (mucositis that results from some conventional therapies) of the skin or mouth. Goldenseal may also be beneficial in treating diseases of the digestive tract because it can contact the affected area directly. Because berberine is concentrated in the bladder, goldenseal may be useful for bladder infections. For pets with side effects from conventional therapies involving the bladder (as may occur in dogs taking the chemotherapy drug Cytoxan) or gastrointestinal system, goldenseal may be recommended by your veterinarian.

> *Goldenseal may be recommended for pets with side effects from conventional cancer therapies involving the bladder or gastrointestinal system.*

Due to similar medicinal qualities and the fact that goldenseal is an endangered plant, Oregon grape (see page 140) can be used in place of goldenseal.

Goldenseal appears to be safe when used as directed. It has not been established as safe to administer to young children, pregnant or nursing women, or people with severe liver or kidney disease; similar precautions in pets are probably warranted. Side effects of goldenseal taken orally are uncommon, although there have been reports of gastrointestinal distress and increased nervousness in people who take very high doses. Goldenseal should not be given to pregnant animals or to pets with low blood sugar (as it lowers blood sugar). Long-term use of goldenseal may cause hypertension and may overstimulate the liver. Do not use in pets with jaundice or liver disease due to the potential for overstimulation of the liver.

Hawthorn *(Crataegus oxyacantha)*

Hawthorn is a well-known heart and vascular tonic, often prescribed for pets with early congestive heart failure. Because of its antioxidant properties (due to the flavonoid and proanthocyanidin content), it may be a useful herb for pets with cancer.

Doctors may prescribe hawthorn for pets undergoing chemotherapy, especially when the drug chosen for chemotherapy may produce cardiac side effects, as is the case with doxorubicin.

Hawthorn is very safe. Formal studies suggest that caution is warranted in pets with low blood pressure and hypertrophic cardiomyopathy, although holistic doctors have not reported problems when prescribing hawthorn for pets with these disorders. In people, side effects are rare, mostly consisting of mild stomach upset and occasional allergic reactions (such as skin rash).

It has not been established safe to administer to young children, pregnant or nursing women, or people with severe liver, heart, or kidney disease. Similar concerns in pets are probably warranted.

Hoxsey and Essiac Formulas

The Hoxsey and Essiac herbal formulas are commonly recommended for people with cancer. There are two types of Hoxsey formulas: the first contains the herbs burdock, red clove, poke-weed root, prickly ash bark, bloodroot, licorice, stillingia, bar-berry, and potassium iodide; the second contains all the herbs in the first formula plus potassium iodide and an extract of the digestive enzyme pepsin. Despite the popularity of the Hoxsey formulas, scientific evidence of their effectiveness is lacking. However, their antioxidant properties may offer some benefit. There is probably minimal toxicity, unless other herbs have been introduced by the manufacturer.

A modified Hoxsey formula is currently being used by Dr. Steve Marsden as part of a protocol for treating various cancers, including osteosarcoma (see pages 209–212 in chapter 7 for a discussion of Dr. Marsden's protocol). (One supplier of the formula used in the Marsden protocol is Peter Byram at N.E. Herbal, in Connecticut, phone 800-745-6051.)

Essiac is the anagrammatized last name of Rene Cassie, the Canadian nurse who created the formula. The original formula is a well-guarded secret but is believed to contain burdock, sheep sorrel, turkey rhubarb, and slippery elm bark. As with the Hoxsey formula, there are no conclusive studies to support the use of the Essiac formula in the treatment of cancer. Additionally, there is controversy over whether any of the commercially available products contain the exact in-gredients in the original formula made by Cassie. Like the Hoxsey formula, there is probably only minimal toxicity, un-less other herbs have been added by the manufacturer, and the antioxidants in the formula might be of benefit to cancer patients.

A modified Hoxsey formula may be useful as part of a protocol for treating canine osteosarcoma.

While these formulas may be safe in pets, there are no controlled studies to show whether they are effective in dogs and cats. Consult with your veterinarian prior to using either the Essiac herbs or Hoxsey formulas.

Licorice Root *(Glycyrrhiza glabra, Glycyrrhiza lepidota)*

Licorice is a fast-acting anti-inflammatory agent. Licorice is also known for its antimicrobial and immune-stimulating properties. Many herbalists regard it as "nature's cortisone" because of its glycyrrhizin content. Licorice root inhibits inflammatory prostaglandins and leukotrienes, so it acts much like corticosteroids. Because licorice also exhibits mineralocorticoid as well as glucocorticoid activity, it has been suggested for use in Addison's disease. Licorice has antioxidant properties and and boosts the immune system by enhancing interferon and T cell production.

The use of licorice may allow pet owners to reduce the doses of more potent corticosteroids. For owners refusing chemotherapy for their pets, licorice can be tried as a substitute for the corticosteroids that would normally be used in chemotherapy regimens. However, there is no proof that licorice is as effective as corticosteroids as a chemotherapeutic agent for pets with cancer. Additionally, because of its steroid-like effects, licorice should not be used when steroids are part of the chemotherapy protocol.

Deglycyrrhizinated licorice (DGL) is a special extract made by removing the glycyrrhizin molecule, leaving the flavonoid components. In people, DGL is used for treating ulcers of the mouth and small intestine, as well as for treating inflammatory bowel disease. The antiulcer effects in people are as significant as are antacid medications such as Tagamet. DGL is also recommended as an herbal ulcer preventive (similar to drugs such as misoprostol) for people taking nonsteroidal medications and corticosteroids. However, it is not clear that DGL provides all the same benefits as whole licorice for other problems.

When used in large doses and for extended periods, licorice can produce similar cortisone-like effects as steroid medications can produce, including high blood pressure. Do not use in pregnant animals. If licorice is used for more than two weeks at a time, side effects can include decreased potassium (supplementing with potassium is recommended), fluid retention, high blood pressure, and increased sodium (increased sodium excretion may be needed). Caution is therefore warranted when administering to pets taking certain cardiac drugs (digitalis) and pets with high blood pressure, heart disease, diabetes, or kidney disease. Dandelion leaf can be added to the regimen to raise potassium and lower sodium levels. In people, side effects occur commonly at levels above 400 mg per day.

DGL is believed to be safe, although extensive safety studies have not been performed. Nevertheless, side effects are rare.

Neither form of licorice has been established to be safe for young children, pregnant or nursing women, or people with severe liver or kidney disease. Similar precautions are probably warranted in pets. Licorice could increase blood clotting time. Licorice induces cytochrome P-450 enzymes in the liver, which may alter the metabolism of other drugs, decreasing their serum levels.

Marshmallow *(Althaea officinalis)*

Marshmallow is useful for irritation of the skin or mucous membranes. The herb contains very high levels of large sugar molecules called mucilage, which appear to exert a soothing effect on mucous membranes. Marshmallow also has antibacterial and immune-stimulating properties, which makes it useful for pets with ulcers of the mouth that may occur with some types of cancers and as a rare side effect of chemotherapy and radiation therapy.

Marshmallow is believed to be safe. It can slightly lower blood sugar levels. For this reason, it should not be used in animals receiving hypoglycemic therapies. People with diabetes should use caution when taking marshmallow. Its safe use has not been established for young children, pregnant or nursing women, or people with severe liver or kidney disease. Similar cautions are probably warranted in pets.

Milk Thistle (Silybum marianum)

Milk thistle is well known for treating liver disease due to its silymarin content. Milk thistle compounds are usually standardized to 70–80 percent silymarin.

The active ingredients in milk thistle appear to be four substances, known collectively as silymarin, of which silibinin is the most potent. Studies suggest that milk thistle can protect the liver against many poisonous substances; it is often recommended to reduce toxicity from chemotherapy. Silymarin appears to function by displacing toxins trying to bind to the liver, and by helping the liver regenerate more quickly. It scavenges free radicals and stabilizes liver cell membranes.

> *Milk thistle is helpful for supporting liver function in cancer patients.*

Silymarin protects the liver as an antioxidant (it is more potent than vitamin E) by increasing glutathione levels (glutathione is a potent antioxidant) and by inhibiting the formation of damaging leukotrienes. Silymarin also down-regulates cancer genes in certain cancers.

A new form of silymarin, in which the compound is bound to phosphatidylcholine, has been shown to have greater bio-availability than unbound silymarin.

The standard dosage of milk thistle in people is 200 mg two to three times a day. In people, the best results are seen at higher doses (140–200 mg three times daily of an extract standardized to contain 70 percent silymarin); the bound form is dosed at 100–200 mg twice daily. In dogs and cats, a recommended dose is 100 mg per 25 pounds of body weight, given twice daily.

Do not use milk thistle in pregnant animals. High doses may cause diarrhea. On the basis of its extensive use as a food, milk thistle is believed to be safe for pregnant or nursing women, and researchers have enrolled pregnant women in studies. However, the safe use of milk thistle as a drug has not been formally established for young children, pregnant or nursing women, and individuals with severe kidney disease. Similar precautions in pets are probably warranted.

Mistletoe (Viscum album)

Mistletoe, and specifically an extract called Iscador®, has been suggested as a cancer therapy (homeopathically, Viscum album is a well-known cancer treatment and is mentioned on page 151). Iscador was first marketed in Switzerland in 1917 and is a popular alternative therapy in Europe. Iscador is a water extract from the mistletoe plant. Mistletoe grows on many different types of trees, such as pine (Pini-Iscador P), oak (Quercus-Iscador Qu), and apple (Mali-Iscador M). The extract contains a variety of chemicals, including lectins (the main one is ML1-3), viscotoxins, polysaccharides, and polypeptides. It has been found that different types of cancers respond better to mistletoe from specific host trees; for example, mistletoe from pine trees (Iscador P) may be helpful for skin cancer. Mistletoe extracts are commonly administered by injection. Studies have shown that the extracts protect DNA, stimulate the immune system, encourage cell death (apoptosis), and possess antitumor and antimetastatic properties. In people with a variety of cancers, survival times did improve when Iscador P was included in their therapy. In this study, an important benefit of Iscador P administration was increased survial time through patient self-regulation, defined as the intrinsic activities of a person to achieve inner well-being and a feeling of competence by controlling stressful situations. Many people using Iscador P as part of their cancer treatment report an improved quality of life (feeling better) and less need for pain medication. The only reported side effects of mistletoe in people are an occasional increase in heart rate and blood pressure. An injectable extract (Qu FrF) produced fever, eosinophilia (an increase in a type of white blood cell), fatigue, and flu-like symptoms in some patients (the severity of side effects increased as dosage of the extract injected increased). These side effects were similar to those seen in people treated with biological response modifier medications (recombinant IL-2, IL-3, and IL-6).

*Oregon Grape (*Mahonia aquifolium, Berberis aquifolium*)*

Oregon grape serves as an alternative to goldenseal. Like goldenseal, it has antimicrobial properties due to its berberine content. This herb is also known for supporting liver function, which makes it useful when treating pets with cancer. Oregon grape may be beneficial for cancer patients because it stimulates white blood cell production from the bone marrow. Animal studies suggest the possibility of anticancer properties.

While safe, Oregon grape should not be administered to animals that are diabetic or that have acute liver disease. At high doses, it may inhibit B vitamin absorption.

Red Clover *(Trifolium pratense)*

Red clover is used as a tonic, diuretic, and blood cleanser. It contains a number of nutrients (including B and C vitamin complexes and protein) that act synergistically to help pets with various disorders. The bioflavonoids and phytoestrogens (including quercetin) in red clover may help pets with cancer, and the plant is included in the popular herbal anticancer formulas Hoxsey and Essiac (pages 135–136). Genistein and daidzein (natural isoflavones) are also found in red clover. For pets with skin cancer, red clover can be taken internally, or a poultice of the flowers can be applied directly to skin cancers.

Red clover should not be used in pets with clotting disorders (due to the presence of coumarin), hormonal disorders involving estrogen, in pregnant or lactating animals, or in pets sensitive to aspirin. This is because red clover contains small amounts of salicylic acid, the active ingredient in aspirin (only a tiny amount of salicylic acid exists in normal doses of red clover). The safe use of red clover has not been established for young children or for people with severe liver or kidney disease; similar precautions are probably warranted in pets. Large amounts of red clover are toxic in grazing animals, such as sheep. The amount found in most herbal supplements is unlikely to be harmful. However, since there is no federal standard for quality control, the actual amounts of herb can vary widely among supplements.

Turmeric *(Curcuma longa)*

The volatile oils and curcumin are the active ingredients of turmeric, which is well known as a spice in curry powder and as an herb in Chinese and Ayurvedic medicine.

Curcumin, the yellow pigment in turmeric, inhibits the growth of cancer and induces cancer cell death (apoptosis), inhibits MMP-2 and MMP-9 enzymes (which normally induce cancer to spread), inhibits nitrosamine formation, increases glutathione levels, is anti-inflammatory (by inhibiting the COX-2 enzyme), is an antioxidant (it exhibits free-radical scavenging effects), and stimulates the immune system. Similar to glycyrrhizin and silymarin, curcumin shows protective effects on the liver. The antioxidant effects are comparable to BHA, BHT, and vitamins C and E.

It is better absorbed in an oil-based form. It can protect the heart against damage by chemotherapy medications. A recommended dose is 15–20 mg per pound per day.

Do not use in pets with bile duct obstruction, gall bladder stones, or gastrointestinal upset. High doses should not be given to pets taking anticoagulants. The safe use of turmeric has not been established for young children, pregnant or nursing women, or people with severe liver or kidney disease; similar precautions are probably warranted in pets.

Wormwood (Artemisia absinthium)

Wormwood, also called Artemisinin, is a well-known herb commonly prescribed for killing parasites (particularly the malarial parasite in people). It works by forming toxic and cell-killing free radicals in the presence of iron; cancer cells typically concentrate iron, which they need to reproduce their DNA when they divide. Artemisinin destroys cells with high levels of iron while posing little or no danger to the normal cells. Test-tube studies have shown selective killing of cancer cells when Artemisinin is administered along with supplemental iron (holotransferrin). The following precautions should be observed:

- Artemisinin should not be used within twenty days of radiation therapy, because radiation spreads or leaks iron into the surrounding tissues.

- Supplemental iron may be needed prior to taking Artemisinin if iron levels are low (more of a problem in people than in pets).

- Laboratory testing is needed to monitor the therapy; recommended tests in people include a complete blood count, reticulocyte count (which may drop initially but normalizes after a few weeks), liver function tests, test of ferritin levels, Total Iron Binding Capacity, Erythrocyte Sedimentation Rate, C-reactive protein test, and tests for appropriate tumor markers (which might increase during the initial stages of tumor death).

Therapeutic dosages in people are 1,000–1,600 mg per day or higher. Artemisinin should be taken with food; using an essential fatty acid (such as flax oil or fish oil) will increase absorption. High doses of pancreatic enzymes (on an empty stomach), CoQ-10 supplementation, and a detoxification program should be used during Artemisinin therapy.

Based upon the large numbers of people who have used Artemisinin for antimalarial therapy, the supplement appears safe when used as directed.

Being a "bitter" herb, wormwood can be helpful in controlling infections and strengthening immunity, especially if the patient is anemic or malnourished. When not properly administered, wormwood can be a very toxic herb (due to its neurotoxic thujone constituent). Like all of the supplements discussed in this chapter, wormwood should be used with caution under veterinary supervision.

Yellow Dock (Rumex crispus)

Yellow dock is a cleansing herb that stimulates liver function and evacuation of the bowels to remove wastes from the body. As a result, yellow dock is useful for cancer therapy because cancer is considered to be a toxin within the body. It can also be used as a remedy for anemia due to its high iron content. It is most commonly used short term, as its action is often quick and dramatic, particularly at the beginning of therapy, to get a "quick cleansing." Excess yellow dock can lead to intestinal cramping, vomiting, and diarrhea; it should not be used during pregnancy or in pets with intestinal blockages. It should not be used in pets in which excess iron could be harmful.

HERBS OFTEN RECOMMENDED FOR PETS WITH CANCER

Alfalfa	Hoxsey & essiac formulas
Aloe vera (acemannan)	Licorice
Astragalus	Marshmallow
Burdock root	Milk thistle
Dandelion leaf and root	Mistletoe
Echinacea	Oregon grape
Flax	Red clover
Garlic	Turmeric/curcumin
Ginseng	Wormwood
Goldenseal	Yellow dock
Hawthorn	

HOMEOPATHY

Homeopathy, first proposed by Dr. Samuel Hahnemann in 1790, is the science of like curing like. Conventional medicine uses drugs to reduce symptoms, correct metabolic problems, and replace physiologic substances; using the medications appears to cure illness. Often, however, sickness recurs or different, more serious ailments appear. Homeopathic veterinarians believe that symptoms are the body's attempt to heal an underlying energy imbalance. (For example, a symptom such as mild fever stimulates the production of white cells and the viral-fighting chemical interferon.) Homeopathic treatment is an energy medicine aimed at stimulating the body to effectively heal itself by working with the symptoms, not against them. The result can be a true cure, in which the animal's symptoms disappear and never reappear, and the pet feels happier, more active, and more interactive than ever before. Sometimes an animal is too ill to fully heal its energetic imbalance and will improve but not be truly cured. In those cases (often seen when an animal has cancer), homeopathy can gently support the body to be as normal as possible for as long as possible, before finally succumbing to the cancer.

With homeopathic therapy, extremely dilute substances are administered to promote healing. Homeopathic doctors believe that the same substances that can cause a disease may, in a diluted form, cure the disease or improve the pet's condition. The more dilute the homeopathic compound, the stronger it is in the treatment of the disorder.

Homeopathic remedies are so dilute that no molecules of the original substances are present. Even if the original ingredients are toxic, they are so diluted that there isn't a trace of any toxins, poisons, or other dangerous substances in the remedies, and therefore they can be used safely. However, because of their powerful impact on a pet's energy field, the more potent remedies should be prescribed only by trained practitioners.

For those who are hearing about homeopathy for the first time, this concept can sound quite strange. As a doctor trained in conventional medicine, I too was surprised when I first heard about the concept of like curing like. When homeopathic compounds are prepared, there is often no trace of the original ingredient. In effect, it seems like all we're giving the pet is water and alcohol (for liquid preparations), or simply the lactose carrier (for pill and tablet preparations). Certainly, drinking water and alcohol or ingesting lactose pills alone will not make pets better.

> *Homeopathy uses the energy of dilute solutions to help the body heal.*

Yet many pets do get better. No, it's not 100 percent effective in every pet, but homeopathic remedies do work.

Skeptics may point to a placebo effect. Certainly, placebo effects are powerful in human medicine. You want to get better, you want the treatment to work, so it works. However, this placebo effect is all but impossible to reproduce or observe in pets. For example, when treating your arthritic dog with homeopathy, you can't tell him that the homeopathic remedy he's taking will make him stop limping, as if he might understand what you've said and stop limping! The treatment either works or fails on its own merits.

Because the more potent homeopathic remedies impact so strongly on the core energy system of the body, they should be carefully prescribed when treating severe diseases like cancer. While homeopathic remedies do not have side effects as conventional medications do, they can stimulate the body to produce new symptoms or temporarily worsen current symptoms.

It is important not to panic and use other treatments in these cases, because the new symptoms may be indications of the body resolving its diseased energy field. Especially in treating animals with cancer, a trained homeopathic practitioner can advise pet owners as to whether the remedy is healing at a deep level while more superficial symptoms (diarrhea, skin rashes, vomiting) are worsening, or if the animal is getting more ill. Homeopathy used incorrectly for months can cause an animal's condition to worsen.

Is there any science supporting the use of homeopathic remedies? Homeopathic practitioners know that remedies are effective in some cases and not in others. They attribute the lack of effectiveness in some cases to their failure to find the correct remedy for the patient, or to an inability of the particular animal to respond to the homeopathic remedy, or to other drugs interfering with the treatment. They often refer an animal to another homeopathic veterinarian whose different perception of the animal may lead to an effective remedy selection, or to another holistic modality, or to conventional treatment if holistic methods have failed.

Many of my clients swear that their own illnesses have been helped by homeopathic remedies prescribed by their doctors. I have seen a number of pets improve with homeopathy as well. However, as with any therapy, there are those cases for which no treatment is effective. Additionally, I rarely practice "pure homeopathy," in which only one or two homeopathic remedies are used as the treatment. Most of my patients are prescribed a number of therapies, in addition to homeopathic remedies since these pets have chronic, often severe conditions. When they respond, it is impossible to say which particular therapy was effective. In many cases there is probably a positive effect from the combination of treatments. Certainly, there is enough positive response in some of my patients to indicate an improvement above a simple placebo effect.

> *Many studies have shown positive effects*
> *in patients treated with homeopathic remedies*
> *when compared to placebos.*

The current medical literature shows increasing objective evaluation of various homeopathic remedies for treatment of various medical problems. Of course, more studies are available in human medicine than in veterinary medicine. As is true with many complementary therapies, there will be individual variation in response.

There is much clinical research, historical evidence, and in vitro laboratory experiments indicating that homeopathic remedies alleviate symptoms in some people and animals, and can be effective in the treatment of diseases.

Homeopathic medicines are tested only on people. These studies have been conducted for two hundred years, and many of them today are designed in compliance with the FDA's requirements for new drug testing.

On September 20, 1997, the British medical journal *The Lancet* published a review of eighty-nine double-blind controlled trials on people showing that homeopathic medicines were 2.45 times more effective than placebo. Laboratory research into the mechanism of action of homeopathy is rapidly increasing.

A few recent monographs are summarized here. Drs. Vittorio Elia and Marcella Niccoli, of Italy, wrote "Thermodynamics of Extremely Diluted Aqueous Solutions." In this study, when a substance was diluted and shaken thirty times (similar to how homeopathic remedies are prepared), it had a higher temperature than controls where only water was used. In five hundred repetitions, the temperature difference was maintained weeks after the dilution had been made. Dr. Philippe Belon, of France, showed that white blood cells called basophils had different activity when homeopathic dilutions were applied ("The Pharmacology of High Potencies: Applied to the Activation of Basophils"). The structure of water molecules compared to homeopathic remedies made in water is explored in "Complexes of Short Hydrogen Bonds: The Active Ingredient in Homeopathy?" More research information is available from Homeopathic Education Services (mail@homeopathic.com) and the Homeopathic Research Network jjacobs@igc.apc.org).

While skeptics of homeopathy point to the fact that there are few double-blind studies, David Eddy of Duke University has published data revealing that not all current conventional medical treatments have been subjected to controlled, double-blind studies, either. Meeting with groups of specialists, Eddy found that these specialists often based their treatment choices on personal experience rather than scientific data. A recent summary of twenty-three studies, selected because of their rigorous use of scientific method, found positive responses to homeopathic treatment in fifteen of those studies.

When possible, I prefer to combine homeopathy with other therapies, including conventional therapies. (Veterinarians specializing in homeopathy find greater success in most cases using just homeopathy and nutritional supplements.)

While homeopathy can be an effective part of the therapy for pets with cancer, it is important to work with a qualified veterinarian and not simply treat your pet on your own. My primary concern with homeopathy is that pet owners may decide to skip going to a veterinarian for a proper diagnosis and treatment, opting instead to treat their seriously ill pets with over-the-counter (OTC) remedies. This would be ineffective and could result in worsening illness, or even death.

> *Over-the-counter homeopathic remedies
> should not be used in pets with cancer.*

Let's take a look at some of the homeopathic therapies for pets with cancer. One word of caution: the less dilute (and therefore weaker) therapies are available for purchase at many health food stores, and pet owners might be tempted to try using these potentially inadequate homeopathic remedies on their own. Before trying any of these therapies on your pet, be sure to consult with a holistic practitioner and get a diagnosis first. There are several reasons for this:

First, many of the OTC remedies are combination potions rather than pure homeopathic remedies. With homeopathy, it is preferable to use just the one or two remedies that most closely match your pet's constitution and symptoms.

Second, the OTC remedies are the least dilute and therefore the least potent. While the dilute remedies are not usually harmful, the more powerful prescription varieties available through your doctor are more likely to be effective.

Third, and most important, a proper diagnosis is needed before using homeopathy or any therapy. Failing to seek trained medical help and relying on home remedies can be dangerous. While homeopathy can be helpful, you should only treat pets homeopathically under a doctor's supervision!

Homeopathic Remedies

As a holistic veterinarian, I never use homeopathic remedies without also trying nutritional therapy, dietary therapy, and herbal therapy. I believe in treating the pet, not just the disease!

Homeopathy is just one of the many components of successfully treating a dog with cancer.

There is no one right remedy, and a thorough examination, history, and laboratory tests must be performed to assist the homeopathic veterinarian in selecting the correct remedy or remedies. I have found the following two homeopathic remedies quite helpful for some pets with cancer:

- *Arsenicum album/Viscum album*: These remedies are often used in pets with solid tumors, such as mammary tumors.

- *Thuja occidentalis* (white cedar): This remedy may be useful for a variety of tumors, warts, and cancers, especially any that might be related to recent vaccinations.

HOMOTOXICOLOGY

Like homeopathy, homotoxicology is based on the concept of using minute doses of remedies to assist in healing. Though both disciplines use diluted substances that are similarly prepared, the focus for each is somewhat different. Classical homeopathy is a single-remedy, single-dose strategy, based on precise determination of individual predispositions to disease states. Homotoxicology, while utilizing the same remedies and dilutions, is usually based on a "symptom picture," which is a mixture of various factors and presentations. It is geared toward treating the underlying body mechanisms that are primarily based in the matrix (mesenchyme), which is the "gel between the cells"; the matrix nourishes the cells, carries information between them, and removes the waste products of cellular metabolism. Homotoxicology and homeopathy can be used together, because homotoxicology prepares the system for the homeopathic "constitutional remedy." An in-depth discussion on the utilization of homotoxicology can be found in Appendix G on pages 260–266.

Remedies for Pets Receiving Radiation Therapy

Several remedies may be helpful in minimizing side effects from radiation therapy. The homotoxicologic protocol must be completed four days before the start of such treatment.

- First day of therapy: Ubichinon compositum with Traumeel, Engystol, and Hepeel

- Second day of therapy: Galium-Heel, Traumeel, Engystol, Hepeel

Ubichinon compositum is indicated, possibly daily and in particular after each application of radiotherapy. For the prevention of disorders of the bladder (cystitis) after radiation.

Reneel tablets are also taken on the day of the radiation, alternating with Causticum compositum every fifteen to thirty minutes. For other painful conditions, the possibly unrestricted use of opiates is recommended to ease the pain, with the side effects (depressed breathing) being compensated by Ubichinon compositum (possibly one vial daily). Ubichinon compositum, in addition, has a favorable influence on the pain resulting from the cancerous condition, and has been used with some success in painful cancers such as osteosarcomas.

Traumeel ointment has proved effective in the treatment of skin damage from radiotherapy.

Remedies for Pets with Cachexia

Cachexia is a marked state of ill health and malnutrition, which increases the rate of illness and death in pets with cancer, and in general reduces the patient's quality of life.

The treatment of cachexia is not easy, and it is best to prevent the condition in the first place. However, several homotoxicologic remedies may be helpful in the treatment of cachexia.

- For treatment of symptoms of general cachexia:
  Funiculus umbilicalis suis (in Thyreoidea compositum,
  Tonsilla compositum, and Ubichinon compositum),
  Naphtoquinone (in Ubichinon compositum), and
  Pancreas suis (in Hepar, Mucosa comp, and Szygium
  compositum)

- For progressive cachexia: Conium (in Cerebrum compositum, Thyreoidea compositum, Tonsilla compositum, and Ubichinon compositum)

- For cachexia with great weakness: Zincum metallicum
  (in Echinacea compositum, Testis compositum, and
  Zincum metallicum)

- For cachexia from cancer: Hydrastis (in Ginseng compositum, Ubichinon compositum, and Mucosa
  compositum) and Thuja (found in Galium-Heel,
  Cerebrum compositum, Echinacea compositum,
  Psorinoheel)

In the next chapter, we'll discuss other complementary therapies that may prove helpful in treating dogs with cancer.

CHAPTER SEVEN

COMPLEMENTARY THERAPIES *for* CANCER: NUTRITIONAL SUPPLEMENTS

IN THIS CHAPTER, I'll review the most commonly used and recommended nutritional supplements for treating pets with cancer. I do not make any recommendations as to specific supplements, because any recommendation depends upon many factors, including ease of administration, cost, type of cancer, and other health issues. Your holistic veterinarian and oncologist can determine the best selection of supplements for your pet's specific condition.

> *No matter how much chemotherapy, radiation therapy, or surgery the pet with cancer receives, if its immune system does not function properly, it will die. The use of supplements in addition to a proper diet are critical in order to have a properly functioning immune system.*

ANTINEOPLASTON THERAPY

Antineoplaston therapy was developed by Dr. Stanislaw Burzynski in the 1960s and was formerly called the Burzynski Therapy. It is currently being evaluated by the FDA as a cancer therapy. This complementary therapy purports to "normalize" cancer cells by repairing damaged DNA using chemicals called antineoplastons, which are amino acid and peptide derivatives. In the past, the antineoplastons were isolated from the blood and urine of healthy people. However, with the advent of new genetic technology such as sequencing, Dr. Burzynski is now able to synthesize the antineoplastons in the lab.

Formerly, it was believed that only people without cancer had antineoplastons in their blood. However, it has now been discovered that cancer patients also have antineoplastons but in markedly deficient levels (patients don't have enough to inhibit cancer growth).

Antineoplastons interrupt the activity of the ras oncogene, which causes cancer cells to divide endlessly. Antineoplastons also stimulate p53 tumor suppressor genes, which are needed for cancer cells to undergo programmed cell death. Healthy cells remain unaffected under these processes.

Dr. Burzynski uses other therapies at his Houston clinic besides the antineoplastons, including an oral medication called sodium phenylbutyrate (also called tributyrate and biphenyl), which is a drug commonly used to treat urea disorders. This drug works by breaking down into the same active components as the antineoplastons.

Patients who are not eligible for antineoplaston therapy at a particular time due to the FDA strict protocol guidelines may be put on sodium phenylbutyrate treatment until they are eligible for the clinical trial.

Only those patients admitted into Dr. Burzynski's FDA

trials can receive the antineoplaston treatment. It is unlikely that this therapy will be available to pets in the near future, as antineoplastons are species specific, and there are no clinical trials in pets being conducted at this time.

ANTIOXIDANTS

Specific chemicals, including various vitamins and minerals, function in the body to reduce oxidation, which is a chemical process that occurs within the body's cells. Oxidation creates cellular by-products, such as peroxides and free radicals, that accumulate in the body and are toxic to the cells and surrounding tissue. The body removes these by-products by producing additional chemicals called *antioxidants*.

In disease, excess oxidation can occur and the body's normal antioxidant abilities can therefore be overwhelmed. This is where supplying antioxidants can help. By giving your pet's body extra antioxidants, it may be possible to neutralize the harmful by-products of cellular oxidation.

High doses of antioxidants act differently on cancer cells versus normal cells in the body. Cancer cells take up more of these higher concentrations of antioxidants than do normal cells. The result for cancer cells is the inhibition of the cellular processes necessary for their growth and reproduction.

> *Antioxidants may neutralize the harmful by-products of cellular oxidation.*

We know that a major cause of death in cancer patients is nutritional depletion. Using antioxidants and the proper diet can help boost the cancer patient's nutritional status and decrease the chance of early death due to tissue starvation.

There are many different antioxidants that can be used as

supplements for pets, including vitamins A, C, and E and the minerals selenium, manganese, and zinc. Antioxidants that may be helpful for cancer and other disorders include superoxide dismutase, glutathione, cysteine, coenzyme Q-10, ginkgo biloba, bilberry, grape seed extract, and Pycnogenol. The most commonly recommended antioxidants are briefly discussed on the next few pages.

In general, vitamins and minerals work best to promote health when given in combination rather than individually. Using them individually can upset the delicate balance of nutrients in the body, and makes the individual vitamin or mineral act more like a drug (with potential toxicity). This is one reason I'm against owners administering their own vitamins and minerals (such as vitamin C or E) without medical supervision.

Owners often ask if pets can receive all of the necessary nutrients in their food; no one would disagree that the best way for people and their pets to get all the proper nutrients is by eating the correct amounts in a well-balanced diet composed of fresh, naturally raised meats and plants. However, it is the rare person or pet who actually eats this ideal diet every day. Even if this were possible, there is no way to compensate for those times of disease or stress when additional antioxidant vitamins and minerals and other antioxidant agents (many of which are not even contained in potent amounts in a person's or pet's diet) are needed. Because of the various pollutants and chemicals our pets encounter each day, it makes a lot of sense to provide an optimum allowance of the important micronutrients to maintain health, rather than a minimum recommended daily amount (RDA) designed to prevent nutritional diseases caused by specific isolated vitamin and mineral deficiencies.

Cancer is one such disease for which antioxidant vitamins and minerals and other antioxidant remedies may be recommended. For acute therapy of the cancer patient, synthetic vitamins and minerals may be used to allow quick stabilization of the patient. For long-term use (prevention, maintenance), food supplements containing natural vitamins and minerals are often preferred. When possible, antioxidants should be provided in their natural states. Finally, a mixture of balanced antioxidants, even synthetic antioxidants, is better than isolated antioxidants for minimizing side effects and maximizing the anticancer effects.

Based upon numerous studies (mainly in people, in laboratory animals, and in test tube-studies), there is no question that antioxidants improve health. As nutritional supplements for fighting cancer, antioxidants:

- increase the cancer-killing ability of conventional treatments (chemotherapy and radiation therapy) while protecting normal cells
- improve the likelihood the patient will survive the cancer
- decrease side effects from conventional cancer therapies

Antioxidants concentrate in cancer cells in much higher amounts than they do in normal cells. Antioxidants:

- prevent cancer cell DNA reproduction
- improve cell-to-cell communication
- turn off cancer genes
- exert antihormone effects
- act as chelating agents, which bind iron
- improve detoxification
- induce cancer cell death (apoptosis)

- block the formation of eicosanoids, such as prostaglandins, that produce inflammation, suppress immunity, and support the growth and spreading of cancer cells
- block enzymes used by cancer cells for growth, local invasion of normal tissue, and the spread of cancer (metastasis).

> *Patients taking supplements are more likely to survive cancer with fewer side effects than those treated with conventional therapies alone.*

Another reason to use the appropriate antioxidant is that not all forms of specific antioxidant vitamins and minerals are effective. For example, let's consider vitamin E, which is composed of several different chemicals called *tocopherols* and *tocotrienols*. While there are many forms of tocopherols, the most common one used in supplements is a synthetic form called *d-alpha-tocopherol*. However, this form is not effective in preventing and treating cancer. Natural d-alpha-tocopherol is the form that is effective. Additionally, d-alpha-tocopherol *acetate* is ineffective against cancer, whereas d-alpha-tocopherol *succinate* is a powerful cancer-fighting antioxidant that helps cancer cells revert back to a more normal state, kills cancer cells (by inducing cell death), and accumulates in cancer cells better than other forms of d-alpha-tocopherol. Mixed tocopherol supplements, containing alpha-, beta-, delta-, and gamma-tocopherols, as well as tocotrienols, provide all forms of vitamin E and are even better at fighting cancer than the individual fractions themselves. For example, while not as powerful an antioxidant as alpha-tocopherol, gamma-tocopherol is the only vitamin E fraction capable of inhibiting reactive nitrogen oxide chemicals. Finally, using high doses of only alpha-tocopherol actually depresses blood levels of gamma-tocopherol (using a balanced supplement containing all tocopherol fractions will increase all tocopherol levels).

While vitamin E is an effective antioxidant, it works best as a fat-soluble antioxidant. However, oxidation also occurs in the water in cells and in between the cells. Simply using vitamin E will not be effective for water-soluble oxidation. Other supplements, such as vitamin C (which is water soluble), are also needed. The best way to get the proper balance of antioxidant supplements is to work with your holistic veterinarian, rather than simply pick and choose on your own.

> *Natural food sources of antioxidants are usually preferred to synthetic products.*

ANTIOXIDANTS AND CONVENTIONAL CANCER THERAPIES: HARMFUL OR HELPFUL?

There is some controversy as to whether pets receiving chemotherapy or radiation therapy should receive high doses of antioxidants, especially synthetic antioxidant vitamins and minerals. Are antioxidants safe for pets with cancer? In general, most doctors believe that antioxidants may be useful for pets with cancer to help achieve greater kill of cancer cells and reduce side effects of conventional therapies. However, some types of chemotherapy (such as doxorubicin) as well as radiation therapy work to kill cancer cells by increasing free radicals and causing oxidation (what Dr. Dan Labriola, in his book *Complementary Cancer Therapies*, calls the "protected zone," when the therapy is most effective at killing the cancer cells). It has been suggested, but certainly not proven, that giving pets high doses of antioxidants at the time of therapy might limit the effectiveness of these therapies because the antioxidants decrease oxidation.

> *By detoxifying free radicals, antioxidants have been shown in many studies to enhance the anticancer effects of chemotherapy and radiation therapy, and to reduce the side effects from these conventional therapies.*

However, despite these theoretical concerns, all of the research and clinical experience to date shows that antioxidants do *not* minimize the effectiveness of conventional cancer therapies. *In fact, antioxidants actually enhance the cancer-killing ability of the medications (including radiation) as well as reduce side effects in patients.* Both in vitro (in the test tube) and in vivo (in the living patient), research in people and laboratory animals supports this belief.

Some anticancer drugs (chemotherapy, in particular) cause the production of free radicals, which can lead to cancer cell death. However, by causing oxidative stress, the free radicals reduce the rate of cancer cell proliferation (reproduction). If cell proliferation decreases during chemotherapy, the chemotherapy may be less effective because chemotherapy depends on rapid proliferation of cancer cells for optimal killing activity. By detoxifying free radicals, antioxidants may therefore enhance the anticancer effects of chemotherapy by encouraging cancer cell growth and reproduction (chemotherapy drugs usually work to kill cancer cells as the cells grow and reproduce). For some antioxidant supplements, actions beyond their antioxidant properties, such as inhibition of topoisomerase II or protein tyrosine kinases, may also contribute to increased effectiveness of conventional therapies. Also, since antioxidants detoxify free radicals, which may cause or contribute to certain side effects that are common to many anticancer drugs, antioxidants may reduce or prevent many cancer therapy side effects.

Most holistic veterinarians, and a growing number of conventional oncologists, support the proper use of antioxidants and other supplements before, during, and after conventional treatment of the pet with cancer.

EXAMPLES OF SPECIFIC ANTIOXIDANTS AND THEIR EFFECTS ON CHEMOTHERAPY AND RADIATION

Beta-carotene has been shown to enhance the cancer-killing ability of melphalan on human squamous carcinoma cells and of cisplatin and dacarbazine on melanoma cells. In mice with transplanted mammary carcinoma, beta-carotene enhanced the antitumor effect of cyclophosphamide.

In-vitro studies with several tumor cell lines have shown vitamin C to enhance the cell-killing activity of doxorubicin, cisplatin, paclitaxel, dacarbazine, 5-fluorouracil (5-FU), and bleomycin. Vitamin C has also been shown to increase drug accumulation and to partially reverse vincristine resistance in human non-small-cell lung cancer cells. Animal studies have shown that vitamin C at 500 mg/kg and 1,000 mg/kg enhances the chemotherapeutic effect of cyclophosphamide, vinblastine, 5-FU, procarbazine, carmustine (BCNU), and doxorubicin, although other studies found that vitamin C was without effect on the activity of doxorubicin when vitamin C was administered at 2 g/kg daily to mice or 835 mg/kg daily to guinea pigs. In mice and guinea pigs, 2,000 mg/kg daily of vitamin C prevented doxorubicin-induced lipid peroxidation and reduced the acute cardiotoxic effect of doxorubicin.

In-vitro studies have shown that vitamin E enhances the cytotoxic (killing) effect of several anticancer drugs, including 5-FU, doxorubicin, vincristine, dacarbazine, cisplatin, and tamoxifen. Studies of laboratory animals have shown the parenteral administration of vitamin E to enhance the anticancer effect of 5-FU and cisplatin, although it had no apparent effect on the tumor-killing properties of doxorubicin. In addition to its activity as an antioxidant, vitamin E enhances cancer-killing activity by inducing cell death by inhibition of protein tyrosine kinases.

In laboratory animals, injectable administration of 20–4,100 IU/kg vitamin E reduced the *acute* cardiotoxicity (heart toxicity) of doxorubicin, suggesting that oxidative stress contributes to this disorder.

Topical vitamin E given to human patients who developed stomatitis/mucositis helped resolve the lesions.

The antioxidant mineral selenium exhibits an important role in reducing oxidation. In laboratory animals, injections of organic and inorganic selenium have been shown to protect against toxicity to the kidneys that may be induced by the chemotherapy drug cisplatin. Protection occurred without decreasing the ability of cisplatin to kill cancer cells.

Selenium has also reduced bone marrow suppression seen with cisplatin administration. However, since selenium can bind with platinum and inactivate cisplatin and carboplatin, which are platinum agents, caution should be used when administering high doses of selenium during chemotherapy with cisplatin and carboplatin until further research has been done. Selenium appears to protect against the *acute* cardiac toxicity that may occur with administration of doxorubicin.

MISCELLANEOUS ANTIOXIDANTS AND THEIR INTERACTIONS WITH CHEMOTHERAPY AND RADIATION THERAPY

Quercetin

Quercetin is a natural water-soluble antioxidant bioflavonoid found in red wine, grapefruit, onions, apples, black tea, and in lesser amounts in leafy green vegetables and beans. In addition to its antioxidant activity, quercetin may increase the effectiveness of some chemotherapy medications by inhibiting topoisomerase II activity and enhancing topoisomerase II-dependent DNA cleavage (similar to the mechanism used by the chemotherapy drug doxorubicin). Quercetin has been shown in vitro (in the lab) to inhibit the growth of some but not all human and animal cancer cell lines. Quercetin also has been shown to enhance the cancer-cell-killing ability of several chemotherapy medications, including cisplatin, nitrogen mustard, busulfan, and cytosine arabinoside. Quercetin reduces cisplatin's side effects to the kidneys and nervous system; it also reduces damage to the heart caused by chemotherapy medications. Quercetin inhibits the LOX and COX-2 enzymes, which contribute to inflammation and cancer. It also inhibits MMP-2 and MMP-9, the enzymes responsible for helping cancer invade surrounding tissue and spread throughout the body. Quercetin inhibits the aromatase enzyme. In people (and possibly pets), this enzyme increases the formation of the estrogen called estrone, which contributes to cancers of the breast, colon, and prostate. In addition, Quercetin can inhibit the attachment of estrogen to its receptor in cells (this attachment is necessary if estrogen is going to cause any effects, including cancer, in the cell).

Quercetin reduces radiation damage to normal tissues and inhibits the cancer growth enzymes ornithine decarboxylase, protein kinase C, and tyrosine kinase (this latter enzyme produces epidermal growth factor, which helps cancer grow). In people, when taken with hesperidin, quercetin protects the lungs from free radical and iron damage that may occur following treatment with busulfan or radiation to the chest. Quercetin protects DNA from damage during radiation therapy. The dose in people is 1,000 mg three times daily taken with food. In pets, doses of 50–400 mg given three times daily is recommended. Quercetin appears to be quite safe. Maximum safe dosages for young children, women who are pregnant or nursing, or those with serious liver or kidney disease have not been established; similar precautions are probably warranted in pets.

N-Acetylcysteine (NAC)

N-acetylcysteine (NAC) is a free-radical scavenger and provides an intracellular source of cysteine, which is needed to synthesize the potent antioxidant glutathione. It also inhibits the cytokine

IL-6, which leads to damage by cancer cells. Finally, NAC lowers TNF-alpha, which can cause muscle loss in cancer patients. However, NAC and glutathione inactivate certain cancer drugs, such as cisplatin, by forming stable covalent compounds with these drugs. Therefore, one should exercise caution when administering NAC during chemotherapy with any electrophilic antineoplastic agent such as cisplatin or carboplatin.

Animal studies have shown that NAC may be beneficial to prevent hemorrhagic cystitis, a severe side effect of treatment with cyclophosphamide. (Hemorrhagic cystitis, which means "hemorrhagic inflammation of the urinary bladder," results from the toxic effect of acrolein, a metabolic product of cyclophosphamide, on the bladder mucosa.) It has been proposed that NAC prevents this side effect by preventing the intracellular depletion of antioxidants, such as glutathione, by acrolein. NAC can be administered with cyclophosphamide and does not impair the cancer-cell-killing activity, as cyclophosphamide is inactive until metabolized by the liver to its phosphoramide mustard metabolites.

NAC has shown to prevent acute doxorubicin-induced cardiac toxicity, without interfering with the antitumor activity of the drug administration.

Glutathione

Glutathione is a major intracellular antioxidant in pets. Glutathione may be provided directly or indirectly through other compounds (such as SAMe, whey protein, or NAC) that are then converted to glutathione in the body. The supplement SAMe (S-Adenosylmethionine) can be used at a dosage of 10–40 mg/kg daily to provide glutathione (Nutramax Labs makes a SAMe supplement for pets).

Like NAC, glutathione can inactivate certain cancer drugs, such as cisplatin, by forming stable covalent compounds with these drugs. Therefore, one should exercise caution when administering glutathione during chemotherapy with any electrophilic antineoplastic agent such as cisplatin or carboplatin.

Glutathione administration reduces the muscle toxicity of cyclophosphamide, and the nerve and kidney toxicity of cisplatin. (Three Rivers Companion Products manufactures a glutathione supplement for pets that is made from an all-natural milk protein isolate.)

> *Glutathione is a major intracellular antioxidant in pets.*

Proanthocyanidins/Bioflavonoids

Proanthocyanidins (also called pycnogenols, bioflavonoids, or simply flavonoids) are a class of water-soluble plant-coloring agent that, while probably not essential to life, may be needed for optimal health. They are naturally occurring polyphenolic compounds found in plants (technically, proanthocyanidins are a type of bioflavonoid made from grape seed or pine bark, whereas bioflavonoids are a general class of antioxidant plant compound that can include proanthocyanidins, quercetin, and isoflavones). These compounds are used for their antioxidant effects against lipid (fat) peroxidation.

More than 5,000 flavonoids have been discovered to date. Quercetin, curcumin, hesperidin, catechins (including epigallocatechin gallate) are among the most potent cancer-fighting flavonoids.

Proanthocyanidins and bioflavonoids also inhibit the enzyme cyclooxygenase (the same enzyme inhibited by aspirin and other nonsteroidal medications); cyclooxygenase converts arachidonic acid into chemicals (leukotrienes and prostaglandins) that contribute to inflammation and allergic reactions. Proanthocyanidins and bioflavonoids also decrease histamine release from cells by inhibiting several enzymes.

The antioxidant properties make them popular among holistic doctors in treating pets with cancer. Proanthocyanidins and bioflavonoids, by potentiating the immune system (via enhancement of T lymphocyte activity and modulation of neutrophil and macrophage responses), are often recommended for use in the treatment of pets with cancer.

The proanthocyanidin Pycnogenol is a patented product that is a Maritime Pine Bark Extract (made from the bark of pine trees native to southern France) and is a mixture of bioflavonoids, which inhibit the prostaglandins that cause inflammation.

Curcumin, the yellow pigment from turmeric, inhibits the growth of cancer and induces cancer cell death; it is also anti-inflammatory (by inhibiting the COX-2 enzyme), inhibits MMP-2 and MMP-9 enzymes (which help cancer to spread), and stimulates the immune system. It is better absorbed in an oil-based form. It can protect the heart against damage from chemotherapy medications. A recommended dose is 15–20 mg per pound per day. The supplement Total Inflam, by Nutri-West, contains curcumin and other anti-inflammatory herbs, and would be helpful for pets with cancer.

Pycnogenol and grape seed extract, by action of their catechin (a flavonoid) content, increase the collagen content of tissues, including blood vessels, that surround cancer cells, making it harder for the cancer to grow and spread. Also, catechins make the cell's basement membrane more resistant to the eroding enzymes used by cancer cells to grow and spread.

Resveratrol, extracted from the skin of grapes, kills cancer cells by activating apoptosis (the "suicide gene") in cancer cells. It also blocks DNA activation by testosterone (as occurs in prostate cancer). Resveratrol protects normal cells from radiation damage while making cancer cells more vulnerable to damage.

In people, a typical dosage of proanthocyanidins is 200–400 mg three times daily. The suggested dosage of proanthocyanidin "complex" in pets is 10–200 mg given daily (divided into two to three doses). The suggested dosage of bioflavonoid "complex" in pets is 200–1,500 mg per day (divided into two to three doses). Alternatively, a dose for proanthocyanidins/bioflavonoids is 20–60 mg per pound per day. The actual dosage of specific products will vary with the product and the pet's weight and disease condition.

Conclusion

Overwhelming research shows that supplementation with antioxidants can enhance the effects of chemotherapy and radiation and reduce side effects associated with these conventional therapies. Here are some concluding points to keep in mind when considering their use.

1. Natural forms of antioxidants seem to be more effective than synthetic forms and are preferred whenever possible, especially for maintenance of the pet beyond the initial treatment period.

2. Individual antioxidant vitamins and minerals should never be used by themselves without medical supervision but combined with other antioxidants (as an example, antioxidant vitamins and minerals appear particularly effective when combined with bioflavonoids).

3. We don't know the "best" antioxidant or "best dosage" for treating the various cancers in pets. We do know in

people that certain organs have higher concentrations of specific antioxidants than others. For example, lung tissue has a high concentration of lutein, whereas breast tissue is high in another carotene called zeta-carotene. It may be that giving additional lutein for lung cancer and zeta-carotene for breast cancer would be the best choice of antioxidants. This tissue specificity of antioxidants probably occurs in pets but has not been studied. It is possible that certain antioxidants work better on certain cancers than others. More research is needed to study this important area. For now, supplementation with several antioxidant combinations is probably wisest. Of course, commonsense should prevail. For example, in pets taking the chemotherapy drug doxorubicin, which can cause toxicity to the heart, the use of the antioxidant coenzyme Q-10 (*after* doxorubicin therapy) has been shown to minimize heart-related side effects.

> *We don't know the "best" antioxidant or "best dosage" for treating the various cancers in pets. Decisions about what to prescribe are based upon clinical experience as well as information obtained from studies in people and laboratory animals.*

Dietary supplementation with antioxidants may provide a safe and effective means of decreasing the incidence of cancer and enhancing the response to cancer chemotherapy. Antioxidants may be important because of their antioxidant properties, as well as for activities such as inhibition of topoisomerase II.

While a diet supplemented with whole food sources of antioxidants is often recommended by doctors for reducing the incidence of cancer, the use of high doses of *selected synthetic antioxidant vitamins and minerals* during conventional treatments remains controversial, is unlikely to be helpful, and may be harmful. As with all complementary therapies, individual antioxidant vitamins and minerals should not be used without veterinary supervision in pets with cancer that are undergoing chemotherapy or radiation therapy.

BETA-GLUCAN

In the 1940s, research at Tulane Medical School found that beta-glucan, a substance isolated from baker's yeast, had immune-stimulating effects. Beta-glucan is an immuno-activating polysaccharide that is a polymer of D-glucose and represents structural components of the cell walls of various bacteria, yeasts, and mushrooms (such as shiitake, maitaki, and reishi). Beta-glucan stimulates tumor necrosis factor-alpha release from macrophages (white blood cells). Other foods, such as barley, oats, and some medicinal mushrooms, contain glucan and other polysaccharides, but they do not activate the specific receptor found on macrophages.

Oral administration of purified beta-1,3-glucan readily binds to protein-based receptors that are on the cell walls of macrophages, and activates them. Once the macrophages are activated, they signal a number of other immune responses with T cells, B cells, cytokines (intracellular hormones that aid in cell communication and transport), interferons, and interleukins. (The host-adhesive glycoprotein vitronectin specifically binds to beta-glucan, which then augments macrophage cytokine release.)

> *Beta-glucan stimulates tumor necrosis factor-alpha release from macrophages.*

Beta-glucan may be useful in killing cancer cells by stimulating tumor necrosis factor and other cytokines. It has been demonstrated that yeast beta-glucan, when injected into subcutaneous nodules of malignant melanoma, showed the absence of melanoma cells on further biopsies; only a collection of activated macrophages was found on the biopsied tissues.

Beta-glucan has been shown to protect macrophages from radiation damage and activate them to protect the body from the effects of radiation by scavenging cellular debris, free radicals, and infections.

As with many supplements, determining the most effective dose is difficult. Too low a dose won't work; too high may depress the immune system (the dose should cause maximal tumor necrosis factor–alpha release; high concentrations may cause apparent suppression of the TNF-alpha activity released). A recommended human dose is listed as 45–200 mg daily. In pets, the most effective dose has not been worked out. A suggested dose in pets is 7.5–10 mg per 30–60 pounds daily. ImmuDyne (800-643-5109, www.immudyne.com) is one manufacturer of a supplement called Macroforce, which contains beta-1,3-glucan. In the human medical literature, it has been suggested that beta-1,3-glucan should be combined with a similar dose of beta-1,6-glucan to enhance its effectiveness. The daily dose should be divided and given on an empty stomach two to three times daily.

BLACK AND GREEN TEAS (*CAMELLIA SINENSIS*)

Black and green teas are made from the same plants. The highest quality teas are derived from the young shoots, which are made up of the first two or three leaves, plus the growing bud; poorer quality teas are made from leaves located farther down the stems. Black tea is oxidized and fermented, resulting in lower concentrations of the antioxidant active ingredients, known as catechins; green tea is not oxidized and contains higher concentrations of the active ingredients. Usually green tea is preferred as more of the active substances remain in the less-processed green form. Green tea contains high levels of substances called polyphenols known to possess strong antioxidant, anticarcinogenic, and even antibiotic properties. The four major green tea catechins are epicatechin, epigallocatechin, epicatechin gallate, and epigallocatechin gallate (EGCG, the most potent and physiologically active antioxidant of the four catechins). A typical cup of green tea contains between 300–400 mg of polyphenols, of which 10–30 mg is EGCG.

Black tea contains theoflavins and theorubigins, which also inhibit cancer-promoting agents and protect against oxidative damage.

Theanine, a component of tea, enhances the effects of doxorubicin in cancer cells while protecting normal cells.

> *Green tea contains high levels of substances called polyphenols (catechins) known to possess strong antioxidant, anticarcinogenic, and even antibiotic properties.*

A growing body of evidence in both human and animal studies suggests that regular consumption of green tea can reduce the incidence of a variety of cancers, including colon, pancreatic, and stomach cancers. Green tea serves to interfere with cancer growth in the following ways: by inhibiting urokinase (uPA, an enzyme used by human cancers to invade cells and spread); by slowing DNA damage (especially from peroxinitrite, a potent free radical not inhibited by most antioxidants); by prohibiting angiogenesis (the formation of new blood vessels used by cancers to grow and spread); by interfering with vascular endothelial growth factor; and by holding in check an NADH oxidase, known as quinol oxidase or NOX (NOX activity is needed for growth of normal cells, and an overactive form of NOX, called tNOX, allows tumor cells to grow; EGCG inhibits tNOX but not NOX); by activating the suicide gene (causing the cancerous cells to die); by preventing iron absorption (when taken with meals).

Giving green tea with the chemotherapy drug doxorubicin decreased the heart toxicity often seen with doxorubicin administration (by decreasing doxorubicin concentration in the heart cells) and increased doxorubicin concentration in cancer cells.

A recent review in the *Archives of Dermatology* suggests that green tea has potential as a preventive therapy for skin cancer and inflammation of the skin. Researchers from the Department of Dermatology at Case Western University in Cleveland reviewed studies of the anti-inflammatory, anticarcinogenic, and antioxidant effects of green tea's active constituents (flavonols, commonly known as catechins) on the skin. Most studies were conducted on mouse skin models. Overall, the studies demonstrated that both oral and topical green tea reduced the inflammatory responses (such as edema and erythema) that are early markers of skin tumor promotion. Green tea protected against the development and promotion of skin tumors. The researchers concluded that green tea is a promising anti-inflammatory and anticarcinogenic agent that "may have a profound impact on various skin disorders in the years to come," but recommended additional human trials.

Green tea has also been shown to maintain white blood cell counts in human patients undergoing radiation or chemotherapy. Other proposed benefits of green tea include: reduced cholesterol and triglycerides; relaxed arterial activity (via an increase in nitric oxide and intracellular calcium); inhibited platelet clumping (via an amino acid in tea that inhibits thromboxane); enhanced immunity (by increased production of B cells); inhibited bacterial enzymes and viral absorption onto cell membranes to prevent infections; lowered blood sugar in diabetic pets (although one study has made the assertion that regular consumption of tea by children increases their risk of developing diabetes); increased antioxidant activity (by increasing levels of seroxide dismutase in the blood and increasing activity of glutathione S-transferase and catalase in the liver); and protection of the liver and kidney.

Studies suggest that people drinking three cups of green tea daily have increased protection against cancer. The typical consumption of green tea in the average Japanese tea drinker is ten cups (the equivalent of 1,000 mg EGCG) per day. However, because not everyone wants to take the time to drink green tea, manufacturers have offered extracts that can be taken in pill form. A typical dosage in people is 100–150 mg one to three times daily of a green tea extract standardized to contain 80 percent total polyphenols and 50 percent EGCG (in pets, a dosage of 5 mg per pound per day has been recommended). Whether these extracts work as well as the real thing remains unknown, although some studies have shown effectiveness. Since pets will not drink this much tea each day, and it is unknown if the extracts are effective, the use of green tea in pets to prevent cancer is speculative at best. Black tea applied topically appears to sooth discomfort in the mouth that is associated with radiation-induced damage (radiation mucositis). Applying black or green tea to pets with gingivitis or oral ulcerations may be soothing. Black and green teas are generally regarded as safe. Tea contains caffeine, although at a lower level than coffee, and can therefore cause insomnia, nervousness, and the other well-known symptoms of excess caffeine intake (decaffeinated tea does not cause these side effects). Smaller pets may show signs of caffeine intoxication if given large amounts of tea or tea supplements, so it is important to work with your veterinarian if tea is part of your pet's treatment protocol. Due to the potential for platelet in hibition and increased bleeding, pets taking anticoagulant medications such as aspirin must be monitored carefully for bleeding. EGCG has provoked asthma attacks in a small number of asthma patients working in a tea factory. Tea has a low sodium but high potassium content; pets with elevated potassium levels (end-stage kidney failure) should not take green tea. Green tea should not be given to infants and young children, as it may cause iron metabolism problems and microcytic anemia; similar precautions probably apply in pets. For pets taking MAO inhibitors, the caffeine in green tea could cause serious problems.

COENZYME Q-10 (UBIQUINONE)

Coenzyme Q-10 (ubiquinone) is a powerful fat-soluble antioxidant that is found in every cell in the body. It plays a fundamental role in the mitochondria, which are the parts of the cell that produce energy. Coenzyme Q-10 controls the flow of oxygen within the cells and functions as an antioxidant to reduce damage to cells from harmful free radicals. Every cell in the body needs CoQ-10, but there is no U.S. recommended dietary allowance because the body can manufacture CoQ-10 from scratch and obtain it from the diet (the richest sources of this vital enzyme are meat and organ meats, such as heart, liver, spleen, and kidney). However, it is hard to get a *therapeutic* dosage from food.

While CoQ-10 is often prescribed for pets with heart disease and gum disease (oral as well as topical application may decrease oral ulcers if they develop from chemotherapy or radiation), it is also valuable as part of cancer therapy.

CoQ-10 is fat soluble and is better absorbed when taken as an oil-based soft-gel rather than as a dry tablet or capsule. In people, the typical recommended dosage is 30–300 mg daily. In pets, the typical recommended dosage is 30 mg every twenty-four to forty-eight hours; however, many doctors, me included, prescribe the higher dosage of 1 mg per pound per day.

CoQ-10 is used in cancer as an antioxidant and also specifically to minimize heart toxicity (acute and delayed) from the chemotherapy drug Adriamycin (doxorubicin), although other chemotherapy medications, including 5-FU, mitoxantrone, and cyclophosphamide, can cause heart toxicity.

While the antioxidant NAC and antioxidant vitamins C and E can help prevent acute toxicity, coenzyme Q-10 is especially helpful in preventing the chronic form of toxicity, which is not prevented by other dietary antioxidants.

The proposed mechanism of the dose-limiting chronic cardiotoxicity seen with doxorubicin involves the production of oxidizing agents (free radicals, specifically, the highly toxic hydroxyl radical) through an iron-dependent process. Free radicals are generated by doxorubicin, which results in mitochondrial lipid peroxidation within myocardial (heart) cells; other effects of doxorubicin on the mitochondria of cardiac cells may also be important. For example, doxorubicin reduces the CoQ-10 content of mitochondrial membranes and inhibits the mitochondrial synthesis of CoQ-10. These effects of doxorubicin on CoQ-10 synthesis and function may explain the acute and chronic forms of doxorubicin-induced cardiotoxicity.

> *CoQ-10 may help prevent*
> *doxorubicin-induced cardiotoxicity.*

This mechanism is also consistent with the observations that chronic doxorubicin-induced cardiotoxicity is not reversible. The resulting congestive heart failure is not responsive to digitalis, and antioxidants such as vitamins E and C do not prevent it.

Supplementation in laboratory animals with injections of CoQ-10 has been shown to reverse doxorubicin-induced enzyme inhibition and prevent acute doxorubicin-induced cardiotoxicity. In contrast to the effects of vitamin E, which does not prevent the development of chronic doxorubicin-induced cardiotoxicity, oral and injectable administration of CoQ-10 has been shown to protect laboratory animals from developing this irreversible cardiotoxicity.

CoQ-10 has been shown not to interfere with the antitumor activity of doxorubicin in mice; it also does not prevent doxorubicin-induced bone marrow suppression in rabbits. *However, since giving CoQ-10 at the same time of doxorubicin may increase the production of the hydroxyl free radical and/or a toxic doxorubicin metabolite, the current recommendation is to administer CoQ-10 after completion of doxorubicin therapy.*

Coenzyme Q-10 has been shown to stimulate the immune system. While CoQ-10 may show indirect anticancer activity through its effect(s) on the immune system, there is evidence to suggest that analogs of this compound are able to suppress cancer growth directly. Analogs of CoQ-10 have been shown to inhibit the proliferation of cancer cells in vitro and the growth of cancer cells transplanted into rats and mice. In view of these findings, it has been proposed that analogs of coenzyme Q-10 may function as antimetabolites to disrupt normal biochemical reactions that are required for cell growth and/or survival, and they may be useful for short periods of time as chemotherapeutic agents.

In 1961, a deficiency was noted in the blood of both Swedish and American cancer patients, especially in the blood of patients with breast cancer. A subsequent study showed a statistically significant relationship between the level of plasma coenzyme Q-10 deficiency and breast cancer prognosis. Low blood levels of this compound have been reported in patients with malignancies other than breast cancer, including myeloma, lymphoma, and cancers of the lung, prostate, pancreas, colon, kidney, and head and neck.

Furthermore, decreased levels of CoQ-10 have been detected in malignant human tissue, but increased levels have been reported as well. It is unknown whether the low levels of CoQ-10 contributed to the development of these cancers, although this is suggested by the studies.

A large amount of laboratory and animal model data on CoQ-10 has been accumulated since 1962. Some of the accumulated data has shown that coenzyme Q-10 stimulates animal immune systems, leading to higher antibody levels, greater numbers and/or activities of macrophages and T cells (T lymphocytes), and increased resistance to infection. CoQ-10 has also been reported to increase IgG (immunoglobulin G) antibody levels as well as the CD4 to CD8 T cell ratio in humans. CD4 and CD8 are proteins found on the surface of T cells, with CD4 and CD8 identifying "helper" T cells and "cytotoxic" T cells, respectively; decreased CD4 to CD8 T cell ratios have been reported for cancer patients. Research subsequently delineated the antioxidant properties of CoQ-10.

According to contributor and veterinary cancer specialist Dr. Kevin Hahn, researchers in one study found that coadministration of CoQ-10 and radiation therapy decreased the effectiveness of the radiotherapy. In this study, mice inoculated with human small-cell lung cancer and then given CoQ-10 and single-dose radiation therapy showed substantially less inhibition of tumor growth than mice in the control group, which received radiotherapy alone. Since radiation leads to the production of free-radicals, and since antioxidants protect against free-radical damage, the effect in this study might be explained by CoQ-10 acting as an antioxidant. As a result, some oncologists recommend that CoQ-10 be administered not during radiation therapy but instead after therapy for its antioxidant/anticancer effects and to reduce stricture and post-radiation scarring. However, these side effects have not been reported in other studies, and they have not been shown to occur in people or pets clinically. This is something to discuss with your veterinarian prior to radiation therapy.

In view of observations that blood levels of CoQ-10 are frequently reduced in cancer patients, supplementation with this compound has been tested in patients undergoing conventional treatment. Reports of CoQ-10 lengthening the survival of human patients with pancreatic, lung, rectal, laryngeal, colon, and prostate cancers exist in the peer-reviewed scientific literature. The patients described in these reports also received therapies other than CoQ-10, including chemotherapy, radiation therapy, and surgery.

Studies in both laboratory animals and people suggest that CoQ-10 may provide a safe and effective means of reducing or preventing the development of the cardiotoxicity associated with chronic administration of doxorubicin without compromising the ability of doxorubicin to kill cancer cells.

Some medications may cause depletion of CoQ-10 and supplementation with CoQ-10 might prove useful for those patients, including patients who are taking cholesterol-lowering statin drugs, such as lovastatin (Mevacor), simvastatin (Zocor), and pravastatin (Pravachol); oral diabetes drugs, especially glyburide, phenformin, and tolazamide; beta-blockers, specifically propranolol, metoprolol, and alprenolol; and antipsychotic drugs in the phenothiazine family, such as tricyclic antidepressants, diazoxide, methyldopa, hydrochlorothiazide, clonidine, and hydralazine. CoQ-10 can reduce the body's response to the anticoagulant drug warfarin. Finally, CoQ-10 can decrease insulin requirements in individuals with diabetes.

Coenzyme Q-10 appears to be extremely safe; no serious toxicity associated with its use has been reported. Doses of 100 mg per day or higher have caused mild insomnia in some people. Liver enzyme elevation has been detected in patients taking doses of 300 mg per day for extended periods of time, but no liver toxicity has been reported. Researchers in one cardiovascular study reported that CoQ-10 caused rashes, nausea, and epigastric (upper abdominal) pain that required withdrawal of a small number of patients from the study. Other reported side effects have included dizziness, photophobia (abnormal visual sensitivity to light), irritability, headache, heartburn, and fatigue. These side effects have not been reported in animals, and animals usually receive lower doses than those reported in human studies.

While usually not associated with side effects, the maximum safe dosages of CoQ-10 for young children, pregnant or nursing women, or those with severe liver or kidney disease has not been determined; the same is true for pets.

COLOSTRUM (LACTOFERRIN, TRANSFER FACTOR, WHEY PROTEIN)

Colostrum is the antibody-rich milk produced by nursing mothers in the first few days following childbirth. It contains lactoferrin, immunoglobulins, peptides, and transforming growth factor-beta (TGF-B). Lactoferrin is a glycoprotein found in milk and whey protein and secreted by cells of the gastrointestinal tract, respiratory tract, and various mucous membranes. Transfer Factor is a patented preparation of small molecules found in blood cells and milk. Colostrum, lactoferrin, and Tranfer Factor are used to stimulate the immune system in order to fight various infectious diseases and assist in cancer therapy. These compounds can prevent the growth and spread of cancers in a number of ways, including reducing inflammation and preventing the binding of iron. Whey protein is a protein found in milk that enhances immunity and increases the antioxidant glutathione in normal cells but decreases it in cancer cells. All of these compounds are safe (make sure they are prepared from certified BSE-free cattle; BSE is the scientific name for mad cow disease). However, because whey protein contains a large amount of glutamate, it should not be used in pets with brain cancer (especially gliomas). A suggested lactoferrin dose for people is 250–350 mg per day of products standardized to 40 percent IgG (immunoglobulin G). Pets can take a similar amount (lower doses for smaller pets).

DMG

Another name for dimethylglycine (DMG) is vitamin B-15. It is found in low levels in foods such as meats, seeds, and grains. Both the human and animal body make DMG from choline and betaine. It is suggested that increased dietary intake of DMG can be beneficial. The metabolic role of DMG is to provide carbon to cells. It is also a precursor of SAMe. DMG appears to enhance oxygen usage, prevent the accumulation of lactic acid, improve muscle metabolism, function as an antistress nutrient to improve the cardiovascular system, and reduce recovery time after vigorous physical activity.

Studies have shown that DMG can improve the immune response by potentiating both cell-mediated and humoral (antibody) immunity. As a result, some holistic doctors recommend DMG for pets with immune disorders such as cancer (at a dosage of 0.5–1 mg per pound daily). For pets with cancer, DMG enhances the immune response (by increasing anticancer cytokines and enhancing the action of natural killer cells), slows down the spread of cancer, improves oxygen utilization, enhances circulation and antioxidant activity, acts as a methyl donor, and reduces lactic acid levels.

DMG is extremely safe. The body converts it into its metabolites, which are either used or excreted as waste.

One product, which combines a patented whey protein isolate (Gluta-Syn) with DMG, is called Gluta-DMG, by Vetri-Science. The product is used for improving immune system function and for producing a sustained cellular increase of the antioxidant glutathione in the body.

EDTA CHELATION THERAPY

Chelation with EDTA, and with other similar products, is often recommended to treat a variety of cancerous conditions. EDTA can inhibit the metalloproteinases that are critical for tumor development and growth. EDTA chelation is well known for its use in cleansing the body of toxins, including toxic minerals, specifically heavy metals like lead and zinc. While EDTA was initially used to treat heavy metal poisoning, some observers felt that other benefits occurred in patients receiving this therapy. Some doctors may recommend this treatment for diabetes, arteriosclerosis, and cancer. In people, twenty or more sessions may be recommended and can cost thousands of dollars.

Since studies of the use of EDTA chelation for treating diseases other than heavy metal poisoning are so far inconclusive, the therapy is not currently used by most holistic doctors. Additionally, serious side effects have been associated with chelation therapy. These include low calcium blood levels, bone marrow and kidney damage, low blood pressure, increased risk of blood clots or bleeding, bacterial infections, seizures, allergic or immune system reactions, heart rhythm abnormalities, and unstable blood sugar levels. Other side effects may include fever, nausea, vomiting, headache, decreased thyroid function, and fatigue. Respiratory arrest and death have been reported. Chelation may be dangerous in individuals with heart, kidney, or liver disease, or in people with conditions affecting blood cells or the immune system. Use during pregnancy or breast feeding or by children may also be dangerous.

ENZYMES

Enzymes are used for a variety of functions in the body. Cellular processes, digestion, and absorption of dietary nutrients are dependent upon the proper enzymes. People tend to think of enzymes as necessary only for the breakdown of food in the stomach. In fact, enzymes produced by the pancreas, intestines, and stomach are all essential for digestion of nutrients in the diet. Once properly digested by pancreatic enzymes, the dietary nutrients can be absorbed by the body.

The pancreas produces amylase, lipase, and various proteases. Amylase is used for digesting carbohydrates, lipase is used for digesting fats, and proteases are used by the body to digest proteins.

While it is true that the pancreas produces enzymes to aid in food digestion, additional enzymes found in the diet contribute to digestion and absorption as well, and these may enhance feed efficiency (maximizing the utilization of nutrients in the diet). Natural raw diets contain a number of chemicals, including enzymes not found in processed diets. Processing often alters the nutrients found in a pet's food, depleting it of important nutrients and enzymes (enzymes are broken down in the presence of temperatures in the range of 120–160°F and in the presence of freezing temperatures). Supplemental enzymes can replenish those absent in processed foods. Even pets on natural raw diets can benefit from additional enzymes, which is why they are often recommended as a supplement.

Additionally, various stressors such as illness, allergy, food intolerance, age (older pets may have reduced digestive enzyme capability), and radiation, in addition to various orally administered medications (antibiotics and chemotherapy) can decrease gastrointestinal function. This results in poor digestion and incomplete absorption of nutrients. Supplying digestive enzymes at these times can improve digestion and absorption.

Enzymes work by liberating essential dietary nutrients. While we don't know all the wonderful things that enzymes do, it is known that certain enzyme supplements can increase the body's absorption of essential vitamins, minerals, and certain fatty acids. Increased absorption of zinc, selenium, vitamin B-6, and linoleic acid have been detected following enzyme supplementation.

Doctors can prescribe either pancreatic, microbial, or mixed enzymes.

Enzymes have been recommended for pets with various disorders, including arthritis, allergies, coat condition problems, bowel disease (especially inflammatory bowel disease), and coprophagia (the ingestion of the pet's own or another pet's feces). For pets with cancer, enzyme supplementation with food can increase the absorption of nutrients and may help counteract the effects of cancer cachexia (the wasting of the body seen in some pets with cancer). Supplemental enzymes serve to replenish the gastrointestinal tract when naturally occurring enzymes are destroyed by chemotherapy and radiation therapy. Giving enzymes without food (several hours before feeding) allows them to work by removing (eating away) break-down products of metabolism. Also, the enzymes can inhibit new blood vessel growth (angiogenesis) needed for cancer to grow and spread. For the pet with cancer, it may be the most beneficial to give enzymes both with food (to improve digestion and absorption of nutrients) and without food (to remove waste products of cellular metabolism and cancer therapy).

I prefer a balanced enzyme product that contains cellulase in addition to amylase, lipase, and protease. Dogs do not normally have cellulase in their bodies, and that's why they can digest only some of the plant material in their diets. Supplementation with enzyme products that contain cellulase in addition to the normal lipase, amylase, and proteases seem to be more advantageous to pets with medical problems, as they liberate chemicals such as zinc, selenium, and linoleic acid that might be bound by fiber.

Since zinc deficiency impairs immunity, it may be that the increased zinc levels in the blood that occur after enzyme supplementation improve the functioning of the immune system in people and pets. Zinc can protect against cellular damage caused by tumor necrosis factor.

Anecdotally, pets (so-called "poor doers") taking enzyme supplements have been shown to have improved energy levels. Since response is dependent on the product used, if one supplement does not help, another one might work better.

Since enzymes are inactivated by heat, they cannot be added to warm food or mixed with warm water. Rather, they simply should be sprinkled as a powder onto food (at room temperature) at the time of feeding or given in a pill or chewable tablet.

Enzyme supplementation is inexpensive, safe, and easy. The only caution is that high doses should not be used after surgery (they may inhibit healing) or during pregnancy (new blood vessel formation is needed to maintain pregnancy). Adding label doses of digestive enzymes to your pet's food, however, is safe following surgery or during pregnancy. Your doctor can help you decide which product is best for your pet's condition.

Miscellaneous Enzyme Supplements

Proteolytic enzymes are one class of enzyme that helps your pet digest the proteins in food. Although the pet's body produces these enzymes in the pancreas, certain foods also contain proteolytic enzymes.

Papaya and pineapple are two of the richest plant sources of digestive enzymes; papain and bromelain are the respective names for the proteolytic enzymes found in these fruits. Since there is some evidence that bromelain may be helpful for pets with cancer, only bromelain will be discussed here.

Bromelain is a collection of protein-digesting enzymes found in pineapple juice and in the stems of pineapple plants. It is thought to be useful for a variety of conditions in addition to cancer. In Europe, it is widely used to aid in recovery from surgery and athletic injuries, as well as to treat osteoarthritis, rheumatoid arthritis, and gout. Bromelain is also useful as a digestive enzyme. Unlike most digestive enzymes, bromelain is active both in the acid environment of the stomach and the alkaline environment of the small intestine. This may make it particularly effective as an oral digestive aid for those pets that do not digest proteins properly. Since it is primarily the proteins in foods that cause food allergies, bromelain might reduce food-allergy symptoms, although this has not been proven.

While most large enzymes are broken down in the digestive tract, those found in bromelain appear to be absorbed whole to a certain extent. This finding makes it reasonable to suppose that bromelain can actually produce systemic (whole body) effects. Once in the blood, bromelain appears to produce mild anti-inflammatory and blood-thinning effects.

It has been suggested as a possible supplement for treating pets with cancer. There is at least one experimental report of bromelain inhibiting the spread of implanted lung carcinoma in mice. No definitive proof exists for its use in the treatment of cancers in dogs. However, since supplementation with any enzymes would not be expected to harm a pet, its use can be safely recommended.

Bromelain appears to be essentially nontoxic, and it seldom causes side effects other than occasional mild gastrointestinal distress or allergic reactions. However, because bromelain thins the blood to some extent, it shouldn't be combined with drugs such as Coumadin (warfarin) without a doctor's supervision. Safety in young children, pregnant or nursing women, or people with liver or kidney disease has not been established; similar precautions are probably warranted in pets as well.

GLANDULAR SUPPLEMENTS
(ADRENAL, THYMUS)

Glandular therapy (cell therapy, tissue therapy) is the use of whole animal tissues or extracts of these tissues for health maintenance and for therapy of mild health problems typically involving the glands of the body. Glandular therapy is tissue specific. In other words, liver extracts benefit the liver, thyroid extracts benefit the thyroid gland, adrenal extracts benefit the adrenal gland, and so forth. Current research supports this concept, that the glandular supplements contain active substances that can exert physiologic effects.

Several studies show that radioactively tagged glandular cells, when injected into the body, accumulate in their target tissues. The accumulation in traumatized body organs or glands is more rapid than it is in healthy tissues, which may indicate an increased requirement for the ingredients contained in the glandular supplements. For example, animals with thyroid cell damage showed rapid uptake of thyroid cells with active regeneration of the damaged thyroids, and liver extracts that were infused into animals caused liver regeneration.

In addition to targeting specific damaged organs and glands, glandular supplementation may also provide specific nutrients to the pet. For example, glands contain hormones in addition to a number of other chemical constituents. These low doses of crude hormones are suitable for any pet needing hormone replacement, but are especially suitable for those pets with mild disease or those that simply need gentle organ support. Pure, chemically produced, full-strength hormones, while beneficial in selected pets requiring quick response to a disease, would not be desired (due to potential side effects) for long-term use in most pets.

Glandular supplements also function as a source of enzymes, active lipids, and steroids that may be of benefit to pets.

Adrenal glandular supplements are whole glandular extracts of the adrenal gland. They may be used by doctors to support the adrenal gland during cancer therapy, particularly if high doses of corticosteroids (which depress the adrenal gland) are used. Other glandular supplements may also be used during the treatment of the cancer patient to offer support for the other glands and tissues of the body. Examples are glandular products to support the function of the liver, thyroid gland, and thymus gland. Thymus glandular supplements (in particular, thymic protein A, an extract) may help pets with cancer by activating cellular immunity and inhibiting the formation of immune complexes formed by humoral immunity, by which cancer cell growth is suppressed.

GLUTAMINE

Glutamine, or L-glutamine, is an amino acid derived from glutamic acid, and serves as a precursor to D-glucosamine. There is no daily requirement for glutamine as the body can make its own. High-protein foods, such as meat, fish, beans, and dairy products, are excellent sources of glutamine. Heavy exercise, infection, surgery, and trauma can deplete the body's glutamine reserves, particularly in muscle cells.

Glutamine plays a role in the health of the immune system, digestive tract, and muscle cells, as well as other bodily functions. It serves as a fuel for the mucosal cells that line the intestines. In people, there is evidence that glutamine supplements might have significant nutritional benefits for those who are seriously ill, as may occur in cancer. Adding glutamine to the feeding formulas of hospitalized pets, including those with cancer that have decreased appetites, might be warranted. Additionally, pets with digestive disturbances (either from the cancer itself or from chemotherapy or radiation therapy) might benefit from supplementation with glutamine.

In people and pets, glutamine is also recommended to reduce the loss of muscle mass, which may occur during injury, stress, or illness, or during high-endurance activities of dogs competing in field trials. While glutamine does not possess antioxidant activity, it serves as a source of glutamate for glutathione synthesis, thus supporting cellular antioxidant systems. It has also been shown to enhance the antitumor effectiveness of methotrexate in laboratory animals. (This may occur as a result of increasing the intracellular tumor concentration of methotrexate.) Glutamine increases muscle mass (muscle wasting can occur as a side effect of cancer), improves white blood cell (lymphocyte) function, and reduces leakiness of the intestines during radiation therapy. Dietary supplementation with glutamine has been shown to protect the heart from doxorubicin toxicity.

Glutamine is a precursor of glutamate. It can increase the aggressiveness of a certain type of brain tumor (glioma); supplementation with glutamine may possibly contribute to this. At this time, it is probably wise to avoid glutamine supplementation in pets with glioma tumors (discuss this with your doctor).

> *Pets with digestive disturbances*
> *(either from the cancer itself or from chemotherapy*
> *or radiation therapy) might benefit from*
> *supplementation with glutamine.*

Glutamine may reduce the gastrointestinal toxicity of some chemotherapy drugs; supplementation during chemotherapy is not harmful and may reduce intestinal damage. Glutamine can also prevent inflammation of the intestinal tract caused by radiation therapy. Glutamine should be considered as a supplement for dogs undergoing half-body irradiation for the treatment of lymphosarcoma.

Glutamine improves immune system function because lymphocytes require a large amount of glutamine to function properly.

While cancer cells also use glutamine to function properly, supplementing with glutamine will not increase cancer growth or spread and is beneficial for pets with cancer.

Glutamine is discussed elsewhere (pages 258–259) as part of the therapy for gastroenteritis or stomatitis (inflammation of the mouth and gums) associated with chemotherapy (specifically with drugs 5-FU and methotrexate) or radiation therapy.

Glutamine is safe when used at recommended dosages. Because many antiepilepsy drugs work by blocking glutamate stimulation in the brain, high dosages of glutamine may overwhelm these drugs and pose a risk to pets with epilepsy. While commonly used supplements are unlikely to be harmful, if your pet is taking antiseizure medications, glutamine should only be used under veterinary supervision. People and pets with glioma tumors (astrocytoma, glioblastoma) of the brain should avoid glutamine supplementation, as glutamine is converted in the brain into glutamate, which can increase the growth of these tumors.

Maximum safe dosages for young children, pregnant or nursing women, or people with severe liver or kidney disease have not been determined; similar precautions are probably warranted in pets. Recommended dosages in pets are 250–3,000 mg daily.

GLYCOPROTEINS/GLYCOCONJUGATE SUGARS (MANNOSE, MANNANS)

Glycoproteins are protein molecules bound to carbohydrate molecules. Glycoprotein molecules coat the surface of every nucleated cell in the body; the body uses the glycoproteins as communication or recognition molecules. These communications may then result in other cellular events, including secretion of bioactive substances (interferon, interleukin-1, complement), ingestion of bacteria and cell debris, inhibition of adherence necessary for bacterial infection, and the spread of cancer.

Scientists have identified eight glycoproteins on human cell surfaces that are involved in cellular recognition processes. These eight glycoproteins that are essential for glycoconjugate synthesis (mannose, galactose, fucose, xylose, glucose, sialic acid, N-acetylglucosamine, N-acetylgalactosamine) can be readily absorbed and directly incorporated into glycoproteins and glycolipids.

Recent research has found specific cell surface glycoforms to be characteristic of many disease conditions. In people with cancer, more than twenty different malignancies are known to be associated with characteristic glycoproteins. Many diseases, including some autoimmune diseases, have been found to be associated with altered cell surface glycoproteins.

Glyconutritional supplements are designed to provide substrates for the body to use in building part of the glycoconjugates on cell surfaces. These supplements, most commonly acemannan and mannose, are designed to make the necessary sugars available to the cells more quickly and in greater quantity.

Acemannan, a mannan isolated from aloe vera, has antiviral properties. It is an immunomodulator that causes activation of macrophages. In the presence of interferon, acemannan induces cancer cell death (apoptosis). It is believed that acemannan exerts its antitumor activity through macrophage activation and the subsequent release of tumor necrosis factor, interleukin-1 and 6, and interferon-gamma, prostaglandin E2, and tumor necrosis factor. Acemannan also enhances macrophage phagocytosis and nonspecific cytotoxicity, which increases the ability of white blood cells (macrophages) to destroy infectious organisms. Acemannan shows bone marrow stimulating activity.

Acemannan has been approved for the treatment of fibrosarcoma in dogs and cats; it may be an effective adjunct to surgery and radiation therapy in the treatment of sarcomas. Intralesional injection into the tumor (2 mg weekly for up to six weeks), combined with intraperitoneal injections (1 mg/kg of body weight given weekly for six weeks, followed by monthly injections for one year), has been recommended to decrease tumor size. Clinically, it has been shown to be effective in some animals in decreasing tumor size (possibly via necrosis and inflammation). However, some of the tumors that had been treated with acemannan injections did not differ from nontreated tumors. The use of acemannan in animals may not be advantageous for every type of solid tumor. At this time, the use of acemannan has limited application for treating tumors in pets; if used, it is probably best reserved as an adjunct to other therapies, in an effort to improve local tumor control and recurrence. Most oncologists do not feel acemannan is of benefit in treating sarcomas.

All eight of the glycoconjugate sugars are readily absorbed by the intestines when taken orally. Studies have shown intact mannose molecules are rapidly absorbed by the intestines of rats into the blood. This elevates the blood mannose levels by three- to tenfold, and mannose is cleared from the blood within hours. The conclusion reached was that mannose was absorbed by the intestinal tract into the blood and from the blood into the cells. These studies suggest that dietary mannose may make a significant contribution to glycoform synthesis in mammals (a popular pet supplement containing mannose is Ambrotose, made by Mannatech Laboratories).

Other human and animal ingestion studies show that mannose is readily absorbed and then cleared from the blood over several hours; some of the mannose is incorporated into glycoproteins. After absorption into the blood, glycoconjugate sugars generally are taken (usually as glycoproteins and glycolipids) into other body fluids, as well as organs and various body tissues.

> *Wound healing can be improved with mannose and acemannan by decreasing tissue damage and inflammation.*

Adverse effects caused by glycoconjugate sugars are rare and usually occur only when they are injected or when doses greatly exceed levels that would be expected in normal diets. For pets being treated with the most commonly used glycoproteins (acemannan and mannose), side effects are not expected. However, in some pets with large tumors (fibrosarcomas) that are treated with acemannan, severe illness could occur as a result of rapid tumor necrosis. Pets receiving injectable acemannan must be monitored closely for side effects that can occur with tumor necrosis. Side effects could include rupture of and seepage from the tumor, infection, or fluid loss. Some patients may require emergency surgery to remove the masses after they start to deteriorate and abscess. Very rarely, shock and sudden death can occur. (Popular glycoprotein supplements used in pets are manufactured by Carrington Laboratories and Mannatech Laboratories.)

GREEN FOODS (SUPER GREEN FOODS)

Green foods most commonly include barley grass, spirulina (blue-green algae), alfalfa, chlorella, wheatgrass, kelp, and chlorophyll and chlorophyllin. Green foods contain a variety of nutrients. Ingestion of these nutrients seeks to prevent and treat illnesses that may be induced by an imbalance of minerals, enzymes, and vitamins in processed diets.

Barley grass contains large amounts of: vitamins A, C, E, B-1, B-2, and B-6; biotin; folic acid; choline; pantothenic acid; nicotinic acid; iron; chlorophyll; potassium; calcium; magnesium; manganese; zinc; proteins; and enzymes.

Spirulina is a high-potency freshwater blue-green algae. It contains the antioxidant superoxide dismutase (a scavenger of free radicals), B complex vitamins, gamma linolenic acid, calcium, iron, magnesium, potassium, boron, molybdenum, mangenese, phosphorus, sodium, zinc, copper, amino acids, other phytonutrients with antioxidant effects, and mixed carotenoids. In-vitro studies show that phycocyanin, the pigment in spirulina, can inhibit cancer colony formation and may enhance the formation of neurotransmitters. Animal studies show that spirulina is an effective immunomodulator, an agent that can affect the behavior of immune cells. For example, spirulina inhibits allergic reactions in rats by suppressing the release of histamine. In cats, spirulina enhances the ability of macrophage white blood cells to kill bacteria; in chickens, spirulina has been demonstrated to increase antibody response as well as the activity of natural killer cells, which destroy infectious cells as well as cancer cells in the body. Spirulina may kill infectious and cancer cells by inducing interferon-gamma and by stimulating interleukin-4 and interleukin-1-beta. Increases in these cytokines (immune stimulating chemicals) helps to protect the body against infectious and potentially harmful microorganisms. Spirulina enhances natural killer cell functions.

One compound isolated from spirulina is C-phycocyanin (C-PC), which possesses potent antioxidant, anti-inflammatory, and anticancer properties. One study found that C-PC induces cancer cell death in a human chronic myeloid leukemia cell line (K562).

> *Green foods contain a variety of nutrients*
> *that may be beneficial for pets with cancer.*

Alfalfa is a well-known herb (see page 119) that is rich in many nutrients (protein and vitamins and minerals) and chlorophyll, which serves as an antioxidant. It is one of the best adjunctive herbal therapies for arthritis and possesses cancer-preventing properties by inactivating chemicals that can cause cancer. Nutritious alfalfa is often fed to animals that need to gain weight.

Chlorella is a warm-water algae that has slightly less protein than spirulina, but more chlorophyll and nucleic acid. It has a tough cell wall that is poorly digested, but may work as a toxin binder. Wheatgrass contains a number of nutrients as well. As with other green foods, it is claimed but not proven that wheatgrass may be helpful for pets with cancer, as it provides extra nutrition, detoxifies the body, helps oxygenate cells, and reduces cell mutations that may become precancerous.

Kelp is a variety of seaweed that contains phytonutrients and marine-based minerals. Some studies have found a radio-protective effect for seaweed and kelp (they protect against radiation damage). Seaweed is a rich sources of sulfated polysaccharides, including heparins. Tumor cells use heparin-digesting enzymes to invade and spread; sulfated polysaccharides impede spread by inhibiting tumor-induced heparin sulfate degradation in the basement membrane of cells. Seaweed contains beta-1, 3-glucan, which alters the enzymatic activity of fecal flora and stimulates the immune response.

The chlorophyll (and a form of chlorophyll called *chlorophyllin*) found in super green foods may assist the body in healing due to its anti-inflammatory properties. Chlorophyllin blocks free radicals, specifically heterocyclic amines and aflatoxins and those generated by sunlight and X-rays. Chlorophyllin can actually prevent free radicals from binding to DNA and causing mutations (and cancer); it also slows down the metabolism of chemicals to prevent them from becoming cancerous.

The enzymes contained in super green foods are not just those that can aid in digestion and absorption of nutrients but those that may also assist in reducing oxidative injury to damaged tissues. Other proposed beneficial effects of super green foods include antitumor effects in laboratory rodents, protective effects against toxin-induced kidney failure, enhanced effects on intestinal microflora, as well as decreases in blood sugar, cholesterol, weight in obese people, blood pressure, and viral activity. In pets, supplementation with super green foods may also improve skin and haircoat conditions.

Another type of green food supplement contains cruciferous vegetables, such as cabbage, brussels sprouts, cauliflower, and broccoli. These vegetables contain indole-3-carbinol (I3C), which has proven effective against hormone-related cancers and environmental cancers (caused by dioxin, aflatoxins, and heterocyclic amines). Meat and dairy products are the main sources of dioxin; cooked meat, especially barbecued meat, is a primary source of heterocyclic amines. I3C works by blocking receptors on the cells that allow the entry of estrogen and dioxin. Other effects of I3C include converting dangerous estrogens into safer estrogens (2-OHE); restoring the function of the p21 tumor suppressor gene; boosting antioxidant activity; enhancing liver detoxification systems; and inducing cancer cell death. In people, suggested doses are 400–600 mg twice daily. Doses for pets are extrapolated from this. I3C is a very safe supplement.

A controversial approach to the treatment of cancer has been proposed by pet owner and author Hulda Clark. Her theory is that all cancer in people (and probably animals) is caused by internal parasites, specifically, the human intestinal fluke. She proposes that people acquire the intestinal fluke and other parasites from undercooked meat and milk, and that the parasites are transmitted between people by close contact such as kissing, sexual activity, and even breast-feeding. In some people, the parasites cause no problem. In people who have the accumulation of isopropyl alcohol (acquired from food and other sources around the house such as cosmetics) and aflatoxins (from moldy foods) in the liver, the intestinal parasites migrate there. This accumulation of parasites in the liver produces a growth factor causing all cells of the liver to multiply and becomes cancerous. Clark also proposes that tumors contain fungi or bacteria in addition to the parasites. Wherever the parasites accumulate, cancer can occur in that location. For example, if adult parasites are present in the liver, and if isopropyl alcohol has also accumulated in the liver, you get liver cancer. With parasites plus alcohol in the pancreas, you get diabetes or pancreatic cancer. In short, Clark blames every disease on parasites plus alcohol.

Her proposed treatment involves killing the parasites, in which case the cancer will be cured. Likewise, by preventing parasites, cancer can be prevented.

Her recommended treatment is herbs (wormwood, black walnut, cloves) to kill all possible parasites. Her herbal therapy is in tincture form (which interestingly contains grain alcohol!). What she does not point out is the potential toxicity of some of these deworming herbs. Her other proposed treatment involves purchasing her specially made electrical device, a "zapping" unit to zap the body and supposedly kill the microorganisms and parasites.

There are several problems with her theories. First, people are usually not infected with animal parasites. Second, how is it, as Clark claims, that some people have isopropyl alcohol in their bodies and not others? Usually, intestinal flukes do not migrate to other parts of the body but stay in the target organ, the intestines. Also, even if we were successfully dewormed, since we can't avoid contact with isopropyl alcohol or infected people, it seems we would need to be dewormed on a daily basis to kill the parasites we would constantly acquire.

While it is true that chronic inflammation of the organs and tissues induced by any parasite, fluke, or aflatoxin may increase the risk of cancer in high-risk populations, there seems to be just as much cancer in low-risk populations. The American Dietetics Association believes that one-third of cancer deaths in humans is diet related, which is in contrast to the Hulda Clark hypothesis. The only known type of cancer to occur in dogs as a result of parasites is the extremely rare esophageal cancer that can occur following infection by the esophageal parasite *Spirocerca lupi*.

Despite Clark's apparent cures, her results have not been confirmed independently. While deworming pets is never a bad idea, conventional dewormers are usually much safer than the herbal therapies used in the Clark protocol. Under your doctor's supervision, you can deworm your pet with cancer, but you should not ignore your pet's illness. If you feel deworming is necessary, don't neglect your pet's main problem; continue with the appropriate therapy for cancer.

HYALURONAN (HYALURONIC ACID)

Hyaluronan is a natural anti-inflammatory agent. It is found in the joints, eyes, brains, skin, and blood of all mammals. It is produced by the body in both high molecular weight and low molecular weight forms and is catabolized by enzymes in the body, producing glucosamine as the by-product.

As mammals age, the amount of hyaluronic acid produced by the body is reduced. This reduction may allow the development of geriatric inflammatory diseases such as arthritis and cancer. Administration of hyaluronan may prevent or be an effective treatment against such geriatric diseases.

Injectable hyaluronan has been used since the 1950s in humans (in cataract surgery) and since the 1980s in animals. During the 1980s, Dr. Karen Brown discovered that hyaluronan could be effective for the treatment of joint problems in horses when injected intravenously. Her research resulted in FDA approval of Legend (Bayer Healthcare, Animal Health Division) for use in horses. Hyaluronan is now routinely used to treat joint problems in people, horses, and dogs.

Hyaluronan, containing important high molecular weight fractions, could not be administered orally until recently. Dermal Research Laboratories Inc. has developed and patented methods of formulation to solve the oral delivery problem. As a result, MVP Laboratories Inc. of Ralston, Nebraska, introduced an oral gel (CholoGel) and a chewable tablet (Cholodin Flex) that are absorbed orally and have been very effective for treatment of arthritis and numerous other diseases and conditions in dogs and cats. While not FDA approved for treating cancer, hyaluronan has been used clinically in pets to shrink tumors. In these pets hyaluronan was injected intramuscularly, and in some cases was also injected along the incision line in pets whose tumors had been removed (to prevent recurrence of the tumor). Hyaluronan may represent another option in treating cancer in pets, and

more research is needed.

IMMUNO-AUGMENTATIVE THERAPY (IAT)

Discovered by Dr. Lawrence Burton, immuno-augmentative thereapy (IAT) analyzes the blood for four proteins that supposedly control mutant cell growth. These proteins can signal the presence of cancer. By analyzing the proteins, a treatment protocol of injections can be designed to boost the immune system and regulate the cancer. IAT is not a cure for cancer but rather a means of restoring the immune system's natural balance, which allows the patient's body to treat itself. IAT is a two-step procedure that involves evaluating and measuring deficiencies of the immune system, and then administering injections that replenish deficient factors. In people, the immune system of each patient is evaluated once or twice daily, five days a week. Blood tests measure relevant immune components. This data reveals the relative activity of the tumor-kill process and immune response. IAT is individualized for each patient. Based on individual serial blood tests, a computer program calculates the amount of therapeutic sera required for each patient to optimize an immunologic response to tumors. Also, IAT therapy may utilize cancer vaccines designed to stimulate the immune system to kill cancer.

Dr. Martin Goldstein has adapted the technique for dogs and cats. While there have been anecdotal cases showing effective treatment of cancer, the therapy has not been subjected to rigorous testing. Because complementary therapies, such as nutritional supplements, are often administered at the same time IAT is prescribed, it is difficult to determine the effectiveness of any individual therapy. The blood testing is done only by Dr. Goldstein, who is based in South Salem, New York, making IAT unavailable on a widespread scale. The therapy can require more than one hundred injections per month, something that would be cost prohibitive and difficult for many pet owners. If cost is not a factor and administering numerous injections is not beyond the ability of the owner, it is a therapy that could prove useful for some. Additional independent studies are needed.

> *Despite anecdotal cases showing its effective treatment of cancer, immuno-augmentative therapy has not been subjected to rigorous testing.*

INOSITOL HEXAPHOSPHATE (IP-6)

Inositol hexaphosphate (IP-6), also called phytic acid or phytate, is a glycoprotein and member of the B vitamin family. It is found in plant fiber and is reported to have anticarcinogenic action, in addition to being a potent antioxidant. It is derived from soybeans, rice, sesame, beans, legumes, and cereal grains. IP-6 is concentrated in the bran of rice, wheat, and rye, so it is removed during milling in the case of processed grains. Polished rice has no IP-6. De-germed corn has little IP-6, because it is concentrated in the germ of the kernel.

IP-6 controls cell division by regulating DNA synthesis, increases the toxicity of natural killer cells, stimulates tumor suppressor genes (thereby reducing cancer growth and spread, making cancer cells more susceptible to chemotherapy), inhibits tumor angiogenesis (blood vessel formation), and works as an antioxidant. Since IP-6 can normalize cell division rate, it has been studied for its effect in animals with various types of active cancers. It has been found to have therapeutic value by causing immature cancer cells to normalize. Further studies have found that IP-6 acts as a blocking agent against tumor promoters in the signal transduction pathways without involving hormone receptors.

There do not seem to be any adverse effects at the recommended animal dosage (taken orally, dissolved in water, given on an empty stomach, otherwise IP-6 attaches to proteins in the food in the stomach and loses its effectiveness). If given in capsule form (not dissolved in water), wait thirty minutes before feeding your pet. Since high levels of IP-6 can lower iron levels in the blood (especially when given with additional inositol), and lower iron levels can reduce immune system functioning, regular blood testing is recommended. A suggested dosage of IP-6 is 25–100 mg/kg one to two times daily.

When injected into soft tissue sarcoma tumors, IP-6 may shrink them. Since an injectable form of IP-6 is not currently available, an injectable solution can be prepared by mixing 500–1,000 mg with 5 ml of sterile saline. When the prepared IP-6 solution is injected into the tumor, it is important to make sure the entire tumor is saturated. For pets with highly vascularized tumors (prostate tumors, hemangiosarcomas, hemagiopericytomas), it is not necessary to inject IP-6 directly into the tumor (blood levels of IP-6 are adequate). While some holistic doctors advocate mixing IP-6 with the patient's serum for injection (autosanguis therapy), there is a chance that IP-6 will bind to the proteins in the serum, rendering it ineffective.

No serious ill effects have been reported for inositol. Iron levels may need to be monitored. Safety has not been established in young children, women who are pregnant or nursing, or people with severe liver or kidney disease; similar precautions are probably warranted in pets. When used as directed, IP-6 does not appear to have any noticeable side effects in cancer patients.

As with all supplements, it is important to purchase a reputable product, because a contaminant present even in small percentages could pose real problems for pets. (One supplement is supplied by PhytoPharmica Natural Medicines, 800-533-2370.)

LAPACHO (PAU D'ARCO, TAHEEBO, IPE ROXO) (*TABEBUIA IMPESTIGINOSA*)

The inner bark of the lapacho tree is used by several indigenous peoples in South American to treat cancer as well as a great variety of infectious diseases. The inner bark is believed to be the most effective part of the plant; unfortunately, inferior products containing only the outer bark and the wood are sometimes misrepresented as "genuine inner-bark lapacho."

One of lapacho's major ingredients, lapachol, possesses antitumor properties. Unfortunately, when administered in humans in high enough dosages to kill cancer cells, lapachol causes numerous serious side effects, such as anemia. At standard dosages, blood levels of lapachol high enough to be deemed effective have not been obtained. Another component of lapacho, b-lapachone, continues to be investigated as an anti-cancer agent since it acts similarly to some chemotherapy medications and may have fewer side effects.

Herbalists believe that the whole herb can produce equivalent benefits as the inner bark but with fewer side effects. However, this claim has never been properly investigated.

While some herbalists recommend lapacho as a treatment for cancer, there is no good evidence that lapacho is effective against the disease. Furthermore, the mechanism by which lapacho possibly works (it has both pro-oxidant and antioxidant properties) may cause it to interfere with the action of prescription anticancer drugs, although this is controversial. While many owners use lapacho, most holistic veterinarians prefer safer and more proven supplements. Do not add it to a conventional chemotherapy regime without consulting your veterinarian.

Lapacho contains many components that don't dissolve in water, so making tea from the herb is not the best idea;

capsulized powdered bark is preferred. In people, a standard dosage is 300 mg three times daily.

Full safety studies of lapacho have not been performed. When taken in normal dosages, it does not appear to cause any significant side effects. However, because its constituent lapachol is somewhat toxic, the herb is not recommended for pregnant or nursing mothers. Safety in young children or in adults with severe liver or kidney disease has not been established; similar precautions are probably warranted in pets.

LARCH ARABINOGALACTAN

Arabinogalactan belongs to a class of polysaccharides derived from the larch tree, mainly the western larch (*Larix occidentalis*). Studies have shown that arabinogalactan may enhance natural killer cells and cause a release of interferon-gamma. For the treatment of cancer, arabinogalactan inhibits the reaction (between the galactose-based glycoconjugate on the cancer cells and a liver-specific lectinlike receptor) that allows cancer cells to spread to the liver. Arabinogalactan thus has strong immuno-stimulating and anti-inflammatory properties.

> *Arabinogalactan inhibits the reaction that allows cancer cells to spread to the liver.*

Arabinogalactan is also an excellent source of dietary fiber and has been shown to increase the production of short-chain fatty acids, principally butyrate, a nutrient that has a particularly important role in the colon. Therefore, it may be useful for the treatment of pets with diarrhea and as protection against cancer-causing compounds. Arabinogalactan has been shown to stimulate natural killer cell activity, stimulate the immune system, and block the spread of cancer cells. Animal studies have shown arabinogalactan to inhibit or block lectin receptor sites in the liver. These sites are thought to be the means by which cancer cells gain entrance to the liver and allow the cancer to spread. Arabinogalactan and mushroom extract are recommended for decreasing liver metastasis and for treating liver tumors.

Larch arabinogalactan is extremely safe; rare episodes of bloating and flatulence have been seen.

Two brand-name pet supplements exist: ImmunoSupport and OncoSupport (supplied by Rx Vitamins for Pets, 800-RX2-2222), both of which contain larch arabinogalactan and other cancer-fighting ingredients. These popular supplements are used safely by many holistic veterinarians.

LYCOPENE

Lycopene is an antioxidant found in tomatoes, watermelon, guava, and pink grapefruit. Like beta-carotene, lycopene belongs to the family of chemicals known as carotenoids. As an antioxidant, lycopene is about twice as powerful as beta-carotene.

In people, there is some evidence that a diet high in lycopene may reduce the risk of cancer of the prostate as well as other cancers. Lycopene may also help prevent macular degeneration and cataracts; it may be very important for optimal health.

Tomatoes are the best source of lycopene, and cooking doesn't destroy the antioxidant. While not all studies agree, some indicate that cooking tomatoes in oil may provide lycopene in a way that the body can use better.

The optimum dosage for lycopene in people and pets has not been established.

In people, lycopene may help prevent cancer, particularly prostate cancer. In observational trials, it is always possible that other unrecognized factors are at work. Animal studies have also found some cancer-preventive benefits with lycopene. The normal diets of dogs rarely contain appreciable amounts of foods that contain lycopene.

Although lycopene is a normal part of the diet for people, there has not been a formal evaluation of lycopene's safety when it is taken as a concentrated supplement. Maximum safe dosages for young children, pregnant or nursing women, or people with severe liver or kidney disease have not been established. No established doses have been formulated for pets, and it is not commonly used as an isolated antioxidant.

MARSDEN PROTOCOL

Holistic veterinarian Dr. Steve Marsden has developed a protocol for treating osteosarcoma cancer in dogs when owners decide against using conventional cancer therapies. While the protocol first worked on osteosarcoma, it seems to work even more reliably on other tumors, such as fibrosarcoma. In general, any highly inflammatory tumor is a good candidate for the Marsden Protocol.

According to Dr. Marsden, the apparent success of the formula suggests that an improperly functioning liver contributes to cancer as the damaged liver fails to remove toxins (such as free radicals that cause oxidation and cell damage) from the body. The core of his therapies for this type of tumor is a modified Hoxsey formula (see pages 135–136 in chapter 6 for a discussion of the Hoxsey therapy). He suggests three parts Oregon grape, two parts (drams) red clover, two parts burdock root, two parts boneset, one part pokeroot, one part stillingia, one part comfrey, one part prickly ash bark, one part cascara, and one part licorice. Also, two parts of alfalfa can be added. The herb boneset helps relieve bone pain, and is excluded from formulas used to treat other malignancies. The dose is sixty drops per 100 pounds of body weight, given three times daily. This formula acts to detoxify the body, relieve liver stress, and, in Chinese-medicine parlance, according to Dr. Marsden, "move blood," "transform phlegm," and "clear heat" from the body. If used inappropriately, the Hoxsey formula could cause gastrointestinal upset.

Dr. Marsden also recommends injections or oral administration of vitamin D-3 (750 IU per pound) and injections of vitamin A (5,000 IU per pound) given once daily, in rapidly progressive tumors, to every thirty days in more stable tumors, in an attempt to promote apoptosis (cell death of the cancer cells) and reduce oxidative stress to the body. Oral supplementation using the injectable form is very well tolerated. Intramuscular injections, however, may cause hypersensitivity reactions; minimize the use of injections (they may also be given subcutaneously to reduce hypersensitivity reactions). For osteosarcoma, the skin over top of the lesion may be clipped, and the daily dose of vitamins A and D applied after being mixed in medical-grade DMSO gel. DMSO is also a cell differentiating agent that can promote cell death in addition to carrying the vitamins directly into the tumor. Improvements are often rapidly visible in osteosarcoma tumors with this type of topical treatment. The only adverse side effect noted has been a transient mild itch where the medication is applied.

Another option in osteosarcoma is to also administer the digestive enzyme bromelain (2,000 IU per day in divided doses, given away from meals) and omega-3 fatty acids (fish oil) at label doses. The goal of this therapy is to enhance cell differentiation and apoptosis already being promoted by the vitamin A and some of the key herbs in the Hoxsey formula.

Exercise must be limited in osteosarcoma; often, cage rest is prescribed for the first month of therapy. This is done to decrease the chance of injury arising from increases in exercise that accompany clinical improvement. Injury promotes inflammation and free radical generation that, in turn, increases oxidative stress and allows tumor regrowth.

> *The Marsden protocol may offer an alternative cancer therapy when owners of dogs with osteosarcoma decline conventional therapy.*

Currently, only a small number of patients have been treated. Approximately 50 percent of these dogs did not improve. Of those that did, they experienced pain relief and survival equal to or better than dogs receiving conventional therapy. In addition to Dr. Marsden's protocol, a hypoallergenic diet (vegetarian or fish and potato) is recommended to improve general health and possibly reduce further oxidative stress (in the event that an underlying food hypersensitivity is present). Dr. Marsden prefers the hypoallergenic diet because it seems to reduce phlegm, which from the perspective of Traditional Chinese Medicine (TCM) leads to circulatory stasis that contributes to tumor formation. Dr. Marsden prefers this diet to special retail preparations or homemade cancer diets. While not proven to do so, he feels the cancer diet increases "dampening" and "heating" (the TCM perspective) and stresses the liver, which may contribute to tumor formation. To date, he has not used any diet other than the hypoallergenic diet in dogs treated with his osteosarcoma protocol. Recently, Dr. Marsden has been experimenting with a modified Gerson's diet regime, which includes a daily shake made of raw liver and leafy greens to increase natural vitamin A in the pet's body.

While this program utilizes high doses of vitamin A (both synthetic and natural), no signs of toxicity have been encountered to date. Hypersensitivity reactions (sometimes severe) can occur, although this is usually associated with intramuscular injections of the vitamins. Finally, Dr. Marsden has used this protocol with positive results in dogs with lymphosarcoma and oral tumors (squamous cell carcinoma). More data is currently being accumulated and will need to be analyzed before the complete picture is available as to its effectiveness in treating these and other cancers.

While the protocol shows some promise, to date the number of patients treated is too small to draw any definitive conclusions. Other researchers are investigating this protocol, and Dr. Marsden is encouraging veterinarians who have patients whose owners have refused conventional therapy to try his protocol and assess the results. He does not suggest that pet owners should avoid conventional therapy or other complementary therapies. But owners who choose not to undertake the standard therapy for the treatment of their pets' osteosarcomas should consider Dr. Marsden's protocol, as it may offer some hope for their pets.

MGN-3

This product is made by combining the outer shell of rice bran with extracts from the shiitake, kawaratake, and suehirotake mushrooms. MGN-3 works against cancer by stimulating the immune system to increase interferon levels, tumor necrosis factor, and the activity of natural killer cells as well as B cells and T cells. In people, the recommended dose is 3 g per day (in divided doses) given on an empty stomach. A pet dosage has not been reported and must be extrapolated from the human dosage. MGN-3 is a safe supplement.

MUSHROOMS

Mushrooms have been used for their purported health benefits for hundreds if not thousands of years. Recent evidence reveals that many mushrooms contain polysaccharide compounds that may have antibacterial, antiviral, and antitumor properties. Some mushrooms are recommended for stimulation of the immune system, as well as for diseases of the liver, kidneys, or heart. Mushrooms and arabinogalactans are recommended to decrease liver metastasis and for treating liver tumors. The active immune-stimulating ingredients in medicinal mushrooms are the beta-glucans.

Of the more than thirty thousand species of mushrooms that exist, approximately fifty or so have been used for medicinal purposes.

Mushroom therapy should be administered only under veterinary supervision. Owners should not simply go "mushroom hunting" or pull "toadstools" from their yards and feed them to their pets, as this could result in the accidental feeding of poisonous species of fungi that can result in death.

Mushroom extracts are usually considered safe when used as directed. Occasional side effects include mild digestive upset, dry mouth, and skin rash. Mushrooms can thin the blood slightly, and therefore should not be combined with drugs such as Coumadin (warfarin) or heparin. Safety in young children, pregnant or nursing women, or people with severe liver or kidney disease has not been established. Dizziness has been reported in people using reishi for several months. These cautions should probably also be applied to pets.

Dosages of mushrooms vary with the product preparation. If you're using fresh mushrooms, a generic dosage of four to six mushrooms can be added to a homemade diet for nutritional support (use one to two mushrooms for smaller pets, and four to six for larger pets). It should be noted, however, that there are no studies showing that routinely feeding mushrooms prevents or effectively treats cancer.

The following is a brief description of the most commonly used medicinal mushroom species.

Almond Portobello (Agaricus blazei)

Traditionally, this mushroom has been used as a health food source in Brazil for the prevention of cancer, diabetes, hyperlipidemia, atherosclerosis, and chronic hepatitis. Analysis of *Agaricus blazei* reveals a number of components that have demonstrated an anticancer effect, including polysaccharides (beta-1,3- and -1,6- glucans; alpha-1,6- and -1,4- glucans; beta galactoglucan; proteoglucans); nucleic acids; lectins; steroids; mannans; fatty acids; and ergosterol. These components inhibit tumor growth, activate cytokines, increase natural killer cell activity, and decrease cancer spread.

Reishi (Ganoderma lucidum)

Contemporary herbalists regard it as an adaptogen, a substance believed to be capable of helping the body to resist stress of all kinds. According to at least one source, reishi is effective only when given by injection.

Shiitake (Lentinula edodes)

Contemporary herbalists regard it as an adaptogen, a substance believed to be capable of helping the body to resist stress of all kinds. According to at least one source, shiitake is effective only when given by injection.

Maitake (Grifola frondosa, Polyporous umbellatus, Grifola umbellatus, Boletus frondosus)

Maitake is a medicinal mushroom used in Japan as a general promoter of health. This appears to be the most effective mushroom to use in pets with cancer, particularly the D and MD fraction. Research has shown that D and MD fractions of maitake stimulate the immune system (natural killer cells, cytotoxic T cells, and the cytokines IL-1 and IL-2). Using the D and MD fractions also improves the results of conventional therapies and reduces side effects from chemotherapy.

Contemporary herbalists classify maitake as an adaptogen, a substance said to help the body adapt to and resist stress. However, as with other adaptogens, definitive scientific evidence to show that maitake really functions in this way is lacking.

NONI (*MORINDA CITRIFOLIA*)

Noni juice is a recently popular remedy made from the South Pacific Noni plant that has been marketed as a cure for just about everything. The juice contains many beneficial ingredients, including sterols, glycosides, anthraquinones, terpenes, amino acids, and proxeronine and proxeronaise (generally regarded as the key ingredients to encourage proper cell function and boost the immune system). Because it may increase the white blood cell count, it has been suggested as helpful for people and pets with cancer. Noni has antioxidant properties and appears to function as a COX-2 inhibitor. Current research is focused on chemoprevention for several types of human cancers; research in animals has shown that Noni juice can reduce the amount of DNA damage from powerful chemical mutagens (cancer-causing agents). When administered at recommended doses, Noni is probably safe despite the lack of any evidence of its effectiveness in treating dogs with cancer.

OMEGA-3 FATTY ACIDS

Fats in the form of fatty acids have recently become a popular supplement among most veterinarians, not just those interested in holistic care. An essential part of every pet's diet, fatty acids were first discovered to work in some pets with allergic dermatitis. Other uses include pets with dry flaky skin and dull haircoats. Recently, they have been advocated in pets with kidney disease, heart disease, elevated cholesterol, and arthritis. Research has shown their effectiveness as a complementary therapy for people and pets with cancer.

The most medically useful fatty acids are the omega-3 and omega-6 fatty acids (omega-9 fatty acids have no known use in treating pets with cancer). Omega-3 fatty acids eicosapentaenoic acid (EPA) and docosahexaenoic acid (DHA) are derived from flaxseed, algae, and the oils of coldwater fish (most commonly salmon, trout, and menhaden fish) and flaxseed, whereas omega-6 fatty acids linoleic acid (LA) and gamma-linolenic acid (GLA) are derived from the oils of seeds such as evening primrose, black currant, and borage.

Flaxseed oil is a popular source of alpha-linoleic acid (ALA), an omega-3 fatty acid that is ultimately converted to EPA and DHA. However, many species of pets (probably including dogs) and some people cannot convert ALA to these other more active, noninflammatory omega-3 fatty acids. In one study in people, flaxseed oil was ineffective in reducing symptoms or raising levels of EPA and DHA. While flaxseed oil has been suggested as a less smelly substitute for fish oil, there is no evidence that it is effective when used for the same therapeutic purposes as fish oil. Therefore, supplementation with EPA and DHA is important, and this is the reason flaxseed oil is not recommended as the sole fatty acid supplement for pets. Flaxseed oil can be used to provide ALA, making it useful as a coat conditioner and as a source of lignans for pets with cancer.

Omega-3 fatty acids are recommended for dogs with cancer.

In transplanted tumor models, omega-3 fatty acids reduced tumor development, while omega-6 fatty acids stimulated tumor development. Omega-3 fatty acids, specifically DHA, have been shown to promote cellular immunity, reduce inflammation, inhibit tumor growth, and decrease the spread of cancer by decreasing the formation of new blood vessels necessary for cancer to grow and spread. Combining DHA with the chemotherapy drug paclitaxel has allowed researchers to use higher doses of the drug (than when the drug has been used by itself) without signs of toxicity; the DHA-paclitaxel combination also has allowed the drug to work longer in the body against the cancer cells than when the drug has been administered alone.

Research on dogs with lymphoma showed increased survival when a diet high in omega-3 fatty acids was combined with conventional chemotherapy compared with dogs treated with chemotherapy and no dietary modifications. Reduced radiation damage in the skin was also seen following supplementation with omega-3 fatty acids.

In addition, Omega-3 fatty acids have been found to inhibit matrix metalloproteinase (MMP) enzymes that play a role in how cancer cells survive and spread in the body.

To prevent fish oils from oxidizing and becoming rancid, some manufacturers add vitamin E to fish oil capsules and liquid products, while others remove oxygen from the capsule.

> *Omega-3 fatty acids have been shown to inhibit tumor growth as well as the spread of cancer (metastasis).*

Fish oil appears to be safe. The most common side effect seen in people and pets is a fish odor on the breath or the skin.

Because fish oil has a mild blood-thinning effect, it should not be combined with powerful blood-thinning medications, such as Coumadin (warfarin) or heparin, except on a veterinarian's advice. Fish oil does not seem to cause bleeding problems when it is taken by itself at commonly recommended dosages (in people, doses of 3–4 g per day and higher may increase bleeding tendencies; high dosages of fish oil cannot be administered with ginkgo biloba due to the high incidence of bleeding disorders). Also, fish oil does not appear to raise blood sugar levels in people or pets with diabetes.

Other Fatty Acids: Flaxseed Oil, Hemp Oil, Salvia

Flaxseed oil is derived from the seeds of the flax plant and has been proposed as a less smelly alternative to fish oil. Flaxseed oil contains ALA, an omega-3 fatty acid that is ultimately converted to EPA and DHA. In fact, flaxseed oil contains higher levels of omega-3 fatty acids (ALA) than fish oil. It also contains omega-6 fatty acids.

As mentioned in the previous section, many species of pet (including dogs) and some people cannot convert ALA to these other more active noninflammatory omega-3 fatty acids. In one study in people, flaxseed oil was ineffective in reducing symptoms or raising levels of EPA and DHA. While flaxseed oil has been suggested as a substitute for fish oil, there is no evidence that it is effective when used for the same therapeutic purposes as fish oil. Unlike fish oil, flaxseed oil has not been proven to be effective for any specific therapeutic purpose.

Because supplementation with EPA and DHA is important, flaxseed oil is not recommended as the sole fatty acid supplement for pets.

Flaxseed oil also contain lignans. Lignans contain seoisoloriciresinol diglycoside and matairesinol, which are active cancer-fighting chemicals. Lignans also contain antioxidants and other chemicals that have antiproliferative, antiestrogen, and antiangiogenesis properties, all of which may slow the growth and spread of cancer.

The essential fatty acids in flax can be damaged by exposure to heat, light, and oxygen (essentially, they become rancid). For this reason, you shouldn't cook with flaxseed oil. A good product should be sold in an opaque container, and the manufacturing process should keep the temperature under 100°F (some products are prepared by cold extraction methods). Some manufacturers combine the product with vitamin E because it helps prevent rancidity.

Flaxseed oil appears to be a safe nutritional supplement when used as recommended.

Hemp seed oil has been referred to as "nature's perfect oil" by several investigators. Its fatty acid ratio is 1:4 of omega-3 to omega-6 fatty acids, a ratio suspected to be that which is naturally found in mammals. It contains 1.7 percent gamma-linolenic acid (GLA) and can be used whenever a combination fatty acid product is needed. However, there are no current studies or recommendations showing any medical benefit of hemp seed oil in pets.

Hemp seed oil appears to be a safe nutritional supplement when used as recommended.

The oil from the seeds of the salvia plant (*Salvia hispanica*) has been proposed as a more palatable fatty acid alternative to fish oil and flaxseed oil. Salvia seed oil can increase omega-3 fatty acid consumption in the diet. Little is known about the use of this supplement and whether it can be of any medical benefit to pets. Studies are needed before salvia seed oil can be recommended as an omega-3 fatty acid supplement.

PURINE PYRIMIDINE NUCLEOTIDES

Purine pyrimidine nucleotides are involved in virtually all cellular processes, and play a major role in structural, metabolic, energetic, and regulatory functions. Like arabinogalactans, they have been shown to stimulate the activity of natural killer cells and may be helpful for dogs with cancer. Purine pyrimidine complexes are the active fractions found in colostrum, the milk mammals produce during the first few days of lactation. Colostrum contains cytokines and other protein compounds that can act as biological response modifiers. Nucleotides also may play an important role in essential fatty acid metabolism, and may have a positive effect on the functions of the gastrointestinal tract and the liver. (For more information on colostrum pages 182–183 in this chapter.)

PROBIOTICS/PREBIOTICS

Probiotics are defined as normal, viable bacteria and yeasts that reside in the intestinal tract and promote normal bowel health. Probiotics are given orally and are usually indicated for use in intestinal disorders in which specific factors can disrupt the normal bacterial population, making the pet more susceptible to disease. Specific factors that can disrupt the normal flora of the bowel include surgery, medications (including steroids and nonsteroidal anti-inflammatory drugs, as well as chemotherapy medications), antibiotics (especially when used long term), birthing, weaning, illness, irradiation (especially full-body irradiation often recommended for the treatment of dogs with lymphosarcoma), and dietary factors (poor quality diet, oxidative damage, stress). Improving the nutritional status of the intestinal tract may reduce bacterial movement across the bowel mucosa (lining), intestinal permeability, and systemic endotoxemia. This is a potential problem in dogs with damage to the intestinal tract that may occur with some types of chemotherapy and radiation treatments, especially if these dogs are temporarily experiencing a low white blood cell count as a result of their therapies.

Probiotics may aid in supplying nutrients to the pet, help in digestion, and allow for better conversion of food into nutrients.

Prebiotics are food supplements that are not digested and absorbed by the host but improve health by stimulating the growth and activity of selected intestinal bacteria (they serve as food for the probiotics).

There are several different probiotic products available that can contain any combination of the following organisms: *Lactobacillus* (*L. acidophilus*, *L. bulgaricus*, *L. thermophilus*, *L. reuteri*), *Acidophilus*, *Bacillus* (specifically a patented strain called *Bacillus CIP 5832*), *Streptococcus* (*S. bulgaricus*), *Enterococcus* (*E. faecium*), *Bifidobacterium* (*B. bifidus*), and *Saccharomyces* (*S. boulardii*, which is actually a beneficial yeast, not a bacterium).

The intestinal tract, especially the large intestine (colon), is home to millions of bacteria and yeasts, most of which are beneficial to the pet. The intestinal bacteria are essential to digestion and the synthesis of vitamin K and many of the B vitamins.

Some of these internal inhabitants are more helpful than others. Acidophilus and related probiotic bacteria not only help the digestive tract function, but they also reduce the presence of less healthful organisms by competing with them for the limited space available.

There are several proposed mechanisms by which probiotics can protect your pet from harmful bowel bacteria: probiotics produce inhibitory chemicals that reduce the numbers of harmful bacteria, and at the same time possibly decrease toxin production by these harmful bacteria; probiotics may block the adhesion of harmful bacteria to intestinal cells; probiotics may compete for nutrients needed for growth and reproduction by harmful bacteria; probiotics may degrade toxin receptors located on intestinal cells, preventing toxin absorption and damage by toxins from harmful intestinal bacteria.

Probiotics are able to survive hydrochloric acid in the stomach. Supplementing with probiotics may stimulate immune function of the intestinal tract.

Antibiotics can disturb the balance of the intestinal tract by killing friendly bacteria; some types of chemotherapy and radiation therapies may injure or kill intestinal epithelial cells. When this happens, harmful bacteria and yeasts can move in, reproduce, and take over. Conversely, it appears that the regular use of probiotics can generally improve the health of the gastrointestinal system.

Cultured dairy products such as yogurt and kefir are good sources of acidophilus and other probiotic bacteria. However, many yogurt products do not contain any living organisms or contain only small numbers of organisms. Some pets will eat these foods, and others won't. Also, if a pet has any lactose intolerance, eating yogurt may produce diarrhea (although this is rare). Most doctors recommend supplements to provide the highest doses possible of probiotics, while avoiding any lactose intolerance.

Because probiotics are not drugs but living organisms, the precise dosage is not so important. Dosages of acidophilus and other probiotics are expressed not in grams or milligrams, but in billions of organisms. A typical daily dose in people should supply about three billion to five billion live organisms. One popular pet supplement provides five hundred million viable cells to be given per 50 pounds of body weight. The suggested dosage range of probiotics for pets is approximately twenty million to five hundred million microorganisms.

Some doctors recommend that when administering antibiotics (or any oral medications), the probiotic should be started at least one to two hours later, dosed at several times per day.

And when the antibiotic treatment has been completed, owners should double or triple the probiotic dose for seven to ten days.

The downside of using a living organism is that probiotics may die on the shelf. The container label should guarantee living acidophilus (or bulgaricus, and so on) at the time of purchase, not just at the time of manufacture.

There is evidence that probiotics may protect the bowel from cancer. The proposed mechanisms for this include inhibiting bacteria in the bowel from converting procarcinogens into carcinogens, inhibiting tumor cell formation directly, and direct binding to or inactivating of bowel carcinogens.

> *Probiotics may protect the bowel from cancer.*

There are no known safety problems with the use of acidophilus or other probiotics. Occasionally, some people notice a temporary increase in digestive gas (the same could occur in pets).

In addition to taking probiotics, it is often suggested that patients take fructo-oligosaccharide (FOS) prebiotic supplements that can promote thriving colonies of helpful bacteria in the digestive tract. Fructo-oligosaccharide is a naturally occurring sugar found in many fruits, vegetables, and grains. (Fructo means "fruit," and an oligosaccharide is a type of carbohydrate.) This complex carbohydrate resists digestion by salivary and intestinal digestive enzymes, and enters the colon where it is fermented by bacteria such as *Bifidobacterium* and *Bacteroides spp*.

The most beneficial effect of FOS is the selective stimulation of the growth of bifidobacterium, which significantly enhances the composition of the colonic microflora and reduces the number of potential pathogenic bacteria. Lactobacillus, another beneficial bacteria, is also seen to proliferate with the addition of FOS supplements. Because FOS increases the colonization of healthy bacteria in the gut, it is considered to be a prebiotic rather than a probiotic.

The typical daily dose of fructo-oligosaccharide for people is between 2 and 8 g. The correct dose for pets has not been determined. One supplement contains 50 mg per dose for a fifty-pound dog; research on FOS has shown positive benefits at a dosage of 0.75–1 percent of the food, when fed on a dry matter basis.

Other reports describing the benefits of FOS suggest that it can suppress triglyceride and cholesterol levels, can control glucose metabolism, and may inhibit the formation of precancerous lesions in the colon.

SALVES

Topical salves made of various products (such as bloodroot and zinc) are often recommended as they have been reported to eat away tumors. While they may be helpful, they are difficult to apply in some instances. They are not of any use if the pet licks off the salve. Also, some products can be toxic, so salves should not be used without veterinary supervision.

SHARK CARTILAGE

Shark cartilage is among the most controversial of the supplements available for people and pets with cancer. It has been recommended based upon the book *Sharks Don't Get Cancer*; however, sharks do develop cancer.

Shark cartilage contains chemical compounds (antiangiogenesis chemicals) that in test-tube studies prevent new blood vessel growth (neovascularization); several test-tube experiments have found that shark cartilage extracts prevent new blood vessels from forming in chick embryos and other test systems; developing drugs to prevent blood vessels from forming in tumors is an exciting new approach to treating cancer. This potential for inhibiting blood vessel formation has made shark cartilage a popular recommendation for pets with cancerous tumors.

There is conflicting evidence as to its effectiveness. In several small and very controversial clinical observations in Mexico, cancerous tumors in human patients did show regression (reduced size of the tumors). Other studies showed questionable benefit or no benefit. A study in mice bearing transplanted tumors showed that the mice administered shark cartilage lived longer; some of their tumors showed histologic evidence of the effectiveness of shark cartilage. This study has also been criticized, however.

Currently, few holistic veterinarians recommend shark cartilage. Some fear it may contribute to a measurable decline in shark populations, while others simply don't believe it is worth the expense, considering that other supplements work more effectively and consistently. It is possible that specific ingredients will someday be extracted from shark cartilage that could be helpful in people and pets. Until then, it's wiser to spend your money on better therapies. Ongoing research is attempting to identify the chemicals in shark cartilage that prevent new blood vessel growth so that this compound can be synthetically synthesized and used for people and pets with cancer.

SOY PROTEIN/ISOFLAVONES

The soybean has been prized for centuries in Asia as a nutritious, high-protein food with many potential uses. Today, soy protein is popular for people as a cholesterol-free meat and dairy substitute. Epidemiologic studies in humans and animals suggest that consumption of soybeans and soy-based foods may lower the risk of various cancers. Soy contains isoflavones (such as genistein and daidzein) that may benefit a pet with cancer. For example, some studies have shown that isoflavones may inhibit the aromatase enzyme, which produces harmful estrogen that can stimulate the growth of tumors of the genital system. However, the aromatase effect is dose dependent. At commonly used doses it stimulates enzyme function and at higher doses it suppresses the enzyme.

Additionally, some studies reveal that isoflavones can stop the growth of breast cancer cells by blocking receptor sites from circulating estradiol, the natural estrogen that promotes some breast cancers. However, other studies have shown that genistein acts as an estrogen in normal breast tissues and may stimulate the growth of estrogen-receptor-positive breast cancer cells.

At this time, the use of soy products in the treatment of cancer is quite controversial. While there is some evidence showing the anticancer benefits of soy and soy extracts, most of the studies used soy components that are removed with processing, so the cancer-fighting benefits of the whole bean are unclear.

One of the major problems with soy (especially textured soy and soy protein isolate) is that soy is high in glutamate, which is a powerful excitotoxin. When hydrolyzed, the glutamate is free and capable of producing nervous system toxicity. Brain atrophy in people has been associated with the increased consumption of soy products, possibly due to the glutamate levels. The high glutamate level may enhance tumor growth for a number of tumors and may stimulate tumor invasion and metastasis.

In addition, all soy products are very high in manganese and fluoride, which can be toxic to the body. In whole soy products these negative effects may be overridden by the anti-tumor isoflavones. Unfortunately, these isoflavones may be removed to prevent toxicity, bloating, and malabsorption.

In addition, soy contains one of the highest levels of lipoxygenase, which increases lipid peroxidation and cancer formation. Most of the naturally occurring omega-3 fatty acids in soy are destroyed in processing.

It appears that many of the anticancer effects reported for soy are occurring because it's being administered at concentrations far above those used in human nutrition or supplementation. Or it could be that the anticancer effects are resulting mainly from isoflavone (rather than raw soy) supplementation. Since there are many other supplements discussed in this book that don't have this level of controversy surrounding them, it would be best to use these other supplements as part of a natural approach to treating cancer.

As you can see, there are many supplements that may be beneficial in treating pets with cancer. The best approach is to work with your holistic veterinarian and oncologist in determining which supplements may work best for *your* pet. *Due to potential side effects and toxicity associated with some supplements, you should not administer any supplements on your own.* Regardless of which supplements are selected, they work best when combined with the proper diet. Selecting the proper diet for the pet with cancer is the focus of chapter 8.

CHAPTER EIGHT

DIET *and* CANCER

WHILE THERE ARE MANY TREATMENT OPTIONS for the various malignancies experienced by our patients, we often overlook the simple aspect of nutrition. In the next decade, prevention and treatment of cancer in veterinary medicine will most likely include a focus on nutrition, just as it does in the human medical field. But for now, dietary therapy is often neglected for pets with cancer, even though eating the proper diet is very important for dogs undergoing cancer treatments.

Cancer patients have deranged nutrient metabolism that can negatively affect the outcome of conventional therapies. Also, studies demonstrate that both people and pets with inadequate nutrition cannot metabolize chemotherapy drugs sufficiently, which predisposes them to toxicity and poor therapeutic response. This makes proper diet and nutritional supplementation an important part of cancer therapy.

DIETARY CONSIDERATIONS
FOR DOGS WITH CANCER

Fewer Carbohydrates and More Protein

There are several metabolic abnormalities that occur in the cancer patient. First, cancer patients often have hyperlactatemia, which is high levels of lactic acid in the blood. Since the metabolism of simple carbohydrates in the diet produces lactate, a diet low in these carbohydrates is preferred.

Also, weight loss often occurs in cancer patients as a result of wasting, also known as cancer cachexia. It occurs as a result of depleted body-fat stores. Tumor cells, unlike normal healthy cells, have difficulty utilizing lipids (fats) for energy. Dogs with lymphoma that were treated with conventional chemotherapy and fed diets high in fat had longer remission periods than dogs fed high-carbohydrate diets (the typical dog food is high in carbohydrates and low in fat).

Amino Acid Supplementation

Research has shown a pronounced decrease in specific amino acids, such as arginine, in the blood of cancer patients. If left uncorrected, these amino acid deficiencies could result in serious health risks to the patient. A diet including supplements of the deficient amino acids might improve immune function as well as treatment and survival rates.

The amino acid arginine decreases tumor growth and spread (metastasis); supplemental arginine (647 mg/100 kcal of food or 500–3,000 mg per day) is useful for pets with cancer. The amino acid glutamine (up to 250 mg per pound per day) may retard the wasting seen in many pets with cancer, and it may help protect against intestinal injury. While rare, episodes of nausea, vomiting, and diarrhea can afflict some pets being treated with chemotherapy or radiation; glutamine supplementation may help in this regard, as it is a complementary therapy commonly employed for pets with gastrointestinal disease and disturbances. I usually add it to my regimen of supplements, along with probiotics and other supplements, to protect the gastrointestinal tract if a pet is undergoing chemotherapy. However, glutamine should probably not be used if the pet has a brain tumor, as it may worsen this type of cancer.

Omega-3 Fatty Acids and Antioxidants

Additions of omega-3 fatty acids and antioxidant vitamins and minerals to the diet may help improve survival rates of cancer patients, and possibly decrease the chances of healthy pets ever contracting cancer.

The use of omega-3 fatty acids (particularly fish oil), which can promote weight gain and may have anticancer effects, warrants special mention. In people with cancer, the use of omega-3 fatty acids, such as those found in fish oil, improves their immune response, metabolic function, and clinical outcomes. These fish oil supplements decrease the duration of hospitalization and complication rates in people with gastrointestinal cancer. In animal models, omega-3 fatty acids inhibit the formation of tumors and the spread of cancer (metastasis). Finally, in addition to their antiwasting effects, the omega-3 fatty acids in fish oil can reduce radiation damage to the skin.

Antioxidants can be added to the diet and are often recommended by holistic veterinarians for treating pets with cancer (see pages 157–172 in chapter 7 for a discussion of antioxidants). Recommendations include adding, as daily antioxidant supplementation, 60–100 mg of coenzyme Q-10, as well as vitamin E at 500 mg per 450 kcals of food. Remember, always consult with your veterinarian prior to giving your pet any supplements.

Fresh Vegetables and Vegetable Supplements

Many holistic veterinarians add fresh vegetables (especially those high in indoles and antioxidants) such as broccoli, kale, and cabbage, in addition to fresh garlic, to the diet of pets with cancer. The vegetables contain antioxidants and phytonutrients that may be of benefit to pets with cancer, and are unlikely to interfere with cancer therapy. Garlic is known for a whole host of benefits, including supporting the immune system for pets with cancer.

Other supplements, such as herbs and medicinal mushrooms, can be used as needed. Your veterinarian can decide which supplements might be helpful after consultation with you and a thorough examination of your pet. (Supplements are discussed more thoroughly in chapters 6 and 7.)

CANINE N/D

Recently, Hill's Pet Food Company introduced the first cancer diet for dogs, called Canine n/d. The diet contains reduced levels of carbohydrates relative to other dog foods, and high levels of protein and fat, omega-3 fatty acids, and arginine. The following is the approximate nutritional composition of the diet.

- protein: 37 percent
- fat: 32 percent
- carbohydrate: 21 percent
- omega-3 fatty acids from fish oil: 7 percent (1,518 mg/100 kcal)
- arginine: 3 percent (647 mg/100 kcal)

In controlled studies, dogs with lymphoma (lymphosarcoma) that were treated with chemotherapy and fed Canine n/d had increased survival times when compared with dogs treated with the same chemotherapy medications and fed a controlled maintenance diet. Similar findings were found for dogs with nasal and oral cancers that were treated with radiation therapy and fed Canine n/d. This study concluded that survival time increased 56 percent; quality of life improved due to decreased pain after radiation treatment; periods of remission were longer; and typical metabolic changes were reversed.

> *While no diet can prevent or cure cancer, improving the quality of the diet can improve a pet's clinical response to cancer treatment and has been shown to prolong survival in certain instances.*

While these findings are impressive, there is no research evidence that Canine n/d helps dogs with other forms of cancer. However, despite this lack of research, it is likely that a pet with *any* type of cancer could benefit from this or similar diets (see below for further discussion). I recommend this diet or one like it to every one of my cancer patients.

While the Canine n/d diet has helped dogs with cancer, there are four potential problems with it. First, it is an expensive diet, especially for owners of large breed dogs. Second, it is available only in a canned variety, due to the high fat content. This makes the diet especially palatable but increases the cost. Third, this diet is very rich due to the high fat and protein content; some dogs cannot eat the diet without experiencing gastrointestinal upset (usually diarrhea). This can be minimized by slowly adding Canine n/d, to the dog's existing diet, while reducing the amount of the existing diet fed. The n/d is added until the dog is eating only n/d, or until gastrointestinal problems occur, in which case the amount of n/d is reduced to the proportion that didn't cause digestive problems. The fourth potential problem is that the protein source in Canine n/d is an animal by-product (beef lung). Owners who desire the most holistic and natural diet possible might object to this protein source.

In my practice, many owners will prepare their own anti-cancer diet made from wholesome protein sources and mix the homemade diet with Canine n/d to get the benefit from both foods. While the n/d diet does not have the most wholesome protein source, it is unlikely that the pet will be harmed by it, and the benefits appear to outweigh these concerns. Egg, poultry, lamb, venison, rabbit, buffalo, tofu, fish, and beef are all high-quality sources of protein.

For dogs that won't eat or can't tolerate n/d, or for owners who prefer a more natural diet, a holistic brand of canned cat food is a good choice (cat food is higher in fat and protein than most dog foods). Brands I like and recommend include Eagle Pack, Nature's Variety, Wysong, California Naturals, Innova, Halo, Nutro, and Old Mother Hubbard.

> *The ideal cancer diet is high in omega-3 fatty acids and protein, and low in carbohydrates.*

HOMEMADE ANTICANCER DIET FOR DOGS

Another choice is to create a homemade diet that approximates Canine n/d. However, due to the high level of omega-3 fatty acids in the food, it is difficult (if not impossible) and expensive to prepare at home. Nevertheless, I have included a recipe that tries to approximate this anticancer diet.

My homemade anticancer diet for dogs approximates the nutrient levels found in Canine n/d — protein: 35–40 percent,

fat: 30 percent, carbohydrate: 20 percent. Most
diets do not meet this nutrient profile and in fact ha
profiles (high levels of carbohydrate, low levels of j
very small or no amounts of omega-3 fatty acids).

This diet, taken from my book *The Natural Health Bible for
Dogs & Cats*, was formulated to feed to normal cats. However,
since the normal cat diet is high in protein and fat, which is just
what is required by dogs with cancer, I have included it here.
Check with your veterinarian to see which diet is best to feed
your dog.

$1/_2$ pound ground meat (turkey, chicken, lamb, or beef)
$1/_2$ cup potato (cooked with the skin), rice, or macaroni
4 tsp chicken fat, canola oil, or olive oil
$1/_8$ tsp potassium chloride (salt substitute) or $1/_{10}$ tsp salt
1 Multivitamin-mineral supplement

This recipe provides 775 kcal and supports the daily needs
of a 25-pound dog. It also provides 43.9 g protein and 22 g fat.

RECIPE OPTIONS
- Adding 2 tbsp canned sardines increases the protein
  content by 6.2 g and the fat content by 4.6 g.

- Arginine can be added at 647 mg/100 kcal of food.

- Omega-3 fatty acids (fish oil) can be added (at 1,518
  mg EPA/DHA/100 kcal). This is very difficult to do
  because the average omega-3 fatty acid capsule contains
  180–300 mg EPA/DHA. Work with your doctor to
  increase the fatty acid content as much as possible
  (adding fish such as salmon to the diet can help
  achieve this goal).

- $^1/_2$ cup raw tofu and 1 cup cooked lentils can be substituted for the ground meat.

- Adding fresh raw or steamed vegetables can increase the level of natural vitamins and minerals, as well as add flavor. Most vegetables provide approximately 25 kcal per $^1/_2$ cup.

- For calcium and phosphorus, add 4 bonemeal tablets (10 grain or equivalent) or 1 tsp bonemeal powder, along with a multivitamin and mineral supplement; I like Vim & Vigor, from Pet Togethers (www.pettogethers.net/healthypet) as my vitamin source.

BONES AND RAW FOOD (BARF) DIETS

I am often asked by owners what I think about feeding raw diets (particularly raw meat) to pets with cancer. Many owners like to feed their dogs a BARF (bones and raw food) diet to approximate the natural diet of the dog's ancestors. While we don't have any convincing research, and while some of my colleagues may disagree, I am a bit uncomfortable with feeding pets with cancer raw meat. Many pets with cancer have suppressed immune systems (especially when taking chemotherapy), and there is always the possibility of raw meat spreading infections or parasites to cancer patients as a result of their compromised immune systems. Since controlling any type of infection is of prime importance in pets with cancer, I prefer not to feed my patients any type of raw meat. If you desire to feed vegetables, make sure they are thoroughly washed and maybe even slightly cooked (steamed) to minimize infection from the vegetables. Following chemotherapy, and during the use of supplements to boost the immune system, a BARF diet may be appropriate (and more safely fed), provided your pet can handle the richness of such a diet. Discuss this topic with your veterinarian if you wish to feed your pet a diet that includes raw meat.

At this point, we've covered a lot of information about dealing with cancer in dogs. In chapter 9, I'll help you tie it all together so that you can begin working with your veterinarian to develop a treatment plan for your dog that incorporates the information presented.

CHAPTER NINE

TYING IT ALL TOGETHER

THERE IS NO ONE UNIVERSAL THERAPY that is right for every dog with cancer. It is important to consider all options in deciding which approach is best for your dog. In most cases, this means a sensible combination of both conventional and complementary therapies. It also means working with several health care providers, usually your regular veterinarian, an oncologist, a radiation specialist, a surgeon, and a holistic veterinarian. Communication among all health care providers is important.

Here is my general strategy for both minimizing the chances of cancer and treating cancer, summarized from my book *8 Weeks to a Healthy Dog*.

CANCER PREVENTION

It is important to understand that there are no guarantees and no way to totally prevent cancer. Even if you follow these recommendations, there is always a chance your pet may still get cancer. What I can say with certainty is that this protocol will minimize the chances of your pet getting cancer and other degenerative disorders.

PROVIDE A PROPER DIET: Minimize animal and plant by-products and chemical preservatives in your pet's diet. When possible, a homemade diet using quality ingredients is best; a holistic, organic processed food would be a second option.

MINIMIZE VACCINATIONS: While they are not always completely reliable, antibody titer tests, which are simple blood tests that give information about an individual pet's antibody status in relation to specific diseases, can help your doctor to immunize your pet only when necessary. When possible, pets should be vaccinated only for those diseases for which they are most at risk, rather than receive every vaccine available. And pets with cancer should not receive any extra vaccines if at all possible! (See the section on vaccinosis on page 267 for an in-depth discussion of a holistic approach to vaccinations and the possible relationship between vaccinations and cancer.)

MINIMIZE EXPOSURE TO TOXIC CHEMICALS: When possible, use natural products to prevent or treat diseases. For example, choose natural flea products over chemical insecticides; if chemical insecticides are required, they should be used only when needed rather than year round. Similarly, if natural products such as glucosamine or hyaluronic acid can be used for pets with arthritis, they are preferred to the extensive use of conventional medications such as NSAIDs.

PREVENT OTHER DISEASES: Take preventative measures. For example, give your dog monthly oral heartworm medication. This will prevent the dog from becoming infected and requiring harsher chemicals for treatment. (Unfortunately, we do not currently have any proven natural methods for preventing heartworm infection and disease.) Also, early spaying and neutering can, for many pets, eliminate the chances of developing most cancers of the reproductive organs, and if you own a light-haired pet, limiting sun exposure can decrease the chances of some types of skin cancer.

VISIT YOUR VETERINARIAN REGULARLY: Regular examinations that include laboratory testing of blood and urine are the best way to ensure early diagnosis of cancer if it occurs. If you suspect cancer, ask your veterinarian for other diagnostic tests, such as X-rays and EKGs. Every lump and bump needs to be aspirated by your veterinarian to rule out cancer; otherwise, that lump could grow and spread, and kill your pet! I recommend annual examinations for pets under five years of age, and semiannual examinations for pets five years of age and older.

PRACTICE A HEALTHY LIFESTYLE: Don't expose your pets to tobacco smoke or other toxins.

USE NUTRITIONAL SUPPLEMENTS: As your pet ages, oxidative stresses increase and degenerative changes occur. Many supplements can mitigate these changes, including supplements of fatty acids (I like a product called Ultra EFA, by Rx Vitamins for Pets), health maintenance formulas (Vim & Vigor, by Pet Togethers; www.pettogethers.net/healthypet), and antioxidant supplements (such as Proanthozone, by Animal Health Options).

CANCER TREATMENT

If your pet is diagnosed with cancer, I recommend taking the following steps to give your pet the best chance for survival and a good quality of life during treatment.

PROVIDE A PROPER DIET: Using the cancer diet discussed in this book (pages 229–237) may increase the death of cancer cells and decrease the chance of cancer spreading throughout the body of your pet.

STOP VACCINATIONS: A pet with cancer does not need vaccinations! Pets in remission may come out of remission when vaccinated. Do not ever vaccinate your pet after cancer has been diagnosed. The only exception is dogs that are afflicted with benign tumors, warts, or cysts, and dogs that have had their small cancerous tumors surgically removed (and the pet is cured). Even then, vaccinate using the results of antibody titers to avoid unnecessary immunization. Since rabies vaccination varies with local laws, discuss your options with your pet's veterinarian. While I don't usually vaccinate dogs with cancer against rabies, I will do so if required by local law (often followed by a homeopathic detoxification protocol).

MINIMIZE EXPOSURE TO TOXIC CHEMICALS: When possible, natural products should be used on your pet. For example, natural flea products are preferred to chemical insecticides. If chemical insecticides are required, they should be used only when needed rather than year round. Similarly, if natural products such as glucosamine can be used for pets with arthritis, they are preferred to conventional medications such as NSAIDs.

PREVENT OTHER DISEASES: Preventing heartworm infection through the use of monthly oral preventive medication is preferred to your pet becoming infected and requiring harsher chemicals for treatment. Don't let your pet die from another disease while being treated for cancer!

VISIT YOUR VETERINARIAN REGULARLY: For pets being treated with cancer, frequent follow-up visits, from once a month to once every three months depending on the cancer treatment, are essential to closely monitor the pet's health and any recurrence of cancer for pets in remission.

PRACTICE A HEALTHY LIFESTYLE: Don't expose your pets to tobacco smoke or other toxins.

COMBINE CONVENTIONAL AND COMPLEMENTARY THERAPIES WHEN POSSIBLE: Don't refuse surgery, chemotherapy, or radiation just because these treatments do not fit your definition of holistic. If surgical removal of a tumor will cure your pet, have the surgery. If chemotherapy or radiation can decrease pain and increase the longevity of your pet, by all means consider these treatments. Of course, complementary therapies can be used to enhance the body's ability to kill cancer as well as to minimize side effects from conventional therapies. I've discussed many different complementary therapies in chapters 6 and 7, and obviously you can't use all of them. There is no right or wrong approach, or right or wrong supplement. Listen to all of the available options presented by the doctors on your pet's cancer team before making a final decision. Because therapy for cancer can be expensive, you must commit to a certain budget and then decide how best to use that budget to maximize your pet's chance of improvement. This needs to be done *before* any therapy is begun.

DO NOT SELF-TREAT: Too many pet owners waste their time and money on questionable supplements and therapies. Work with your holistic health provider, spend money on high-quality supplements (not the least expensive ones you can find), and let the experts guide your decisions.

USE NUTRITIONAL SUPPLEMENTS: Dietary supplements may improve the quality of life of patients before, during, and after chemotherapy and radiation therapy; many of the supplements discussed throughout this book can reduce or prevent chemotherapy-induced and radiation-induced side effects.

The diagnosis of cancer can be frightening for pet owners. By learning all you can, maintaining an open mind, and working with your pet's team of specialists, you can have a positive influence on your pet's life!

SUPPLEMENT MANUFACTURERS

THERE ARE MANY REPUTABLE MANUFACTURERS of nutritional supplements that may help pets with cancer. But be aware that there are also supplement producers that do not have good reputations for quality control. I have found the products in the list below to be helpful for supporting pets with cancer. In this listing, I have included only general supplements, not specific supplements (I customize my recommendations for each pet based upon a number of factors that may be unique in each case). Supplements should only be administered under veterinary supervision. These are just a few of the many supplements I use; your veterinarian may have other favorites that have worked well.

OMEGA-3 FATTY ACIDS: I like the product Ultra EFA, by
   Rx Vitamins for Pets.

ANTIOXIDANTS: I like Proanthozone, by Animal Health Options, and OPC Synergy, by Standard Process.

HEALTH MAINTENANCE FORMULA: Vim & Vigor, by Pet Togethers (www.pettogethers.net/healthypet), is useful to balance the diet and support the immune system as a basic supplement. I also use it in healthy pets to minimize diseases such as cancer.

DETOXIFICATION: Homotoxicologic supplements, by Heel, and herbs, by Evergreen Herbs, plus Hepatosupport, by Rx Vitamins, make up my basic detoxification protocol.

WHOLE FOOD SUPPLEMENTS: I use a variety of immune-boosting supplements, including those by NutriWest.

CANCER SUPPORT: In my practice, I use a variety of custom-made herbs. Two products available to veterinarians are ImmunoSupport and OncoSupport, both made by Rx Vitamins. Additionally, Cellular Forte with IP-6, by PhytoPharmica, is very helpful, as are the following products by Thorne Research: Curcumin, Immugen, Moducare, and Myco Immune.

The following companies offer a variety of prescription supplements that may benefit pets with cancer: Rx Vitamins for Pets, VetriScience, Animal Health Options, Heel, NutriWest, and Nutramax, and Thorne Research.

PAIN CONTROL *for the* CANINE CANCER PATIENT

DOGS DIAGNOSED WITH CANCER may have chronic pain. Conventional medications are often used to make life more comfortable for these pets. Medications that may be helpful to reduce pain include opioids and NSAIDs (nonsteroidal anti-inflammatory drugs).

There are several medications available within the family of opioids that include butorphanol (given orally or by injection, with effects last from two to four hours), burpenorphine (given orally or by injection every eight to twelve hours), fentanyl (the patch is placed on the shaved skin and effects may last up to seventy-two hours), and nalbuphine hydrochloride (given by subcutaneous injection in a typical dose of 0.5–1 mg/kg, with effects lasting three to four hours).

NSAIDs such as piroxicam (Feldene) have antitumor effects; in *very rare* instances, dogs receiving piroxicam have been miraculously cured of their cancers! For this reason, many veterinarians prefer piroxicam to other NSAIDs, such as Rimadyl or EtoGesic, although in animal models several NSAIDs have shown varying degrees of antitumor effects on various cancers. Caution should be taken in chemotherapy protocols that use corticosteroids (such as prednisone and prednisolone), because the use of NSAIDs and corticosteroids together may cause ulcers or perforations of the gastrointestinal tract (corticosteroids and NSAIDs can cause ulcers when used by themselves). The medication Cytotec (misoprostol) can be prescribed to minimize the chance of gastrointestinal ulcers when piroxicam is used. Cytotec is expensive, and certainly most pets not taking this medication do not develop ulcers.

Radiation therapy may be useful for pain relief for metastatic bone lesions as well as primary tumors.

Finally, antitussive (anticoughing) medications, such as butorphanol, may be useful for pets with respiratory tumors, and antiemetic (antivomiting) medications, such as metoclopramide, can make life more comfortable for pets with gastrointestinal distress.

SUPPORTING *the* CANCER PATIENT

Sometimes pets with cancer need general support during their treatment. The following suggestions may be helpful.

Anorectic pets, or those with decreased or no appetite, may need supplemental feeding, either hand-feeding by the owners or *short-term* tube feeding. Owners can easily learn the proper technique for hand-feeding their pets, and there are several diets that can be used. Some pets prefer their food warmed to room temperature. When a pet can't or won't eat, a feeding tube can be placed down the esophagus or into the stomach, which is usually performed under sedation or anesthesia with minimal risk. The diet and supplements for feeding through a tube must be carefully selected to avoid clogging the tube and to ensure the pet is getting enough calories and liquid to maintain body weight (if the tube becomes clogged, you can use water or soda to dissolve the clog). Additionally, various medications (corticosteroids, oxazepam, cyproheptadine, B vitamins) can be given that may stimulate appetite in some pets.

Pets with bone cancer (osteosarcoma) that have not been treated with limb amputation can be made comfortable with walking casts to prevent fractures of the affected bone. Ramps make it easier for the pet to get in and out of the car and the house.

Animals with limited mobility can develop decubital ulcers over pressure points, usually the elbows and ankles. These ulcers can be reduced or avoided through the judicious use of padding, waterbeds, air beds, or egg crate mattresses. Frequent and complete cleaning of the pet's coat and skin is important if the pet is soiling itself with urine or feces; diapers may also be needed. Immobile pets should not be left outdoors unattended, because they are susceptible to maggot infestations and skin infections.

Dogs with transitional cell carcinoma of the bladder may develop incontinence or bloody urine. Urinary incontinence can be managed with extra bedding or by putting diapers on the pet. If bloody urine is severe, additional therapy might be needed to minimize bleeding. One technique that has been reported in the medical literature is medication administered by a veterinarian directly into the pet's bladder under anesthesia. The medicine is a mixture of 1 percent solution of formalin with a vial of Synotic (containing DMSO), which is instilled into the bladder through a urinary catheter. The solution is kept in the bladder for ten to fifteen minutes and then removed; this is intended to flush out any blood clots. This procedure may reduce the bloody urine for seven to ten days, and it may be repeated as needed.

Dogs with brain tumors may need medication to control their seizures. Diazepam suppositories introduced into the rectum may terminate the seizure. The flower essence called Rescue Remedy may help as well; five to ten drops are placed in the mouth or on the gums, and repeated as needed. One holistic treatment for terminating seizures is to place an ice pack over the dog's back, from the middle of the rib area extending back to the first few lumbar vertebrae (have your doctor show you this location); the ice pack should be placed over this spot for two to three minutes while the pet recovers from the seizure.

Severe vomiting may be controlled with Reglan or Zofran injections. After being trained by their veterinarians, most owners can be shown how to safely administer injectable medications at home.

WARNING SIGNS
of CANCER

OWNERS OFTEN WONDER whether there are any signs that might indicate cancer in their pets. The following signs, while not definitive for cancer (they may also be seen with other diseases), should arouse suspicion about the *possibility* of cancer. In general, any of the following signs that persist despite what seems to be appropriate therapy should prompt consideration of cancer. *Diagnostic testing is the only reliable way to rule out cancer; if there is any question as to whether your pet has cancer, make clear to your veterinarian that you want diagnostic tests for conclusive evidence.* The clinical signs that might indicate cancer are listed below; the bracketed text lists other more common disorders that may cause similar signs.

- Lumps and bumps, especially new ones and those that grow quickly; those that appear, decrease in size, or disappear altogether and then reappear or enlarge;

and those that change color or easily bleed [fatty tumors, cysts, abscesses]

- Skin sores or irritated areas [bacterial or fungal infections, immune disorders]

- Red spots on the skin, gums, or mucous membranes [platelet disorders, infectious diseases]

- Wounds that do not heal [immune disorders, infections]

- Weight loss or gain [inflammatory bowel disease, thyroid disease, any systemic illness]

- Lack of appetite or decreased appetite [any disease]

- Abdominal enlargement/potbellied appearance [heart disease, liver disease, protein disorders]

- Weakness or exercise intolerance [heart disease, respiratory disease]

- Excessive panting or heavy breathing [heart disease, respiratory disease]

- Collapse [heart disease, respiratory disease, seizures]

- Pale gums and mucous membranes [anemia]

- Bad breath [dental disease, kidney disease, gastrointestinal disease, liver disease]

- Bleeding or chronic discharge from wounds or from any body orifice [platelet disorders, infectious diseases, bladder stones]

- Chronic diarrhea and vomiting, along with a change in bowel habits [inflammatory bowel disease]

- Blood in the urine or urinary incontinence, along with a change in urinary habits [bladder infection or inflammation, bladder stones, polypoid cystitis]

EUTHANASIA *for the* PET *with* CANCER

MOST PET OWNERS PREFER that their beloved pets pass away quickly and quietly at home. Unfortunately, the slow decline of a pet with cancer often necessitates intervention with euthanasia to prevent unwanted suffering at the end of life. While saying good-bye to a beloved family member is never easy, the owner should take comfort in knowing that death is a normal part of the "circle of life" experienced by all creatures. While difficult for the pet owner, euthanasia is a selfless act that puts the pet's best interests above the needs of the owner, who doesn't ever want to lose a companion.

There are many questions that must be addressed in considering euthanasia, the most important of which is, "How will I know when the time comes?" The answer to this question lies with the pet. Many pets will give some sign, such as unrelenting vomiting or diarrhea, yelping or whimpering, exhibiting lethargy, not eating, and simply shutting down (having more bad days than good days). *In short, the pet's quality of life is poor or nonexistent.* The pet can no longer enjoy life with the owner, and the owner can no longer enjoy the pet in its current condition. Many of my patients "have that look in their eyes" that tells me they are ready to be released from this life. Pet owners should take comfort in knowing that if they must make the difficult decision to euthanize their pets, they are not giving up on their pets but rather accepting the reality of their condition. The decision is both humane and correct. Understandably, pet owners never like to think of death or euthanasia, but I prefer to approach the subject with clients who are open to the discussion shortly after the diagnosis of cancer. While we always hope death will be months or years away, it's easiest to think about it, discuss it, and plan for it long before death becomes a reality. In the early stages of cancer treatment, plans can be made for the euthanasia procedure (for example, which family members would like to be present) and for the disposal of the pet's body (such as cremation or burial).

While always emotionally painful for family members and caregivers, the process of euthanasia is actually quite painless for the pet. Simply put, the pet is given an intravenous overdose of anesthetic. The pet quickly loses consciousness, and death occurs within seconds. To make the intravenous injection easier, your veterinarian may need to first insert an intravenous catheter (this is more likely for weak animals or obese pets with veins that might be difficult to find and inject).

While most euthanasia procedures occur smoothly, sometimes complications can arise. For example, the animal may jerk its leg after only a portion of the anesthetic is injected, causing excitement rather than unconsciousness. Sometimes an unconscious pet will have involuntary, jerky movements of its limbs or bodies. Occasionally, an unconscious pet will lose bowel or bladder control. Very rarely, a pet will be given an additional injection if it requires a higher-than-expected amount of euthanasia agent. While these problems are rare, owners should be prepared for them, as they can add to the owner's grief.

Following euthanasia, the owner has to decide how to dispose of the pet. Several options are available, including private burial or communal cremation and burial (check with your doctor for specifics). Most of my clients choose private cremation with the return of the ashes to the family.

SIDE EFFECTS *from* CONVENTIONAL CANCER THERAPIES *and the* SUPPLEMENTS THAT MAY COUNTERACT THEM

SIDE EFFECTS ARE VERY RARE IN PETS during or after chemotherapy or radiation therapy. If they do occur, there are supplements that might be beneficial in their treatment. In the following list of possible side effects, I've made specific recommendations based on what has been successful in my own practice.

DECREASED BLOOD COUNTS: In addition to medications such as erythropoetin and colony stimulating factor, supplements including curcumin, folate, vitamin B-12, niacinamide, vitamin C, and vitamin E are recommended.

DIARRHEA: Probiotics, enzymes, ginger, and glutamine may help. (Please note that glutamine should be used cautiously if at all in pets with brain tumors.)

HAIR LOSS: Other than in an area irradiated during radiation therapy, hair loss very rarely occurs in pets. Administering antioxidants (including quercetin, curcumin, green tea, and hesperidin) and biotin may help.

HEART TOXICITY: This most commonly results from cumulative doses of the chemotherapy drug doxorubicin (and in people, mainly cyclophosphamide, 5-FU, and mitoxantrone). Administering vitamins C and E, selenium, omega-3 fatty acids, hawthorn, and N-acetylcysteine can reduce acute heart damage. These supplements can be administered before, during, and after doxorubicin therapy. Administering coenzyme Q-10 *after* doxorubicin therapy is completed can help prevent delayed heart damage.

KIDNEY TOXICITY: Some medications that may be helpful are curcumin and Panax ginseng. N-acetylcysteine is helpful for hemorrhagic cystitis, a condition involving bleeding from the bladder in pets taking cyclophosphamide. Intravenous glutathione may be helpful for pets treated with cisplatin.

LIVER TOXICITY: Liver detoxification using homeopathics, milk thistle, curcumin, indole-3-carbinol, MSM, and mixed carotenoids is recommended.

LUNG TOXICITY: In people, busulfan and bleomycin may cause pulmonary fibrosis. Rutin, quercetin, hesperidin, green tea, vitamin E, boswellia, and curcumin may help alleviate toxicity in pets.

MOUTH OR THROAT SORENESS/ORAL ULCERS: Chemotherapy or radiation therapy of the head and throat may cause oral ulcers. Grapefruit seed extract (mouth rinse), Traumeel (a homeopathic remedy from Heel), coenzyme Q-10 (prepared and swallowed as a mouth wash), vitamin E (rubbed on the ulcerated areas), and glutamine (taken orally) may reduce the incidence of ulcers as well as heal ulcers.

NAUSEA/VOMITING: These may occur following direct damage to the stomach or intestinal lining, or from stimulation of the vomiting center in the brain. Medications such as Reglan or Zofran are often prescribed. Supplements that soothe the gastrointestinal tract include ginger, marshmallow, slippery elm, and deglycyrrhizinated licorice root. Glutamine helps heal damaged intestinal cells, *however, it should be used cautiously if at all in pets with brain tumors.*

NERVE TOXICITY: Protecting the nervous system from free radical damage of DNA may be accomplished by administering alpha lipoic acid, curcumin, quercetin, milk thistle, and coenzyme Q-10. Ginkgo biloba, an herb known for its ability to reduce cognitive degeneration, would be helpful as well. However, since pets with cancer are usually treated with high doses of omega-3 fatty acids, the combination of ginkgo plus fish oil can cause possibly fatal hemorrhagic stroke and is not usually recommended.

HOMOTOXICOLOGY

THE PRINCIPLES OF HOMOTOXICOLOGY are based on the research findings of Dr. Hans-Heinrich Reckeweg, who created the discipline. It provides an effective and systematic paradigm that can serve as a powerful tool in interpreting the progress of disease, including its neoplastic phases. The table (on pages 262–263) showing the Six Phases of Homotoxicology defines the development of disease according to homotoxicology, with the dedifferentiation, or cancer, phase (shown in last column) as the last stage in the progression of serious cellular pathology. Many steps precede this slide into cellular disease and death, as evidenced by the stages to the left of the dedifferentiation phase.

Neoplastic (cancerous) phases are the final phases of all homotoxicosis development. These phases represent a disorder of cellular nature. Homotoxicologic remedies are capable of effectively promoting the discharge of toxins and of cleansing the ground substance. Additional medicinal agents and nosodes that are effective in cancer therapy include those that activate cell metabolism and that support organ regeneration. All of these medication possibilities provide effective support in cancer therapy, and can often be combined with conventional treatments.

The following is a summary of homotoxicologic remedies that may be useful in treating the pet with cancer (based upon treating the neoplastic phases of the disease). Your doctor will decide which remedies are most suitable.

These biotherapeutic/antihomotoxic preparations promote the discharge of toxins:

- Lymphomyosot

- Hepeel

- Reneel

- Chelidonium-Homaccord

- Heel-Chol

- Nux Vomica-Homaccord

- Berberis-Homaccord

- Galium-Heel

The following substances activate the cell metabolism:

- Coenzyme compositum

- Ubichinon compositum

- Glyoxal compositum

THE SIX PHASES OF HOMOTOXICOLOGY

	HUMORAL PHASES		MATRIX
ORGAN SYSTEM	EXCRETION PHASES	INFLAMMATION PHASES	DEPOSITION PHASES
Tissue Damage	No enzyme damage; excretion principle; natural healing tendency		
Skin	Episodes of sweating	Acne	Naevi
Nervous System	Difficulty concentrating	Meningitis	Cerebrosclerosis
Sensory System	Tears, otorrhea	Conjunctivitis, otitis media	Chalazion, cholesteatoma
Locomotor System	Joint pains, myalgia	Epicondylitis, acute sprain	Exostosis, myogelosis
Respiratory Tract	Cough, expectoration	Acute bronchitis	Silicosis, smoker's lung
Cardiovascular System	Functional heart complaint	Endocarditis, pericarditis, myocarditis	Coronary heart disease
Gastrointestinal System	Diarrhea, vomiting	Gastroenteritis, acute hepatitis	Diverticulosis, fatty liver
Urogenital System	Polyuria	Urinary tract infection	Bladder stones, kidney stones
Blood	Reticulocytosis	Leukocytosis, suppuration	Polycythemia, thrombocytosis
Lymph System	Lymphedema	Lymphangitis, tonsillitis, lymphadenitis	Lymph-node swelling
Metabolism	Electrolyte shift	Lipid metabolism disturbance	Gout, obesity
Hormone System	Globus sensation	Thyroiditis	Goiter, adenoma
Immune System	Susceptibility to infection	Weak immune system, acute infection	Weak reactions

| PHASES | CELLULAR PHASES | |
IMPREGNATION PHASES	DEGENERATION PHASES	DEDIFFERENTIATION PHASES
Enzyme damage; compensation principle; chronic diseases		
Allergy	Scleroderma	Melanoma
Migraine	Alzheimer's disease	Gliosarcoma
Iridocyclitis, tinnitus	Macular degeneration, anosmia	Amaurosis, malignant tumor
Chronic rheumatiod arthritis, fibromyalgia	Spondylosis, osteoarthritis, muscular dystrophy	Osteosarcoma, chondroma, myosarcoma
Chronic (obstructive) bronchitis	Bronchiectasia, emphysema	Bronchial carcinoma
Heart failure	Myocardial infarction	Endothelioma
Duodenalulear gastritis, chronic hepatitis	Ulcerative colitis, chronic disease	Stomach cancer, colon cancer
Chronic urinary tract infection	Renal atrophy	Cancer of the bladder or kidneys
Aggregation disturbance	Anemia, thrombocytopenia	Leukemia
Insufficiency of the lymph system	Fibrosis	Hodgkin's lymphoma, non-Hodgkin's lymphoma
Metabolic syndrome	Diabetes mellitus	Slow reactions
Hyperthyroidism, glucose intolerance	Menopausal symptoms	Thyroid cancer
Autoimmune disease, immunodeficiency, chronic infection	AIDS	Slow reactions

- Thyreoidea compositum
- Tonsilla compositum
- Pulsatilla compositum

These preparations provide general support:

- Galium-Heel
- Psorinoheel
- Lymphomyosot
- Phosphor-Homaccord

Give Ginseng compositum and Molybdan compositum at the start of the treatment for two to three weeks, one to two tablets three times daily, then only once daily, and subsequently one tablet two to three times weekly (every second or third day).

A general guideline is that the pet takes eight to ten drops of each together six times daily. After eight weeks, the remedies are taken four times daily, and after another eight weeks the remedies are taken three times daily.

The following offer cancer support specific to the tissue involved:

- Nux Vomica-Homaccord and Veratrum-Homaccord: cancer of the intestine
- Gynacoheel, Lamioflur, and Hormeel: uterine cancer and cancer of the surrounding tissues
- Chelidonium-Homaccord: liver and gall bladder cancer
- Graphites-Homaccord: cancer of the small intestine

- Phosphor-Homaccord: laryngeal cancer
- Duodenoheel and Spascupreel: cancer of the small intestine and pancreatic cancer
- Lamioflur: cancer of the nose, mouth, and genitals
- Mezereum-Homaccord: cancer of any mucous membranes
- Reneel and Spascupreel: cancer of the urinary system
- Apis compositum: cancer of the kidneys
- Schwef-Heel: epithelioma cancer
- Bronchalis-Heel (also Droperteel, Phosphor-Homaccord, Husteel and Tartephedreel): Lung cancer
- Hormeel: cancer of the glands and genitals

Due to the continual attack by intermediary homotoxins (cancer-causing agents, tumor antigens, lactic acid), a chronic state of stress exists, and the exhaustion of the cortices of the adrenal glands is increasingly intensified. Therefore, it is advisable to utilize the remedy Berberis-Homaccord continuously. Strumeel and Thyreoidea compositum may also be indicated to stimulate the functions of the thyroid gland.

In sarcoma cancers, Galium-Heel (orally and/or by injection) may also be helpful.

These preparations offer cancer support for the symptoms specified:

- Nux Vomica-Homaccord and Veratrum-Homaccord: straining to evacuate the bowels
- Colocynthis-Homaccord: nerve disorders

- Gelsemium-Homaccord and Spigelon: nerve disorders

- Spascupreel and Atropinum compositum: shooting pains and spasms

- Drosera-Homaccord, Husteel, Droperteel, Bronchalis-Heel, Tartephedreel: cough

- Mercurius-Heel and Traumeel: ulcers

Other supportive therapies that may be helpful include the following.

- Arsuraneel has a generally calming action on the toxin level; likewise Cruroheel on the connective tissue structures. These two preparations should, therefore, be used daily in frequent doses.

- Rendimax treats acidosis, a common condition in pets with cancer (cancer thrives in an acidic environment).

- Auto-Sanguis Sequence Therapy is potent homotoxicologic therapy. This therapy involves drawing a small amount of blood from the patient, diluting it in the appropriate remedies, and giving the mixture back to the patient, usually by injection. The mixtures can be given subcutaneously (under the skin), in acupuncture points, and even orally in some cases. The patient's blood serves as a carrier for the remedies, making this a potent form of therapy.

VACCINOSIS:
ARE VACCINES CAUSING
CANCER *in* OUR PETS?

VACCINOSIS IS THE TERM given to the chronic reaction of the body against repeated immunizations. Many holistic veterinarians and holistic-minded owners are concerned about the frequent (and most likely unnecessary) immunization of pets for just about every disease imaginable.

As discussed in my book *The Natural Health Bible for Dogs & Cats*, a number of serious conditions have been linked to excessive immunization, and animals run the risk of adverse reactions as increasing amounts of foreign antigens are injected into them. Since vaccination involves altering the immune system, it is not surprising that occasionally it can cause serious adverse effects, including injection-site sarcomas, an aggressive cancer of cats that occurs roughly once for every 1,000 to 10,000 injections; vaccines are implicated more than other injectable medications for causing cancer. Injection-site sarcomas have been reported in only a handful of dogs (four dogs as of this writing). Other complications caused by vaccines include decreased red blood cell count (autoimmune hemolytic anemia) and decreased platelet count (thrombocytopenia), liver failure, kidney failure, bone marrow suppression, immune suppression, systemic lupus erythematosus, rheumatoid arthritis, and food allergy. Vaccinations are also linked to atopic dermatitis, an allergic disease caused by an augmented immune response to vaccines or by other allergens or immugens, the so-called allergic breakthrough phenomenon. Vaccines are also linked to different types of immune kidney diseases (glomerulonephritis/renal amyloidosis), seizures, bloating, hypothyroidism, and hyperthyroidism.

Both killed vaccines (containing adjuvant to stimulate a greater immune response) and modified live vaccines have been implicated in adverse vaccine reactions. Many reactions seem to occur following booster immunization with vaccines containing several antigens, such as five-way vaccines or seven-way vaccines.

Currently, many doctors still follow the recommendation to administer most immunizations at least annually. Unfortunately, there is no scientific basis for this recommendation.

Rabies is usually a three-year vaccine, meaning that immunity lasts at least three years (some state laws require annual immunization, even though the three-year vaccine is used). Canine bordetella intranasal vaccine is usually administered every six months.

There are ongoing research projects that seek to determine the maximum duration of immunity of vaccines in pets. This presents quite a challenge, as there are many vaccines to be tested. The results of these tests will most likely need to be repeated to verify their accuracy. Results of the tests (and retesting) will probably take at least five to ten years or more before current vaccination protocols can be changed with confidence. However, current research and recommendations are that vaccines (in most cases) produce immunity that lasts longer than twelve months.

Some doctors follow updated recommendations, giving vaccines every three years, unless it is determined that a more frequent interval should be followed. An alternative to routine vaccination of every pet is the use of vaccine (antibody) titers. I prefer this approach, as it allows me to individualize and personalize my recommendations for every patient, which is the ultimate goal of holistic pet care.

Titers test a pet's antibody response to various vaccines. In simple terms, antibodies are proteins made by the pet's white blood cells, specifically B lymphocytes. These antibodies are made whenever a pet contracts an infectious organism (virus or bacteria, as a result of a natural infection) or is vaccinated; the vaccine introduces low doses of infectious organisms, tricking the immune system to form protective antibodies without causing disease as might occur in a natural infection. Using a titer test reveals the pet's antibody status. The results are then interpreted to determine whether the pet is adequately protected against a specific infectious disease and whether the pet requires additional immunization (more on titers can be found in my book *The Natural Health Bible for Dogs & Cats*).

Pets with chronic immune disorders such as cancer may be at increased risk for further immune damage from exposure to harsh chemicals typically found in flea products, preservatives in most commercial pet foods, and antigens in vaccines. While their recommendations are controversial, most holistic doctors do not administer vaccines to pets with chronic, serious disorders, especially those involving the immune system. Pets in remission from cancer have been known to relapse following immunization; as a rule, most doctors do not recommend ever revaccinating pets with cancer.

REFERENCES

Altman, R., and M. J. Sarg. *The Cancer Dictionary: An A-to-Z Guide to Over 2,500 Terms*. New York: Facts On File, 1992.

American Cancer Society's Guide to Complementary and Alternative Cancer Methods. Atlanta: American Cancer Society, 2000.

Bateman, K. E., P. A. Catton, P. W. Pennock, and S. A. J. Kruth. "Radiation Therapy for the Palliation of Advanced Cancer in Dogs." *Journal of Veterinary Internal Medicine* 8, no. 6 (November–December 1994): 394–99.

Bergman, P. "Chemoprevention." *Proceedings of the 1999 American College of Veterinary Internal Medicine Forum in Chicago*: 115–18.

Blaylock, R. *Natural Strategies for Cancer Patients*. New York: Kensington Publishing, 2003.

———. "A Review of Conventional Cancer Prevention and Treatment and the Adjunctive Use of Nutraceutical Supplements and Antioxidants: Is There a Danger or a Significant Benefit?" *Journal of the American Nutraceutical Association* 3, no. 3 (fall 2000): 17–35.

Block, J. "Clinical Evidence Supporting Cancer Risk Reduction with Antioxidants and Implications for Diet and Supplementation." *Journal of the American Nutraceutical Association* 3, no. 3 (fall 2000): 6–16.

Bostock, D. C. "The Prognosis Following Surgical Removal of Mastocytomas in Dogs." *The Journal of Small Animal Practice* 14 (1973): 27–40.

Bratman, S., and D. Kroll. *The Natural Health Bible*. New York: Prima/Random House, 1999.

Buerger, R. G., and D. W. Scott. "Cutaneous Mast Cell Neoplasia in Cats: 14 Cases (1975–1985)." *Journal of the American Veterinary Medical Association* 190 (1987): 1440–44.

Center, S. "New Approach to Managing Hepatic Dysfunction, Roundtable on the Therapeutic Use of S-Adenosylmethionine, Part I." *Veterinary Forum* (November 2000): 40–45.

Choen, S. P., and C. E. Fudin, eds. "Animal Illness and Human Emotion." *Problems in Veterinary Medicine* 3, no. 1 (March 1991).

Chretin, J. D., N. A. Shaw, K. A. Hahn, G. K. Ogilvie, K. M. Rassnick, and A. S. Moore. "Prophylactic Trimethoprim-sulfdiazine during Chemotherapy Induction: A Double-Blind Placebo-Controlled Study." *VCS Annual Conference 2000 Proceedings Pacific Grove* 47: 75–82.

Day, C. *The Homeopathic Treatment of Small Animals, Principles and Practice*. London: C. W. Daniel, 1992.

Downing, R. *Pets Living with Cancer: A Pet Owner's Resource*. Lakewood, CO: American Animal Hospital Association Press, 2000.

DVM Newsmagazine. "Study Suggests Hormones Linked to Bone Cancer." Press Time. January 2001.

Ford, S. "Compassionate Therapeutics for Senior Oncology Patients." *Veterinary Forum* (November 2000): 58–61.

Goldstein, M. "Modalities for Cancer Therapy." *Proceedings of the 2000 American Holistic Veterinary Medical Association Conference*: 128–30.

———. *The Nature of Animal Healing*. New York: Knopf, 1999.

Gorter, R., M. van Wely, M. Reif, and M. Stoss. "Tolerability of an Extract of European Mistletoe among Immunocompromised and Healthy Individuals." *Alternative Therapies* 5, no. 6 (November 1999): 37–48.

Graf, E., and J. W. Eaton. "Dietary Suppression of Colonic Cancer: Fiber or Phytate?" *Cancer* 56 (1985): 717–18.

Grossarth-Maticke, R., H. Kiene, S. Baumgartner, and R. Ziegler. "Use of Iscador, an Extract of European Mistletoe (*Viscum album*), in Cancer Treatment: Prospective Nonrandomized and Randomized Matched-Pair Studies Nested within a Cohort Study." *Alternative Therapies* 7, no. 3 (May–June 2001): 57–78.

Hahn, K. A. *Veterinary Oncology: The Practical Veterinarian Series*. Philadelphia: Butterworth-Heinemann, 2002.

Hahn, K. A., and R. C. Richardson. *Cancer Chemotherapy: A Veterinary Handbook*. Boston: Lippincott Williams & Wilkins, 1998.

Holt, S. "Antiangiogenesis: A Role for Natural Therapies." *Proceedings of the 2000 American Holistic Veterinary Medical Association Conference*: 95–109.

————. "The Power of Cartilage." *Kensington Health* (1998): 72–128.

————. "Soya for Health." *Liebert* (1996): 13–28.

————. "The Soy Revolution." *Dell Health* (1998): 163–74.

Homewood, A. E. *The Neurodynamics of the Vertebral Subluxation.* Parker Research Foundation, 1962.

Hoskins, J. "Feline 'Triad Disease' Poses Triple Threat." *DVM Newsmagazine.* February 2000: 45–75.

Hunt, L. E. *Angel Paw Prints: An Anthology of Pet Memorials.* Pasadena, CA: Darrowby Press, 1998.

Jeffery E., and A. Keck. "Enhancement of Detoxification Systems with Brussels Sprouts Prepared by Standard Process Inc." *Whole Food Nutrition Journal* 20 (2001): 78–83.

Jones, K., K. Hughes, L. Mischley, and D. McKenna. "Coenzyme Q-10: Efficacy, Safety, and Use." *Alternative Therapies* 8, no. 3 (May–June 2002): 42–55.

Katiyar, S. K., N. Ahmad, and H. Mukhtar. "Green Tea and Skin." *Archives of Dermatology* 136, no. 8 (2000): 989–94.

King, G. K., K. M. Yates, P. G. Greenlee, et al. "The Effect of Acemannan, Surgery, and Radiation on Spontaneous Canine and Feline Fibrosar-coma." *Journal of the American Animal Hospital Association* (1995).

Knapp, D. W., et al. "Measurement of NK Activity in Effector Cells Purified from Canine Peripheral Lymphocytes." *Veterinary Immunology and Im-munopathology* (1992): 212–14.

————. "Phase I Trial of Piroxicam in 62 Dogs Bearing Naturally Occurring Tumors." *Cancer Chemotherapy Pharmacology* 29 (1992): 214–18.

————. "Piroxicam Therapy in Twenty-four Dogs with Transitional Cell Carcinoma of the Bladder." *Proceedings of the 1991 American College of Veterinary Internal Medicine Forum*: 140–43.

Labriola, D. *Complementary Cancer Therapies.* New York: Prima/Random House, 2000.

Lagoni, L., D. Morehead, and C. Butler. "The Bond-Centered Practice: The Future of Veterinary Care." *Proceedings of the 1999 American College of Veterinary Internal Medicine Forum in Chicago.*

Lamson, D., and M. Brignall. "Antioxidants and Cancer Therapy II: Quick Reference Guide." *Alternative Medicine Review* 5, no. 2 (2000): 152–63.

Life Extension Foundation. "Anti-Cancer Foods and Supplements" *Life Extension Magazine* (February 2003): 55–62.

————. "Chlorophyllin and Cancer Prevention" *Life Extension Magazine* (February 2003): 66–68.

————. *Disease Prevention and Treatment*, exp. 4th ed. Hollywood, FL: Life Extension Foundation, 2003.

————. "Theanine Enhances Chemotherapy and Reduces Side Effects." *Life Extension Magazine* (July 2002): 35–36.

Liska, W. D., E. G. MacEwen, F. A. Zaki, et al. "Feline Systemic Mastocytosis: A Review and Results of Splenectomy in Seven Cases." *Journal of the American Animal Hospital Association* 15 (1979): 589–97.

MacEwen, E. G., and K. Young. "Canine Lymphoma and Lymphoid Leukemias." In *Small Animal Clinical Oncology*, edited by S. Withrow and E. G. MacEwen, 451–79. Philadelphia: W. B. Saunders, 1996.

Macleod, G. Dog: *Homeopathic Remedies*. London: C. W. Daniel, 1994.

Marsden, S. "Naturopathic Treatment of Canine Osteosarcoma." *Proceedings of the 2000 American Holistic Veterinary Medical Association Conference*: 59–62.

McKenna, D., K. Hughes, and P. Jones. "Green Tea Monograph." *Alternative Therapies* 6, no. 3 (May 2000): 61–84.

Messonnier, S. P. *8 Weeks to a Healthy Dog*. New York: Rodale, 2003.

————. *The Natural Health Bible for Dogs & Cats*. New York: Prima/Random House, 2001.

Mills, S., and K. Bone. *Principles and Practice of Phytotherapy*. Philadelphia: Churchill Livingstone, 2000.

Monti, D. J. "Pawspice: An Option for Pets Facing the End." *Journal of the American Veterinary Medical Association* 217, no. 7 (October 1, 2000): 969.

Nelson, R., and C. G. Couto. *Manual of Small Animal Internal Medicine*. Philadelphia: Mosby, 1999.

Ogilvie, G. K. "Hospice and Bond-Centered Practice: The Future of Veterinary Care." *Proceedings of the 1999 American College of Veterinary Internal Medicine Forum in Chicago*: 231–37.

Ogilvie, G. K., and A. S. Moore. *Managing the Veterinary Cancer Patient: A Practice Manual*. Trenton, NJ: Veterinary Learning Systems, 1995.

Patniak, A. K., W. N. Ehler, and E. G. MacEwen. "Canine Cutaneous Mast Cell Tumors: Morphologic Grading and Survival Time in 83 Dogs." *Veterinary Pathology* 21 (1984): 469–74.

Rawlings, J. "Percutaneous Placement of a Midcervical Esophagostomy Tube: New Technique and Representative Cases." *Journal of the American Animal Hospital Association* 29 (1993): 562–630.

Rogers, P. A. M. "Immunologic Effects of Acupuncture." In *Veterinary Acupuncture: Ancient Art to Modern Medicine*, edited by A. Schoen, 250–52. Philadelphia: Mosby, 1994.

Rubin, P. *Clinical Oncology: A Multidisciplinary Approach for Physicians and Students*. Philadelphia: W. B. Saunders, 1993.

Shen J., N. Wenger, J. Glaspy, et al. "Electroacupuncture for Control of Myeloablative Chemotherapy-Induced Emesis: A Randomized Controlled Trial." *JAMA* 284 (2000): 2755–61.

Singh, N. and H. Lai. "Selective Toxicity of Dihydroartemisinin and Holotransferrin toward Human Breast Cancer Cells." *Life Sciences* (June 2001): 343–45.

Tantivejkul, K., Z. S. Zhang, I. Saied, I. Vucenik, A. M. Shamsuddin. "Inositol Hexaphosphate (IP6) Inhibits Growth of Human Hepatocellular Carcinoma." *Proceedings of the 1998 American Association for Cancer Research* 39: 314–15.

Tizard, I. R., R. H. Carpenter, B. H. McAnaley, et al. "The Biological Activities of Mannans and Related Complex Carbohydrates." *Molecular Biotherapy* 1 (1989): 290–96.

Turrel, J. M., B. E. Kitchell, L. M. Miller, et al. "Prognostic Factors for Radiation Treatment of Mast Cell Tumor in 85 Dogs." *Journal of the American Veterinary Medical Association* 193 (1988): 936–40.

Vail, D., and S. Withrow. "Tumors of the Skin and Subcutaneous Tissues." In *Small Animal Clinical Oncology*, edited by S. Withrow and E. G. MacEwen, 167–91. Philadelphia: W. B. Saunders, 1996.

Villalobos, A. E. "Conceptualized Hospice for Pet's Last Days: Pet Pawspice. *Proceedings of the 2000 American Veterinary Medical Convention in Salt Lake City*: 322–25.

———. "Oncology Outlook: Chemoprevention: Can Food Fight Cancer?" *Veterinary Product News* (March 2000).

———. "Oncology Outlook: On Bladder and Prostate Cancer." *Veterinary Product News* (January 2000).

———. "Oncology Outlook: Pet Hospice Nurses the Bond." *Veterinary Product News* (September 1999).

———. "Oncology Outlook: Quality of Life Scale Helps Make Final Call." *Veterinary Product News* (September 2004).

———. "Oncology Outlook: Those Stubborn Cats That Won't Eat." *Veterinary Product News* (August 1999).

———. "Pawspice." *Journal of the American Veterinary Medical Association* 217, no. 7 (October 1, 2000): 969.

Vucenik, I., V. J. Tomazic, D. Fabian, and A. M. Shamsudin. "Antitumor Activity of Phytic Acid in Murine Transplanted and Metastatic Fibrosarcoma." *Cancer Letters* 65 (1992): 9–13.

Vucenik, I., T. Kalebic, K. Tantivejkul, and A. M. Shamsudin. "Inositol Hexaphosphate (IP6) Inhibits the Growth of Human Rhabdomyosarcoma." *Proceedings of the 1997 American Association for Cancer Research* 38: 96.

Willoughby, S. "Chiropractic Care." In *Complementary and Alternative Veterinary Medicine: Principles and Practice*, edited by A. Schoen and S. Wynn, 185–200. Philadelphia: Mosby, 1998.

Withrow, S. J., and E. G. MacEwen. "Soft Tissue Sarcomas." In *Small Animal Clinical Oncology*, 2nd ed., edited by S. J. Withrow and E. G. MacEwen, 211–26. Philadelphia: W. B. Saunders, 1996.

Wulff-Tilford, M., and G. Tilford. *All You Ever Wanted to Know about Herbs for Pets*. Irvine, CA: Bowtie Press, 1999.

INDEX

Page numbers given in *italics* indicate material in tables.

ABOUT *the* AUTHOR

DR. SHAWN MESSONNIER graduated in 1987 from Texas A&M University with his Doctor of Veterinary Medicine degree. In 1991, he opened Paws & Claws Animal Hospital, the first referral hospital for dogs, cats, and exotic pets in Plano, Texas.

Dr. Messonnier writes a regular column on holistic veterinary medicine for *The Dallas Morning News*; his popular column is distributed across North America by Knight Ridder News Service. For several years, he was host of Fox television's *4 Your Pets* pet care show. He now hosts *The Natural Vet* on Martha Stewart Living Radio, part of the Sirius Satellite Radio Network.

In addition to practicing medicine, Dr. Messonnier serves on the board of the prestigious international journal *Veterinary Forum*. He has shared his thoughts on integrative pet care with millions of pet owners as a contributor to various pet publications, including *Dog Fancy, Cat Fancy, Cats, Veterinary*

Product News, *Whole Dog Journal*, *Animal Wellness*, *Veterinary Forum*, *Whole Cat Journal*, *AKC Gazette*, *Vegas Dog*, *Dog Nose News*, *Body & Soul*, *Natural Horse*, and *Pet Business*.

Also, Dr. Messonnier has authored a number of books for both pet owners and veterinarians. His recent contributions to the field of natural pet care include *The Arthritis Solution for Dogs*, *The Allergy Solution for Dogs*, *8 Weeks to a Healthy Dog*, and the award-winning *The Natural Health Bible for Dogs & Cats*.

Dr. Messonnier is a speaker and consultant. His popular lectures teach veterinarians and pet owners how holistic approach can reduce the cost of veterinary care and help pets live longer, healthier lives.

You may contact Dr. Messonnier about speaking and consulting, or about setting up a telephone consult at:

2145 West Park Boulevard
Plano, Texas 75075

Phone: 972-867-8800

Email: shawnvet@sbcglobal.net
Website: www.petcarenaturally.com or
www.pettogethers.net/healthypet